GANGLAND

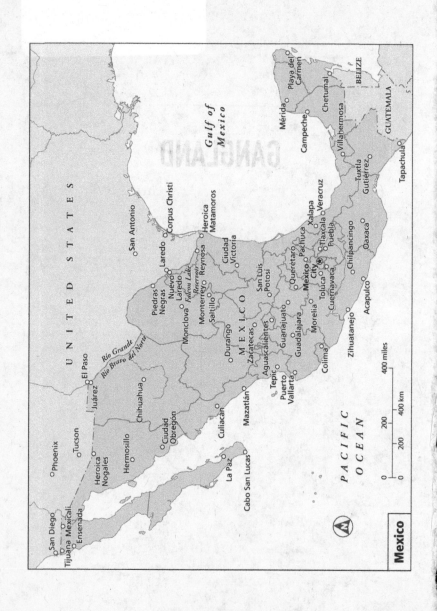

GANGLAND

THE RISE OF THE MEXICAN DRUG CARTELS FROM EL PASO TO VANCOUVER

JERRY LANGTON

HarperCollins Publishers Ltd
2 Bloor Street East, 20th Floor
Toronto, Ontario, Canada
M4W 1A8

www.harpercollins.ca

Library and Archives Canada Cataloguing in Publication
information is available upon request

ISBN 978-1-44342-775-3

Printed and bound in the United States of America
RRD 9 8 7 6 5 4

To the Langton–Cowan Organization:
La Salchicha, El Dida and El Hoohoo.

CONTENTS

CONTENTS

ACKNOWLEDGMENTS

In addition to the many brave people mentioned in my sources, I would also like to thank the team at John Wiley & Sons for their support and enthusiasm: editor Don Loney, marketer Robin-Dutta Roy, production editor Elizabeth McCurdy, publicist Erika Zupko, and national account manager for Indigo and Online, Paul Coulombe. Special thanks to Michael Nicholson, whose enthusiasm and encouragement were vital to this project and to Brian Rogers. Thanks also to Leta Potter, who wields considerable clout in all things. And, of course, I must thank my wife and kids for their infinite patience, good humor and creativity.

CHAPTER 1
Deadly Playground

It wasn't always this way. Just a few years ago, El Paso and Juárez were like one big city, the border more a formality than anything else to most people. "You'd go to Juárez for a good time; we'd go pretty much every weekend," said Tim McNeill, an El Paso resident who hasn't been across the border in five years. "It was fun; you could drink and have a good time, buy things that weren't allowed over here . . . it was where you went to blow off steam." El Paso was the nice, but straight-laced neighborhood, and Juárez was the poorer, more religious, maybe a little more dangerous cousin where residents from either side of the border could let their hair down and enjoy themselves.

But times changed. Economic challenges have deeply impoverished the Mexican side, especially compared to their neighbors just a few yards to the north. Mexicans have long been poorer than Texans, but failures in the economy at the end of the 20th century made the distinction even sharper. That economic hardship has sent literally millions of Mexicans north, looking for better lives. Because the United States is a very difficult country for foreigners to live and work in legally, most of the Mexicans who have moved there are undocumented—what are referred to for the purposes of this book as illegal immigrants. Unprotected by many of the laws U.S. citizens and legal immigrants take for granted, illegal immigrants lead a shadow life, aware at any moment they can be deported back to Mexico. Many of these people feel betrayed by the Mexican government and ignored by the American government.

Other factors have changed the landscape. Drugs, both legal and illegal, have long been a reason for Americans to cross over into Juárez. You can buy many popular prescription drugs (Viagra is a favorite) over the counter without a prescription in most of Mexico, which has long been drawing Americans and American dollars over the border. And although the laws on recreational drugs like marijuana had largely been the same in Texas and Mexico until recently, they have long been much more tolerated in Juárez, where the police rarely ever got in anyone's way. Not surprisingly, Juárez and other border cities have become funnels for drugs being shipped into the U.S.

It is a situation both countries basically tolerated, if not officially approved. The drug trade—which was illegal, but largely peaceful—flourished in Juárez and other border cities for decades. Then Richard Nixon declared a War on Drugs in 1972, working to intercept drugs coming into the country. Using sophisticated detection methods and applying harsh penalties, the Americans drove the drug trade farther underground. The increase in danger led to an increase in rewards as drug users paid higher prices for smaller quantities. The new rewards attracted organized crime, and the tougher border led them to employ illegal immigrants. A new equilibrium was established as drug traffickers got rich and the drug trade became a much bigger part of the economy. *Narcocorridos*—danceable songs celebrating the exploits of drug traffickers—became popular. Kids started emulating the drug runners and their gangster bosses.

Then it changed again. When the Mexican government cracked down on the drug cartels—the crime organizations that had evolved from street gangs acting as mules, ferrying product between drug lords in Colombia and retailers in the U.S. and Canada—in 2006, they fought back. In the few years since, thousands of people have been killed, much of Mexico is considered too dangerous for North Americans to enter and the nation itself is said by experts (including the U.S. State Department) of being in danger of absolute collapse.

• • •

In the old days, there were signs everywhere hawking products to North Americans the moment you entered Juárez. And as soon as you crossed the border, a *taxista* would offer you a ride or a hawker would appear hoping to sell something—oranges, prescription drugs, or maybe just a free ticket to the kind of strip show you'd never see north of the Rio Grande. That's all gone now. The signs are almost all graffiti now, some hailing Che Guevara and other champions of anti-imperialism, others exhorting the locals in Spanish to go to church and read their bibles. Nobody approaches the visitors from the north anymore. Instead, the first thing you see is the military, soldiers wearing masks so the cartels can't identify them and threaten their families. They're everywhere in Juárez, doing their best to keep the peace.

Two blocks south of the bridge over the Rio Grande—at the corner of Juárez and Azucenas—you can see vestiges of what Juárez used to be like. On one corner is a massive, windowless bar called Tequila Derby, across from it the Centro Juarcz Liquor Center and on the other side is the Juarez Race & Sports Book, a gambling franchise. Next to it is Drug Discount Pharmacy—with the slogan "The Best Price in Town"—offering all kinds of medicines over the counter. Many of the other shops, like discount opticians and dentists, are also clearly aimed at Americans. All the signs are in English, with prices given in dollars as well as pesos. Many of the shops are now shuttered and there's little traffic, either walking or driving. There are a few juice and shaved-ice vendors, but everywhere you look there are collections of men, mostly young, just hanging around, apparently with nothing better to do. On almost every pole, there is a sign taped up, appealing for information about a missing woman.

On the next block there is a collection of bars catering to American customers. From the outside, the Kentucky Club doesn't look like much. It's just a one-level storefront between a fancy restaurant and a pharmacy selling Viagra and Cialis by the pill. The building is painted light green and it has a dark green awning to shade the front windows from the desert sun. On the awning there is orange and yellow art deco script reading "World Famous Kentucky Club Since 1920." Above that is an old red, white and blue sign sponsored by Tecate, a popular beer brewed in another Mexican border city.

Its exterior plainness belies its rich history. The bar claims that it is the birthplace of the margarita, although that's been widely disputed. In its heyday during the 1950s and '60s, it was incredibly popular with famous Americans: Ronald Reagan is said to have enjoyed drinking there, as did John Wayne. Richard Burton and Elizabeth Taylor were semi-regulars there, and both Jim Morrison and Bob Dylan dropped by the Kentucky Club when they were searching for some lyrical inspiration. Most famously, Marilyn Monroe bought a round of drinks for the whole bar to celebrate her divorce from Arthur Miller.

Inside, it's lavish in a retro-fancy way. The ceiling is white with black beams and hanging metal chandeliers, the bar is wooden and majestic and all of the staff are required to wear white shirts, ties and vests.

But for all its style and romance, the mood inside the Kentucky Club is somber these days. The phone has been disconnected (most downtown businesses have gotten rid of their phones because the only calls they get anymore are extortion threats), and business has decreased as both Americans and Mexicans alike are afraid to walk the streets of Juárez after dark. It's hard to blame them, the murder rate of the city of just over 1 million is higher than that of Baghdad and Kandahar combined.

But unlike so many other establishments in the area, the Kentucky Club has been free of violence. "In a way, I feel calm because we pay the *cuota* [protection] not to have problems," said a doorman who goes by the name Raul. "Many businesses have been burned and shot up. But here, they protect us and the customer—because we pay."

And, although it is forced to close early now, and is usually surrounded by masked soldiers with assault rifles, the staff of the Kentucky Club wants Americans to know that it's still open for business. "We want to remind our customers that just like Juárez doesn't give up, neither will we," said waiter Arturo Sanchez Ontiveros. "We will stand with our city as long as we can."

• • •

It's bold talk, my Mexican friends and contacts tell me, but few think the Kentucky Club or Juárez itself can hold up to the beating they are taking for that much longer. They are a collection of journalists, former journalists and others who have been directly related to the violence in Mexico. One of them has been kidnapped, most of them have been shot at, all of them have been threatened. It's a hard place and a hard time to be a journalist.

In many parts of Mexico, drug-related killings are not reported upon because journalists have been killed for what the cartels have called "collaborating" with authorities. Juárez has been the hardest hit. It has become so dangerous, in fact, that the front page of the September 19, 2010 edition of *El Diario*, the city's largest circulation daily newspaper, was devoted entirely to an open letter to the cartels. In it, the editors of *El Diario* asked the drug cartels what they were allowed to write. "We do not want more deaths," it said. "We do not want more injuries or even more intimidation. It is impossible to exercise our role in these conditions. Tell us, then, what do you expect of us as a medium?" After the murders of two of their reporters in one week, the editors had no choice but to admit who was boss. "You are, at present, the de facto authorities in this city," the letter read, "because the legal institutions have not been able to keep our colleagues from dying."

I ask the Mexicans where to start. How can I tell North Americans what's going on in Mexico and in Juárez in particular in a way they can understand. "You could start with Miss Sinaloa," one said, referring to the brilliant article, "Mexico's Red Days," written by Arizona-based reporter Charles Bowden for *GQ*. In it, he described in vivid detail how a Mexican beauty pageant winner arrived in Juárez and suffered almost unbelievable torture at the hands of the cartels simply because they could get away with it. Others want me to tell other individual stories, about how this cartel killed these people, about the drug kingpin who delighted in melting the bodies of his enemies or another whose signature was hanging beheaded bodies from traffic overpasses. They want me to speak of car bombs, crooked cops, 14-year-old assassins or gold-plated AK-47s. Everyone, it seems, has their own way to understand the Mexican Drug War.

But there was one voice that really reached me. Nuria J is a Juárez poet, librarian and women's rights activist. She is tireless in her own war against the Drug War. She told me that to understand Mexico, to understand Juárez, to understand why the violence and terror have become as rampant as they have, it is imperative to know about the missing women of Juárez. It would tell people how Mexico works: its people, its authorities and its criminals.

LAS MUERTAS DE JUÁREZ

Susana Chávez was a remarkable young woman. She started writing poetry in earnest at the age of eleven, and decided to make it her life's work. Even while still very young, she read her work before crowds and was included in prestigious exhibitions. Later, she earned a degree in psychology at the Universidad Autónoma de Ciudad Juárez.

As a young adult, she turned the focus of her work to the growing number of women who had been murdered in and around Juárez. It was a strange and chilling phenomenon, even in what has since become one of the most violent cities in the world. Beginning in 1993, the bodies of women began showing up on the streets, alleys, vacant lots and garbage dumps of Juárez. Most of the victims were between the ages of 12 and 22, and many of them showed obvious signs of torture and rape. Some of them were intentionally left in degrading poses.

The majority of them were workers in *maquiladoras*, factories usually owned or associated with large corporations (invariably reported in the media as American, but they are just as likely to be Spanish, Korean or Japanese) that take advantage of Mexico's low minimum wage and relaxed enforcement of labor and environmental regulations. The factories generally employ far more women than men (sometimes exclusively so) because of a widespread belief that they are more reliable and trustworthy, and less likely to cause any trouble. Many of the victims were migrants from other parts of Mexico and Central America, attracted to the border region by the abundance of job opportunities.

Although about 400 bodies had been recovered, some estimates have claimed as many as 5,000 young women from the area have gone missing since 1993. The number of missing women is often under-reported because until recently Mexican police did not begin searches for missing persons until they had been gone for at least 72 hours, and their searches are often cursory at best. As one Mexican police commander told reporters: "It's not a crime to disappear." Sometimes families are afraid to report their daughter missing. Sometimes they just don't know.

Locals referred to the missing women as *las feminicidios* (the femicides) and *las muertas de Juárez* (the dead women of Juárez). Outraged by the horrific atmosphere of fear and violence against women in her hometown, Chávez became an activist, using her poetry and other methods to raise awareness and push the authorities to do a better job of investigating the murders. She became famous in the area—a leading member of the advocacy group Nuestras Hijas de Regreso a Casa (Bring

Our Daughters Home)—and her phrase *Ni una más* (Not one more) became a rallying cry for the entire movement.

And then she became one of the victims. On Wednesday, January 5, 2011, Mexicans were celebrating *Día de los Santos Reyes*, a traditional, non-statutory holiday marking the arrival of the Three Wise Men of the Gospels. Early in the evening, 36-year-old Chávez left the house she shared with her parents to go visit friends at a nearby restaurant. She never arrived. "I waited for her all night long, but she never came back," her mother told local media. "On Thursday, we began to search for her. Then we learned she was dead. [The police] showed us some pictures, and that was the way we could identify her."

Police had been called that morning because a Juárez family had found a streak of blood, indicating someone had been dragged into an alley, on a sidewalk near their home. Police then found a severed left hand and, a few feet away, Chávez's body with a black plastic garbage bag tied over her head.

Their subsequent investigation determined that Chávez had met three 17-year-old boys in a bar and decided to drink with them. After some time, the boys convinced her to go to one of their homes. Police said that Chávez went with them, but when she refused their sexual advances, they tied her up, covered her mouth with duct tape and drowned her in a bathtub. They severed her hand with a hacksaw, police said, in an effort to make the murder look like it was the work of organized crime, which, of course, was still running wild in Juárez despite thousands of police officers and soldiers occupying the city.

The Chihuahua state police claimed that her murder was an unfortunate isolated incident, and not the result of the Drug War or Chávez's activism. "Unfortunately, these people were drunk, they were taking drugs, and after hanging out for a while, they decided to kill her," Chihuahua State Attorney General Carlos Manuel Salas told *Milenio*, a national daily newspaper. The boys were, according to police, members of a local street gang called Los Aztecas, but did not have previous criminal records.

Few in Juárez believed the boys were guilty of the crime. Since the murders began in earnest in 1993, many people have been charged with the killings and put behind bars, but the bodies keep showing up.

The first victim identified as one of the missing women of Juárez was 13-year-old Anna Chavira Farel. Her beaten, raped, sodomized and strangled body was found January 23, 1993 in a vacant lot in the city's Campeste Virreyes neighborhood. The next, 16-year-old Angela Luna Villalobos, was found two days later in a similar condition not far away. As more bodies were found and far more young *maquiladora* workers went missing, citizens pressured the authorities to do something about what they were calling "El Depredador" (the Predator). In October 1995, after at least 46 bodies of girls and young women had been found in Juárez, Chihuahua state police arrested a suspect.

He certainly seemed the part. Abdel Latif Sharif was born in Egypt in 1947. A gifted chemical engineer, he emigrated to New York City in 1970. He was fired from his job there for embezzlement and moved to New Hope, Pennsylvania, in 1978.

One of his friends and co-workers, John Pascoe, later told police that he took Sharif on a deer-hunting trip and was surprised to see him torture a wounded buck, laughing while breaking the limbs of the helpless animal until Pascoe put it out of its misery. He also noted that Sharif was often in the company of young women, some of who had disappeared after their contact with him. When Pascoe found the possessions of a girl who had gone missing next to a mud-stained shovel on Sharif's porch in 1980, he severed their friendship.

Sharif's talents led an upstate New York-based building materials company called Cercoa (now part of the giant Ferro Corporation) to create a department specifically for him in Florida in 1981. The job paid him well enough that he could afford to live in Palm Beach. On May 2, 1981, he invited a 23-year-old woman named Molly Fleming, whom he met in a bar, to his house where he beat and raped her repeatedly. When he was finished, he offered to take her to a hospital where he was promptly arrested.

Cercoa bailed him out and paid for his legal defense, which was further complicated in August after he sexually assaulted another woman he met in West Palm Beach. He was sentenced to probation for the first rape and 45 days in prison for the second.

After his release, Cercoa fired him and Sharif moved to Gainesville, a city dominated by the University of Florida. He was married briefly. His wife, Joanne Collins Podlesnik, divorced him after he beat her unconscious. On March 17, 1983, Sharif placed an ad in *The Gainesville Daily Register* looking for a live-in housekeeper. He beat and raped a woman who answered the ad and threatened her by saying: "I will bury you out back in the woods. I've done it before, and I'll do it again." After he was arrested, he escaped from jail, but was quickly apprehended. He was sentenced to 12 years in prison with the understanding that when his sentence was over, Sharif would "be met at the prison gates and escorted to the airport" for deportation to Egypt.

But it didn't work out that way. He was paroled in October 1989 and soon hired by Midland, Texas-based Benchmark Research & Technology, where his work in nonflammable, hydrocarbon-free well drilling materials received praise from the U.S. Department of Energy and influential Senator Phil Gramm. It also earned Sharif a consistent income from patents he registered while working there. But he was arrested again in 1991, this time for driving under the influence. A former co-worker from Florida who had coincidentally moved to Midland saw his name in the paper and called Immigration to investigate Sharif's deportation order.

The case dragged on, and in May 1994, a judge agreed to a deal in which the prosecution would drop all charges if Sharif would voluntarily leave the U.S., never to return. Benchmark then transferred him to one of their *maquiladora* factories in Juárez and rented him a large house in the city's posh Rincones de San Marcos neighborhood.

In October 1995, a worker at the factory accused Sharif of raping her repeatedly. She said he warned her not to go to police or he would kill her and dump her body in Lote Bravo, a stretch of desert just south of Juárez where many bodies of young women had already been found.

Although she later dropped her charges, a detective working the case found out that the 48-year-old Sharif had been dating 17-year-old Elizabeth Castro Garcia, whose beaten and raped body had been found in Lote Bravo on August 19. Sharif was arrested, tried and sentenced to 30 years in prison.

But while the media was trumpeting the arrest of the Juárez Ripper—and pointing out, almost boasting, that he was a foreigner brought to Mexico by the Americans—the killings didn't stop. In fact, they increased. Not only were there more bodies, but those that were found were more and more likely to be mutilated in horrific ways. And the press also neglected to mention that the killings had begun at least 15 months before Sharif had moved to the area.

The citizens—particularly young women—of Juárez were growing increasingly frightened and the authorities were at a loss to explain why taking Sharif off the streets didn't do anything to stop the killings. What happened next would have been rejected if it were the plot outline for the cheesiest crime show in television history.

On April 8, 1996, police questioned a man named Hector Olivares Villalba in connection with the rape, mutilation and murder of 18-year-old Rosario Garcia Leal. Under interrogation, Olivares Villalba admitted that he was indeed one of many young men from a Juárez street gang called Los Rebeldes (the Rebels) who had murdered Garcia Leal on December 7, 1995. Police raided a number of nightclubs associated with the gang and rounded up almost 300 people for questioning. That led to the arrest of gang leader Sergio "El Diablo" (the Devil) Armendariz Diaz, Juan "El Grande" (Mr. Big) Contreras Jurado, Carlos Hernandez Molina, Carlos Barrientos Vidales, Romel Cerniceros Garcia, Fernando Guermes Aguirre, Luis Adrade, Jose Juarez Rosales and Erika Fierro, all members of Los Rebeldes.

Eager to pin the murders on Sharif, police accused the nine members of Los Rebeldes of participating in a sinister plot in which Sharif would pay them to commit rapes and murders using the same methods he had in order to make people believe that he was not the culprit and that the real *depredador* was still at large. Police claimed that Contreras Jurado testified that Armendariz Diaz had once ordered him to visit Sharif in prison and bring back an envelope containing $4,000 in U.S. currency. Once it was received, they said, Armendariz Diaz ordered the gang members to kidnap, beat, rape and murder a young woman known to them only as "Lucy."

All of the accused later recanted their confessions, saying that they were made under torture. They showed reporters burn marks they said came from their interrogators. Charges were later dropped against Ceniceros Garcia, Fierro, Guermes Aguirre, Hernandez Molina and Olivares Villalba. The others—Armendariz Diaz, Contreras Jurado, Carlos Barrientos Vidales, Luis Adrade and Jose Juarez Rosales—went to trial for 17 murders police said were coordinated by Sharif from his prison cell. Armendariz Diaz added some excitement to the proceedings when he pleaded guilty to organizing and participating in the gang rape of a 19-year-old fellow inmate while awaiting trial. Police also said that Armendariz Diaz's teeth were perfect matches to bite marks found on the breasts of at least three victims attributed to Los Rebeldes.

But putting Los Rebeldes in prison didn't do any more to stop the killings than imprisoning Sharif did. The murders continued unabated even though Mexico's own Human Rights Commission openly criticized the state police and their methods, insisting they take the problem more seriously. But still the police and prosecutors clung to the idea that the murders were the work of one extremely proficient serial killer, probably working under the direction of Sharif.

And many in government indicated that the deaths of women on the streets of Juárez were far from a top priority. "Women who have a night life, go out late and come into contact with drinkers are at risk," Chihuahua's former attorney general Arturo Gonzáles Rascón told *El Diario* in February 1999. "It's hard to go out on the street when it's raining and not get wet." Although there was no evidence to support it, other authorities had accused the victims of being prostitutes, or in some way provoking their attackers. "Despite the fact that most of the victims were schoolgirls or workers, there's a persistent belief around town that the targeted women somehow invited the attacks," said American journalist John Burnett. "Nowadays, it's a common joke when two men see a provocatively dressed woman, for one to elbow the other and say: 'She better watch out or she'll end up in the desert.'"

More light was shed on the hundreds of rapes and murders on March 18, 1999, when a badly injured 14-year-old girl named Nancy Gonzalez started banging on a stranger's door in Juárez, screaming and begging for help. When police arrived, she told them that she had been repeatedly raped, beaten, suffocated and left for dead by a man named Jesus Guardado Márquez, known locally as "El Tolteca" (the Toltec), because he looked like he was from that indigenous group. He was a *maquiladora* bus driver, who picked up women from their homes and dropped them off at factories, returning when their shifts were over. The concept behind the buses (which the factories paid for) was to keep the women safe from the predators on the streets. But when Gonzalez—who had falsified her birth date to get her job—finished her shift at 1:00 a.m., she found that she was the last passenger on the bus and that it had taken a turn into the desert. Guardado Márquez then assaulted her and tried to choke her to death.

Upon hearing that Gonzalez was still alive, Guardado Márquez (who had been found guilty of sexual assault once before) fled Juárez with his pregnant wife, but was arrested on April 1 in Durango. Under interrogation, Guardado Márquez admitted to his crimes against Gonzalez and named four other bus drivers—Victor "El Narco" (the Narc) Moreno Rivera; Augustin "El Kiani" (the Persian) Toribio Castillo; Bernardo "El Samber" Hernando Fernandez; and Jose Gaspar "El Gaspy" Cerballos Chavez—who raped and murdered their passengers as a gang called Los Choferes (the Chauffeurs).

Incredibly, state police claimed that their leader, Moreno Rivera, had been hired by Sharif in an effort to clear his name, just as they alleged Los Rebeldes had. They said Sharif had paid the bus drivers $1,200 per murder and that he demanded the victims' underwear as proof.

A British reporter tracked down Sharif in prison (he was in solitary confinement and said he was frequently denied access to his lawyer) and asked him what he thought of the government's story. "They accuse me of everything. They always said I was a genius and very intelligent. How come a genius would make the same mistake twice?" he said. "If I did it with Los Rebeldes, why would I do the same thing the same way? Paying people to kill women outside [prison] is very stupid." Police could provide no evidence of cash transactions, phone conversations or visits to Sharif in prison.

The accused claimed they did not know Sharif and that their confessions were the result of torture. Authorities blamed them for a total of 211 murders, including a ludicrous 191 by Guardado Márquez alone. Media had started calling him "El Dracula." He and the other bus drivers recanted their confessions. Motores Electricos de Juárez, Gonzalez's employer, fired her and sued her for taking a job she was too young for. Sharif's sentence was reduced from 30 years to 20 after the prosecution admitted it had "problems with evidence," and both sides promised to appeal. He died—of what officials called "natural causes"—in prison in 2006.

Not surprisingly, the killings did not stop. By the end of 1999, the phenomenon was making international news. The victims, known as *Las Desaparecidos* (the Disappeared) were drawing a great deal of interest in the United States, including some celebrities who championed their cause and protested what they saw as poor efforts by police and government to stop the killings. Canadian Candice Skrapec, an instructor of criminology at the University of California, Fresno, told newspapers that the killings were likely the work of American Angel Resendez Ramirez, better known as "the Railway Killer." She was wrong. When he was arrested, Resendez Ramirez admitted to a number of murders, but none in Mexico.

When the skeletal remains of eight more victims were uncovered in a vacant lot just a block away from the Maquiladoras Association headquarters on November 5, 2001, police announced the creation of a new task force to investigate the crimes and offered a reward of $21,500 for information leading to an arrest. The area, known as "El Campo Algodonero" (the Cotton Field), had been the site where so many bodies have been buried over the years that it led to a commonly used threat, "I'll leave your body in the Cotton Field."

On November 10, two more bus drivers—Javier "El Cerillo" (the Match) Garcia Uribe and Gustavo "La Foca" (the Seal) Gonzalez Meza—were arrested for the eight murders discovered a week earlier. Again the men confessed and then recanted, saying the confessions were the results of torture.

One of their defense attorneys, Mario Escobedo Anaya, left work on February 5, 2002. He had received death threats before, and when he noticed he was being followed by a Jeep Cherokee, he fled the scene, stomping on his car's accelerator pedal. The Jeep, police claim, was the personal vehicle of state police commander Roberto Alejandro Castro Valles. The police initially reported that Escobedo Anaya had died when his car crashed, but when the autopsy report showed he had actually died as a result of repeated gunshot wounds, they changed their story to say that an officer killed him in self defense. To prove it, they showed local reporters a Jeep Cherokee full of bullet holes. By the end of 2009, the pair's other two lawyers—including Escobedo's father, Mario Escobedo Salazar—had also been killed in mysterious circumstances.

Over the years, things changed. Celebrities from the U.S. and Mexico did their best to raise awareness. Journalists came from all over the world to spread the word. And, in May 2005, the Chihuahua state police dropped their 72-hour waiting period before they would investigate missing persons. But it didn't help the situation for women that violence from the cartels had exploded in the city. Police—who were already overwhelmed by the crime level in the city and were understaffed due to purges of corrupt officers—were suddenly confronted with 10 or 12 murder investigations a day. The mystery of the missing women of Juárez took a back seat to the drug war.

And the bodies still keep coming. There are lots of theories. People in Juárez like to blame groups like Satanists, organ harvesters, even a cabal of wealthy men who pay huge sums to hunt women on the streets of their city for sport. The common thread is that outsiders are to blame.

Academics on both sides of the border blame the *maquiladoras*. They point out that the factories attract vulnerable

women and force them to travel to and from work in dangerous places and at dangerous times. But the places and times
being dangerous are less the fault of the factories than they are
of the place itself. The *machista* culture of many Mexicans has
been deeply unnerved by the fact that many women in border
areas make more money than their fathers, brothers and hus-
bands. "Women are occupying the space of men in a culture of
absolute dominance of men over women," said Esther Chavez
Cano, the best known of all women's right advocates in Juárez.
"This has to provoke misogyny."

Indeed what was happening in Juárez wasn't coming from
outside. It was coming from Juárez itself. Although the sheer
number of murders and missing women suggests many culprits,
there is one group that has been conclusively identified as con-
tributing to the slaughter. The Juárez Cartel employs a number of former and active-duty policemen as an enforcer unit.
They are called *La Linea* (the Line) and are heavily armed and
extensively trained in urban warfare. Because so many police
in Juárez are involved with *La Linea* and the cartel, it's difficult for Mexicans to feel safe when the very people employed
to protect them are also the most likely to prey upon them.
"The Juárez Cartel are the cops," an informant told U.S. federal officials during an investigation about police corruption in
the city. "They've turned Juárez into their deadly playground.
They make their own rules."

In an interview with *The Dallas Morning News*, a former
drug trafficker who had worked in cooperation with *La Linea*
said it was not uncommon to see abducted women at the gang's

parties. And when he did not see the women again, he simply assumed they had been killed. He explained his logic by telling the reporters: "Sometimes, when you cross a shipment of drugs to the United States, adrenaline is so high that you want to celebrate by killing women."

While all of the factors that would appear to contribute to the wholesale violence against women in Juárez also occurs in other border cities, the women in them have not been subjected to anywhere near the same amount of terror. Tijuana has more factories, a largely corrupt police force and just as many entrenched gangs. The conditions in places like Nuevo Laredo, Calexico, Matamoros and other cities are much the same as they are in Juárez, but the women there are not nearly as likely to be victims of rape and murder.

I asked the Mexicans I knew if they had a theory. Only one of them—Miguel G, a journalist who has fled Mexico to work in the U.S. as a graphic designer—did. He told me: "Juárez is just a bad place."

CHAPTER 2
The Eagle Eats the Snake

Mexico is not like the United States or Canada. Of course, it has a different official language, but it also has a state religion, different legal and political systems, and a much more violent history. It is also what economists refer to as a developing nation, what we used to call a third-world country.

And it has a different way of thinking. When the Nobel Prize-winning Mexican poet and diplomat Octavio Paz was asked about the difference between Mexicans and North Americans, he put it bluntly: "The Mexican tells lies because he delights in fantasy, or because he is desperate, or because he wants to rise above the sordid facts of his life; the North American does not tell lies. The North Americans are credulous."

More importantly, Mexico has a long history of unstable governments being replaced by periods of corrupt, one-party rule. It has withstood several violent coups, at least one full-scale revolution, been invaded several times by foreign powers and has even had two emperors. From the time the Mexica nation defeated the Azcapotzalco in 1428 (and probably before that) until the election of Vicente Fox as president in 2000, Mexico had not experienced a single transfer of power to the opposition without violence. A knowledge of the Mexican history that helped incubate it is essential to the Mexican Drug War.

THE MEXICA

Prior to the arrival of the Spanish in 1519, the territory that now forms Mexico was home to anywhere from 6 million to 25 million people (it is still difficult to estimate populations of pre-contact indigenous people). There were dozens of languages and ethnic groups, but much of the area was dominated by a loose alliance of Nahuatl speakers now referred to as the Aztecs. They arrived in Mexico from the north about 1,500 years ago, pushing the hunter-gatherer Otomanguean people farther south. The Aztecs' advanced agriculture, technology and social structure allowed them to establish a very large territory, spanning much of modern-day Mexico from the Gulf of Mexico to the Pacific coast.

One group of Nahuatl speakers who arrived in Aztec territory in the late 14th century and became one of its confederates identified themselves as the Mēxihtli, and are known to history as the Mexica. They asked the permission of the area's dominant people, the Azcapotzalco, to settle in the valley surrounding Lake Texcoco in central Mexico. The Azcapotzalco agreed. According to legend, the Mexica saw an eagle eating a snake on a prickly pear cactus, decided it was a message from above telling them where to settle, and set up their homes at the spot. This image is now reproduced on the Mexican flag. On a marshy island in Lake Texcoco, the Mexica founded the city of Tenochtitlan, and the area they dominated was called Mēxihco or Mexico.

About 100 years later, the Mexica had grown in power and prestige and began to rival the Azcapotzalco as the dominant Aztec group. After an Azcapotzalco murdered the Mexica leader, the Mexica aligned with two other Aztec nations and defeated the Azcapotzalco in 1428. The survivors assimilated into the Mexica.

By the early 16th century, the Mexica had easily grown more powerful than any other Aztec people and were considered the dominant people. Their leader (or "Huey Tlatoani") was a bellicose king who put into effect many laws designed to elevate the noble class above the commoners, including one that forbade commoners from watching nobles eat. His name was Motehcuzōma Xocoyotzin, but he is referred to by historians as Moctezuma II and is more commonly known as Montezuma.

CORTÉS LANDS ON THE YUCÁTAN

At about that time, sailors from Spain made frequent trips to the Americas, particularly around the Caribbean Sea and Gulf of Mexico. One of them—Hernán Cortés de Monroy y Pizarro, commonly known as Hernán Cortés—visited Cuba and what is now the Dominican Republic on the island of Hispaniola. He was part of a group who called themselves *conquistadores* (conquerers) because their primary activity was claiming new territories for Spain, forcing the inhabitants to work for them and to accept their religion.

The governor of Hispaniola hired Cortés to colonize Mexico as the Spanish had Cuba and Hispaniola, but then changed his mind because he decided Cortés was undermining his authority and seeking to claim more glory than he deserved (the two had been rivals in school back in Spain). Defying the governor's orders, Cortés went into considerable personal debt to collect 11 ships, 100 sailors, 530 men (including 12 with guns), a small but undetermined number of women, at least 100 slaves, 13 horses and a few small cannons for his expedition.

He landed on the Yucatán Peninsula in southern Mexico. Unlike the high, dry plateau inhabited by the Aztecs, the jungly Yucatán was home to the Maya, a loosely knit and constantly bickering group of self-determined nations with a common language, but one—unlike the Aztecs—who lacked a dominant group or capital city.

Cortés and his men were not the only Spaniards in Mexico when they landed. An earlier expedition had arrived by accident, lost in a storm and shipwrecked on the Yucatán coast. The survivors were quickly captured by the local Mayans, who distributed them among the area's important families as slaves. By the time Cortés arrived, disease and other fates had killed all but two—Gonzalo Guerrero, who won his freedom from the Maya by showing bravery in battle, and Gerónimo de Aguilar, a Franciscan friar who escaped and was accepted as a free man by a neighboring group of Mayans who had a grudge against his captors.

Cortés and his men lived in relative peace among the Mayans there. Before long, he was told stories of two other white men in the vicinity. He eventually met with both Guerrero and Aguilar and told them of his plan to colonize Mexico for Spain. Aguilar agreed to be his guide and translator, while Guerrero rebuffed him, choosing instead to return to his group of Mayans to fight against the Spanish.

While exploring the Yucatán, Cortés fell in love with a Mayan slave. He was told she was a captured Aztec princess, but modern historians doubt that. Her exact name is also disputed—she is usually called Malinche, Malintzin or Mallinali—but Cortés named her Doña Marina. She would stay with him in Mexico and later had a son by him.

Aware that he had to succeed in Mexico or face the governor and potential execution, Cortés asked the Mayans if they knew of any big cities, preferably those with gold. He was told of such a place, farther north, called Cempoala. This was the capital of the Totonac nation and had about 20,000 people in what is now the state of Veracruz. The Cempoala townspeople welcomed the *conquistadores* and quickly agreed to allow them to build their own settlement nearby. Later, some decided to ally with the Spanish to invade the cities of the Aztecs, where they said the real wealth was. While there, Cortés learned of a conspiracy by some of his men to sail back to Cuba, so he destroyed his entire fleet, forcing his men to stay in Mexico.

Together, the Spaniards and the Totonacs made the long trip northwest. They first reached the territory of a nation called the Tlaxcala. Over the course of the previous century, the Mexica-led Aztecs had launched a series of conflicts later referred to as the Flower Wars, in which they conquered and absorbed most of their neighboring nations. The one exception was the Tlaxcala.

The Tlaxcala didn't trust the newcomers and attacked. They were excellent warriors and surprised the Spanish with their fighting ability, eventually surrounding them. This could have been the end of Cortés and his men, but for some tense negotiations which managed to change the minds of the Tlaxcalteca leaders. Tired of constant conflict and fearing they would be the Mexicas' next victims unless they acted, the Tlaxcala allied with the Spanish and Totonacs and agreed to send a thousand Tlaxcalteca soldiers to help invade the Aztec cities. As part of the deal, the Tlaxcalteca leaders would not pay tribute to the Spanish and would be allowed to build a fortress in Tenochtitlan, and rule it militarily. Fearing an alliance between the Mexica and the Tlaxcala, who shared a language and religion, if he did not acquiesce, Cortés agreed.

By that time, the Aztec leaders in Tenochtitlan had heard of the Spanish advance and sent emissaries with gifts and offers of peace. Cortés accepted and sent two of his own men to speak with the Mexica.

Against the advice of the Tlaxcalteca, Cortés advanced on the city of Cholula. The second-biggest city in Mexico after Tenochtitlan with about 100,000 residents, Cholula was a multi-ethnic religious center with a pyramid and 365 temples. Although greatly influenced by the Aztecs, Cholula was not aligned with any nation and had almost no military, depending instead on the help of the gods—and the goodwill of its neighbors—for defense.

The advancing army arrived peacefully, but not without tension. What happened next is in doubt. Cortés' side of the story is that Doña Marina heard from a Cholulan noblewoman of a plot to murder the Spanish in their sleep. The Tlaxcalteca version is that Cortés had promised them Cholula, and they were enraged when they found out that the Cholulans had tortured their ambassador. It may only have been a rumor. The Aztecs claimed that the Tlaxcala were angry at the Spanish for delaying in Cholula and were ready to attack them unless they did something.

Whatever the reason, Cortés and his men massacred the Cholulans. In his own account, Cortés claimed his men set fire to the city and killed 3,000 people in less than three hours. Another Spaniard who was there put the total number of dead at 30,000.

The massacre sent a shock wave through the area. Terrified of the Spanish and their allies, the local people did not oppose their march through their country. To add to the terror campaign, Cortés sent emissaries to the Mexica, telling them that because the people of Cholula hadn't shown him proper respect, they had had to be punished. He also added that gold would be an appropriate way to show respect.

Arriving at Tenochtitlan on November 8, 1519, Cortés and his men must have marvelled. With 300,000 residents, Tenochtitlan rivalled any European city except Constantinople. Tenochtitlan was built on an island and was accessible only by boat or by one of four narrow causeways. Moctezuma greeted Cortés personally with a great celebration and dressed him in a floral robe, the highest honor his people could bestow.

Moctezuma housed and fed the 3,500 invaders in his brother's palace. Cortés demanded gold, and Moctezuma gave it to him. Cortés insisted on more. Again he was given what he wanted. He demanded that the two most important idols in the main temple pyramid be destroyed and replaced by statues of the Virgin Mary and St. Christopher. Again, to avoid war with the well-armed Spanish and their allies, his will was granted. Sensing tension among the locals, Cortés then took Moctezuma prisoner, telling the Mexica that his life would be spared as long as they did not revolt.

Word then arrived that another, much larger group of Spaniards was in Mexico. Pánfilo de Narváez had been sent by the governor of Hispaniola to arrest Cortés and colonize the Aztecs. Desperate, Cortés led 260 of his soldiers to meet de Narváez and his 900 men. Catching them by surprise, Cortés won a brief but intense battle and took de Narváez (who lost an eye in the fighting) prisoner. Upon hearing about the gold of Tenochtitlan, most of de Narváez's men joined Cortés.

Returning to Tenochtitlan, Cortés was shocked to see the

Spanish who had been left behind being held prisoner by the Mexica. In an effort to calm the situation, Cortés arranged to have Moctezuma appear on a high balcony and give a speech imploring the Mexica to let the Spanish leave peaceably. The crowd started to shout insults and throw stones at Moctezuma. He was hit by some and badly injured, dying a few days later.

Cortés joined his men under siege and started to make a plan. Since the Mexica had removed large sections of each of the causeways, Cortés had his men construct a wooden platform they could use to bridge the gaps. Using both darkness and rain as a cover, the Spaniards snuck out of the palace where they were being held late in the evening of July 1, 1520. They were detected after having crossed the first gap, where the platform got stuck. The Spaniards and their allies were unable to dislodge it before they were set upon by thousands of Mexica soldiers. Cortés and other nobles on horseback (and at least one man on foot) were able to leap over the second gap to safety, but the remaining Spaniards and their allies had to jump into the lake and try to swim to safety. Many of the Mexica were armed with *atlatls*, a spear-throwing device that could accurately send a projectile the length of a football field and, at close range, could penetrate armor. More than 600 of the Spanish, many of their allies, their guns and almost all of their loot were lost in the escape.

What remained of Cortés' army returned to Tlaxcala. After appealing to King Charles I of Spain, Cortés received reinforcements from Cuba, and he and the Tlaxcala again turned their attention to the Aztecs. Over the next year, Cortés managed to subdue—usually, but not always, by force—the entire Aztec nation except for the residents of two cities, the Mexica of Tenochtitlan and nearby Tlatelolco, which was smaller and largely dependent on Tenochtitlan.

When Cortés returned, he launched several ships in Lake Texcoco and cut the causeways that were the only dry-land links Tenochtitlan had with the mainland, as well as the aqueduct that brought in fresh water from the hills because the lake's high salt content made it non-potable. The Mexica held out for eight desperate months, sacrificing 70 Spanish prisoners to their gods, but were no match for the Spanish cannons, starvation, dehydration and a smallpox epidemic that claimed one-third of their population. Finally, on August 13, 1521, the last Aztec emperor, Cuauhtémoc, surrendered Tenochtitlan and Tlatelolco to Cortés.

THE SPANISH LEGACY

Cortés destroyed the city, expelled the Mexica, and built a new one, Ciudad de México (Mexico City), in its place. He was appointed governor of what was named *Virreinato de Nueva España* (the Viceroyalty of New Spain), banned the Mexica from living in Mexico City and demanded the destruction of all statues of the Aztec gods, replacing them with Christian saints.

The story of how Cortés conquered the Aztecs is valuable today not just because it explains how modern Mexico began, but also how many of the factors that were put into play have had a profound effect even today. Many indigenous Mexicans have retained their ethnic identities, particularly in southern states like Oaxaca and Chiapas, which have experienced independence movements and even armed rebellions since the 1990s. Cortés established a strong Christian religious presence and Spanish customs and legal traditions, which still hold to some extent today.

The most important of traditions the Spanish brought was a social system called the *encomienda* (parcelling). Under this system, each Spanish immigrant was assigned a specific number of indigenous people that he was obligated to protect, teach Spanish and instruct in the Roman Catholic faith. In return, they would pay him in crops, gold and other things of value. This custom established a harsh class system based on ethnicity.

Cortés had a mixed-ethnicity son, perhaps the first person born of half-European/half-indigenous American descent. Soon after he was born, Martín Cortés was separated from his mother and sent to live with his father's relatives back in Spain. When he was about 6 years old, his father petitioned the pope to legitimize all three of his illegitimate children, which was granted.

But when he returned to New Spain with his half-brothers (one from a previous marriage and two more from later marriages), Martín Cortés did not enjoy the same legal rights as them. The crown-appointed viceroy, Antonio de Mendoza y Pacheco, had installed a strict caste system that went farther than the *encomienda*. The five basic castes were (in declining order of prestige and rights): *Peninsular*, a person born in

Spain to Spanish parents: *Criollo/Criolla*, person born in New Spain to Spanish parents; *Mestizo/Mestiza*, a person born in New Spain with one Spanish parent and one indigenous parent (later, anyone of mixed European-indigenous ancestry); *Indio/India*, a person of indigenous descent; and *Negro/Negra*, a person of African descent. Martín Cortés is still referred to in Mexico as the "first *Mestizo*."

It was a harsh system. No one but *Peninsulares* could hold public office and the vast majority of New Spain's prosperity that wasn't shipped off to Spain was in their hands, even though they were very few in number. And as time went on, they were relatively fewer in number—in the United States and Canada, the vast majority of immigrants from Europe arrived as families, but in Mexico and much of the rest of Latin America, the bulk of immigrants from Spain were single men.

The few who married other *Peninsulares* had children who were *Criollos* (as did those who married *Criollas*), while those who married *Mestizas* or *Indias* fathered *Mestizo*. Aside from the hunters and trappers of the frozen Canadian North and Alaska, this phenomenon didn't happen in English-speaking North America where indigenous people were segregated, first by law and then by social and economic factors. That difference has led to very different ethnographics. Today Native Americans make up less than 1 percent of the total population of the U.S. and people of mixed indigenous/European roots are fewer still; in Canada, those numbers are 4 percent and a little more than 1 percent. In both countries, indigenous or part-indigenous people generally live away from major population centers and are rarely assimilated into mainstream culture. In Mexico, however, they *are* the mainstream culture: *Mestizos* now make up about three-quarters of the nation's total population, with what used to be known as *Criollos* and *Indios* both at about 12 percent, and others accounting for less than 1 percent.

THE RISE OF MIGUEL HIDALGO

As with many colonies, an independence movement emboldened by the revolutions in the United States (1775–1783) and France (1789–1799) emerged in New Spain. As they grew in numbers, *Mestizos* and *Criollos* became more vocal about their grievances.

The independence movement accelerated when Napoleon Bonaparte, Emperor of France, declared war on Portugal. Claiming he was allied with Spain, Napoleon moved thousands of troops into the country on the pretext he was surrounding Portugal. When he had established a full-size army in Spain in 1807, he dismissed King Ferdinand VII and proclaimed his older brother, Giuseppe Bonaparte, King Joseph I of Spain. After an initially unsuccessful Spanish revolt, Joseph stayed on the throne until Lord Wellington defeated his army in Vitoria, Spain, in 1813. He then moved to New York City (where he sold the Spanish crown jewels), then Philadelphia, before settling in New Jersey. His most notable acts while on the throne were to put an official end to the notorious Spanish Inquisition, and to sign the Spanish Constitution that limited the king's powers.

Joseph's usurpation of the throne caused an uproar in New Spain. The *Peninsulares*, who were loyal to Ferdinand and his Bourbon dynasty, were incensed. In September 1808, they unseated Viceroy José de Iturrigaray and installed a provisional government headed by one of their own, Gabriel de Yermo. The long-term plan was to restore Ferdinand to the throne in New Spain, and eventually in Spain as well.

The most prominent leader of the early independence movement was a *Criollo* priest named Miguel Hidalgo y Costilla y Gallaga Mondarte Villaseñor, better known now as Miguel Hidalgo.

A parish priest from the small town of Dolores in the central state of Guanajuato, Hidalgo worked hard to help the poor people around him, teaching grape farming, bee-keeping and the cultivation of silkworms to help them improve economically. He was outspoken in his criticism of *Peninsulare* politics during the famine of 1808 caused by a drought in the grain-rich state of Durango, when they withheld grain from the poor, speculating that their hunger would boost the price of the staple.

Increasingly fed up with the oppressive *Peninsulares*, on the night of September 15, 1810, Hidalgo sent some of his armed followers to the Dolores sheriff's office to free 80 men he felt were unfairly imprisoned. Aware that he was now officially a revolutionary, the following morning at mass he gave a speech that is now reverently referred to as the "Grito de Dolores" (the cry of Dolores) and considered the first Mexican declaration of independence:

My children, a new dispensation comes to us today. Will you receive it? Will you free yourselves? Will you recover the lands stolen 300 years ago from your forefathers by the hated Spaniards? We must act at once. . . . Will you defend your religion and your rights as true patriots? Long live our Lady of Guadalupe! Death to bad government! Death to the *gachupines*!

Gapuchines was a slang term for *Peninsulares*. Immediately, people, including some *Criollos*, but mostly *Mezitos* and *Indios*, rallied to his support and he soon had an army of 800 men. But Hidalgo had no military training, nor did most of his men. About half of them had horses but few had any weapons more effective than a shovel or hoe. Because Hidalgo was a priest and many of his followers, while uneducated, were deeply spiritual, the army had a religious fervor. A rumor started that they were fighting under Ferdinand's auspices, and many believed it, though the Spanish king was unaware of the revolt.

Hidalgo's plan was to march more than 200 miles southeast to Mexico City to confront the *Peninsulare* government. One of his first stops was the ornate Sanctuary of Nuestra Señora de Guadalupe in Atotonilco (now a World Heritage Site frequently called "the Sistine Chapel of Mexico"). He took one of the chapel's portraits of the Virgin Mary, attached it to his lance and used it as a banner to rally his men. He encouraged his men to make their own banners with political statements like: "Long live Ferdinand VII!" and "Death to bad government!"

At first, it was a very successful operation. Hidalgo and his men would come into a town and convince the inhabitants to join them, frequently imprisoning *Peninsulares* and their *Criollo* supporters. By the end of September, Hidalgo's army had captured several towns and numbered 50,000.

But a lack of discipline led to problems. The men began to loot and terrorize the towns they entered. Prisoners were frequently executed without trial. When they reached Guanajuato, the terrified *Peninsulares* and their *Criollo* supporters holed up in the town's massive public grain storage facility. After two days of heavy fighting, Hidalgo's men overwhelmed the defenses and massacred about 600 people, including many women and children.

Hidalgo's problems magnified. Until then, Hidalgo's army had enjoyed a great deal of support from liberal *Criollos*, many of them comparatively wealthy, but the terrorism of the campaign turned a large proportion of them away from his cause. Hidalgo's second-in-command, a *Criollo* army veteran named Ignacio Allende (one of the few of the men with military experience) was outraged and demanded Hidalgo do something. While Hidalgo admitted the massacre was tragic, he excused it by citing historic precedent, pointing out that all revolutions have been encumbered by unnecessary violence.

In October, Hidalgo's men granted him two titles—generalissimo for his rank as military commander and His Most Serene Highness to show his political and religious leadership. He made himself a splendid multi-colored uniform laced with both silver and gold. He marched on Valladolid, a city bigger than any his troops had encountered before, and took it with little struggle. Hidalgo took advantage of his biggest audience yet and railed against the *Peninsulares*, calling them arrogant and accusing them of keeping the rest of the country oppressed economically, politically and spiritually. He said that the goal of his cause was to "send them back to the Motherland." While he was there, Hidalgo settled an old score, forcing his old friend, the Bishop of Valladolid, to rescind the excommunication order against him for heresy, apostasy and sedition on September 24, 1810.

His army stayed in Valladolid for several days, preparing for an assault on the capital. He negotiated with the local priests and promised not to allow the violence his men had visited upon other cities if he could help it. While there, he declared freedom for all slaves and an end to tribute payments to the government by *Indios* and *Mulattos* (a small sub-caste made up of children from *Criollo-Negro* unions).

But when he found that the local cathedral had been locked to keep him and his men out, Hidalgo was outraged. He didn't let his men run wild as they had in Guanajuato, but he did imprison every *Peninsular* regardless of sex or age, replaced everyone in public office with one of his followers, and raided the city's treasury.

• • •

Hidalgo and his men marched on toward Mexico City collecting men, weapons and money in the various towns in his path, but in the rugged forests of Monte de las Cruces, they were intercepted by Royalist forces. Greatly outnumbered, the Royalists retreated, but not before inflicting huge numbers of casualties among the undisciplined, poorly armed mob.

Worse yet, Hidalgo's men were losing the psychological war. He found the *Mestizos* and *Indios* in the Valley of Mexico to be much better off economically than his supporters and mostly loyal to the crown. The new viceroy of New Spain, a career soldier named Francisco Javier Venegas de Saavedra, was aware of the insurrection and took steps to quell it. He mounted a propaganda campaign warning of violence and instability if the rebels were to arrive.

His well-trained soldiers from Veracruz were commanded by Lieutenant Colonel Torcuato Trujillo Sanchez and augmented by some 500 former slaves who had previously worked at de Yermo's estates. After they retreated from their first encounter with Hidalgo's army, Trujillo Sanchez called for help from General Félix María Calleja del Rey. This larger army defeated elements of Hidalgo's men on several occasions, inflicting serious casualties.

Calleja del Rey and Trujillo Sanchez and their 6,000 soldiers chased the 100,000 insurgents around Mexico finally meeting them on January 17, 1811 at Puente de Calderón. At first, the battle seemed to be going in Hidalgo's favor, but a well-aimed cannonball managed to hit and set fire to one of the insurgents' ammunition wagons and the resulting series of explosions killed or wounded many and threw most of the rest into a panic-fueled confusion. About 13,000 insurgents died in the battle. The more disciplined Royalists then had no problem cutting down the fleeing insurgents, guaranteeing victory.

What remained of Hidalgo's army fled north in hopes they would receive aid from the United States, which was supporting anti-colonial movements around the globe. But they didn't get far. They made it to the mountains outside Santiago de la Monclava in Coahuila, but were tracked down while camping out at the *Norias de Baján* (Wells of Baján) near Monclava, Coahuila on March 21, 1811.

Hidalgo and his top aides—Allende, Juan Aldama, José Mariano Jiménez and Mariano Abasolo—were taken prisoner. After a series of short trials, Abasolo was given a life sentence and died in prison. The others were given death sentences and were shot. Before his execution, Hidalgo was defrocked and excommunicated—under Catholic doctrine, this prevented him from going to heaven. When he faced the firing squad on July 27, Hidalgo thanked the jail staff for their kindness, refused the offer of a blindfold and put his right hand over his heart to show the executioners where to shoot.

The four dead men's heads were removed and placed on poles and displayed in the town square of Guanajuato for 10 years as a warning to other would-be revolutionaries.

MORELOS CONTINUES THE FIGHT

Despite huge losses in manpower and leadership, the insurgent movement did not go away; it just went underground led by a series of guerrilla leaders. The first was one of Hidalgo's colonels, José María Teclo Morelos y Pavón (better known to history as José Morelos). Born a poor *mestizo* in Valladolid, Morelos was a 45-year-old parish priest in Cuarácuaro when he heard of Hidalgo's exploits and joined him.

He was a much better general than Hidalgo, winning twenty-two battles and controlling much of the south Pacific coast and New Spain's most important Pacific port, Acapulco. On September 13, 1813, he organized the National Constituent Congress of Chilpancingo, at which of representatives of the various regions he controlled discussed how they would rule after replacing the Spanish colonists. There discussions were summed up in a document called *Sentimientos de la Nación* (Sentiments of the Nation), and declared Mexican independence, established a tricameral government based on that of the United States and named Roman Catholicism as the official state religion. The document called for the confiscation of all property owned by the colonists, the abolishment of all slavery and torture, the dismantling of the caste system and the name "American" be applied to any Mexican-born individual, regardless of their ethnic ancestry.

The document called for Morelos to be head of the new nation with the title *generalissimo*, and to be addressed as "Your Highness." Morelos asked if he could be called "Siervo de la Nación" (Servant of the Nation) instead, and referred to by his name.

At a second meeting on October 22 in Apatzingán, the congress issued *Decreto Constitucional para la Libertad de la América Mexicana* (Constitutional Decree for the Liberty of

Mexican America). Many of the changes—like having a legis-
lative branch stronger than the executive branch—flew in the
face of Morelos' stated aims, but after some military setbacks
that left much of the territory he had previous conquered in
enemy hands, he knew he was in no position to argue.

He was captured in November at a disastrous battle at
Tezmalaca and brought to Mexico City in chains for a quick
trial. Put before a firing squad on December 22, the attending
bishop lifted his excommunication order at the last minute
because he saw Morelos praying on his way to being shot.

CHAPTER 3
A Mexican-born Emperor

Morelos was succeeded by an even more able military strategist in Vicente Ramón Guerrero Saldaña (commonly known as Vicente Guerrero). Born into a wealthy *Criollo* family not far from Acapulco, Guerrero was a gunsmith by trade and an early proponent of independence, joining Morelos when he was 28.

After taking over the reins from Morelos, Guerrero managed to forge strong alliances with separate anti-colonial armies led by Guadalupe Victoria (a nom de guerre for José Miguel Ramón Adaucto Fernández y Félix) and Isidoro Montes de Oca, with himself as supreme commander.

His Royalist counterpart was Agustín Cosme Damián de Iturbide y Aramburu (better known as Agustín de Iturbide), a conservative *Criollo* who had been brutally efficient in hunting down insurgents led by Hidalgo and Morelos. In fact, he was so zealous that he was briefly relieved of command in

1816 for cruelty after he boasted of summarily executing 300 insurgents as part of an 1814 Good Friday celebration and of imprisoning the mothers, wives and children of known insurgents in an effort to get them to lay down their arms. He was also accused of looting, embezzling and otherwise illegally profiting from his campaigns.

He was reinstated in 1820, but never forgot the humiliation of his dismissal. And he was angry that the government had not given him sufficient funds for the task at hand, forcing him to dip into his own fortune and even steal to make up the difference.

After several defeats, de Iturbide began to seriously doubt he would be able to get the better of Guerrero and his hit-and-run guerrilla attacks. And, like many *Criollos*, he was frustrated at being limited in his potential simply because of the place of his birth. King Joseph I of Spain had signed a constitution that limited royal powers in 1812, in effect granting much more autonomy to New Spain, but when Ferdinand VII returned to power, he threw it out. That pleased the *Peninsulares*, but angered many *Criollos* who were getting more anxious for expanded rights, if not outright independence.

So de Iturbide changed his mind and switched sides. His intentions were almost certainly to lead a Criollo independence movement, but he knew he needed the help of the *Mestizos* and *Indios*, who already outnumbered them by a considerable margin. To effect this, he offered Guerrero and his men full pardons if they would lay down their weapons. To nobody's surprise, Guerrero declined, but he did agree to a face-to-face meeting along with Victoria.

Later called the "Embrace of Acatempán" after the town in which it was held, the February 24, 1821 meeting was cordial and agreeable. The Royalist-turned-rebel de Iturbide showed Guerrero and Victoria his plan for independence which he called the *Plan de Iguala* (Plan of Equals).

Despite its name, the *Plan de Iguala* was a semi-Royalist tract that would be seen as exceptionally racist today. The long-term plan was to bring Ferdinand to New Spain and have him rule as king. If he refused or was unavailable, another member of the Bourbon dynasty would be installed on the throne.

To create public support, de Iturbide included three guarantees: New Spain would be renamed Mexico and would be ruled from Mexico City, not Madrid; Roman Catholicism would be the official state religion; and all citizens of Spanish descent would be equal subjects. All Mexicans other than *Peninsulares* and *Criollos* would still be subject to the upper castes, but the insurgents accepted the plan because it promised independence from Spain, an enforcement of Catholicism and, because it did not involve attacking or expelling the wealthy upper classes, would not destroy the current economy.

The insurgent leaders agreed to amalgamate their armies with his under the name of *Ejército de las Tres Garantías* (Army of the Three Guarantees), and march on Mexico City with de Iturbide in command.

They surrounded Mexico City and were pleasantly surprised to see that most of the Royalist forces were sympathetic to their cause and did not fight. On his 38th birthday, September 27, 1821, de Iturbide marched his men under a new red, white and green banner. The following day, the new military rulers issued the official Declaration of Independence, which was signed by Jefe Político Superior Juan O'Donojú y O'Rian, the viceroy (who interestingly, was of Irish descent, though born in Seville).

The new Mexico did not refer to itself as a country or nation, but as an empire. The plan was to offer the crown first to Ferdinand and, if he declined, to his younger brothers Carlos and Francisco, followed by his cousin, the archduke Charles. If they all declined, the new Mexican parliament—or Cortes, no relation to the *conquistadore*—would then designate a ruler of their own choosing.

Not surprisingly, de Iturbide was elected president of the Provisional Governing Junta and he installed a 36-member cabinet made up almost exclusively of his own men, giving the former insurgents almost no voice in the new government. He had, in fact, done something that would have enraged Hidalgo: instead of granting citizenship for all in his new country, de Iturbide had just made things better for his own people, offering almost nothing to non-white Mexicans.

One of his first acts was to offer the post of Emperor to Ferdinand. Of course, Ferdinand refused, and forbade any of his family from taking the crown either. He also rejected the concept of Mexican sovereignty and pointed out that O'Donojú lacked the authority to grant it and even began half-heartedly to plan a reconquest of Mexico.

Rebuffed by the Bourbons, the Cortes looked for a suitable emperor of regal blood among the Mexicans, but found none.

Fearing the de Iturbide might try to take the throne himself, the Cortes reduced the army's influence. This backfired, however, leading to problems in the economy and social unrest when some rebel groups considered the military weakened. With a throng of followers around him, de Iturbide took the crown for himself, in what many now believe to be a coup.

His coronation—on July 21, 1822—was an elaborate affair in which he put the crown on his own head, just as Napoleon had done, gave himself the title of "Prince of the Union" and styled himself Emperor Agustín I of Mexico. He dissolved the Cortes and sent his political enemies to prison.

These actions made him a lot of new enemies. Anti-imperialist movements—called Republicans because of their shared philosophy of deposing Agustín and installing a repub-lic—sprang up all over Mexico. Even the most conservative *Peninsulares* were greatly offended by this commoner (born in Valladolid yet!) who so pompously wrapped himself in emper-or's robes. But most of his enemies were liberal *Criollos* and *Mestizos*, both of which groups wanted something better than a home-grown dictator. With the Mexican empire stretching from present-day Oregon thousands of miles south to what is now Colombia, the political and economic necessities of such a large and diverse country needed deft government, not a self-involved plutocrat.

One of these insurrections, in Veracruz, was led by a char-ismatic army general named Antonio de Padua María Severino López de Santa Anna y Pérez de Lebrón (now generally just called Santa Anna). A shrewd man with a passion for gambling and little reluctance to change sides when he saw a better offer, Santa Anna had been one of Emperor Agustín's early supporters, calling him "El Libertador" (the Liberator), a move that earned him his rank and a nice hacienda. When he saw the emperor's support waning, however, he threw his lot in with the Republicans, joining with Victoria, one of the signators of the *Plan de Iguala*, who was now deeply embittered with Agustín.

When Agustín sent an army to quell Victoria and Santa Anna, he made a huge mistake. He appointed Colonel José Antonio Echavarri Aldai, an old friend of Santa Anna's, as its leader. It was not long before Echavarri changed sides and the combined armies of Echavarri and Santa Anna were reinforced by Victoria's men.

Agustín sent an emissary to Santa Anna, asking him to meet in Mexico City. Fearing an assassination plot, Santa Anna responded with the *Plan de Casa Mata*, which called for an end to the empire and the establishment of a republic with a written constitution. After the widespread distribution of the plan, Guerrero, who was also angry at the betrayal of the man who called himself emperor, came out of hiding to join their cause. Making matters worse for Agustín, the southern provinces of his empire—the states of Guatemala, El Salvador, Honduras, Nicaragua and Costa Rica—declared their independence from Mexico (and Spain) under the name República Federal de Centroamérica (Federal Republic of Central America) and there were armed independence movements in a number of neighboring states.

Santa Anna and his men marched on the capital, facing little serious opposition. The emperor gathered his few remaining loyal troops, but they were badly outnumbered. On May 11, 1823, Agustín signed the document of surrender that also called for his exile. He sailed for Tuscany, but pressure from their Spanish allies forced him to settle in England. The new Mexican congress named him a traitor, but continued to pay him a small pension.

This new congress abolished the Empire and all other preceding documents, and on March 31, 1823, decided that a triumverate, comprising Victoria, Nicolás Bravo and Pedro Celestino Negrete, a *Peninsular*, would lead the country as Supreme Executive Power. Three alternates—Miguel Domínguez, Mariano Michelena and Guerrero—were named to provide insurance.

Over the next year and a half, the triumverate ruled and put together a government. After a year, the *Constitución Federal de los Estados Unidos Mexicanos de 1824* (Federal Constitution of the United States of Mexico) was signed, calling for a presidential election. Victoria won a large majority and named Bravo as his vice-president.

There were no political parties at the time, but all of the elite were Freemasons, and were divided according to the lodge they attended, the Scottish Rite (*los Ecosses*) or the York (*los Yorquinos*). This caused a lot of internal problems and there were many coup attempts, including one led by Bravo (*an Ecosse*) against the Yorquino Victoria.

And President Victoria had other problems to worry about.

The economy was in a shambles, in part due to a Spanish block-ade. After Mexico was recognized by the United Kingdom, the United States and several other countries who became trad-ing partners and were easily powerful enough to challenge the Spanish, things improved. Mexico also joined Simón Bolívar's Pan-American Union, supplying him with financial support in his attempt to free Peru.

Victoria stepped down in 1829 and was replaced by Guerrero. However, neither he nor any of his immediate successors had much luck staying in office. In fewer than 26 years between April 1, 1829 when Guerrero took power until December 11, 1855, the head of state of Mexico changed 46 times. Santa Anna was himself president 11 non-consecutive times in a span of less than 22 years.

WARFRONT

This kind of instability did little to help the economy or to gain Mexico much respect from its neighbors. Until the 1830s, Mexico had enjoyed good relations with the United States. As English-speaking settlers moved westward with the United States' purchase of almost a million square miles of territory from France in 1803, many settled in the Mexican territory of Tejas, or Texas. By 1829, English speakers outnumbered Spanish speakers. Santa Anna, who had abandoned Republican ideals and established a dictatorship, charged extra taxes on English-speaking Texans beginning in 1834, and prohibited any further immigration of English speakers, but they came anyway.

A Texan independence movement under the leadership of Stephen F. Austin emerged and Santa Anna invaded. He won a major victory at the Alamo but, facing a brilliant strategist in General Sam Houston, was utterly routed at the Battle of San Jacinto in 1836. Retreating, Santa Anna realized he was surrounded by Texans and stripped off his lavish uniform before he was captured. Unfortunately, the combination of his silk underwear and an underling referring to him as "El Presidente" led the Texans to realize whom they had as prisoner. They took him to Houston, who guaranteed him a safe trip back to Mexico if he would withdraw all troops from the territory, cease hostilities and recognize the new sovereign nation of Texas. He agreed, but was quickly out of power again.

In 1845, Texas joined the United States. The Americans, who wanted to establish a Pacific coast colony before the British could, sent a representative down to Mexico City to negotiate a purchase of Mexico's northern territories. It didn't go well. Mexico saw four different presidents, six war ministers and 16 finance ministers in 1846 alone. Popular opinion considered the offer an insult to national pride and there were calls for war. The American envoy agreed.

The United States declared war in 1846 and saw rapid success in English-speaking areas of Mexico. Santa Anna, who had been secretly negotiating with the Americans to effect the sale, offered his services to Mexico as a general stating he had no presidential aspirations. Once appointed general, he double-crossed both the Americans and the Mexican government by making himself president again and fighting to retain the territories.

A naval blockade hindered Mexico's economy and it found few allies. Under the leadership of General Winfield Scott, the Americans launched a huge amphibious landing at Veracruz, taking it quickly. They marched to Mexico City, surrounded it and inflicted terrifying casualties. With the capital under siege, a small number of Americans marched to Puebla, but the people there were so frustrated with Santa Anna they surrendered without a fight. After the battle of Chapultepec at which Bravo led his last loyal troops into a massacre (he was taken prisoner), Mexico City was left undefended and occupied by Scott's men. He forced them to sign the Treaty of Guadalupe Hidalgo which allowed the U.S. to purchase what are now California, Nevada, Utah, New Mexico, most of Arizona and Colorado and smaller parts of Oklahoma, Kansas and Wyoming. In great debt both personally and as president, Santa Anna sold more territory to Washington in 1853 when the Americans found a suitable railway route through the extreme northern part of Mexico.

With peace established with the United States, Mexican internal politics were still not reconciled between Republicans and Royalists, now known as Liberals and Conservatives. The Liberals wanted a democratic vote and a reining in of both the church and military, while the Conservatives opposed these ideas and many even desired a return to a monarchy.

By August 1855, even the staunchest Conservatives could no longer abide Santa Anna's corruption and abuse of power, and he was overthrown, exiled to Cuba and tried as a traitor, with his estates handed over to the new government. This led to a series of liberal presidents and one of them, Benito Juárez (Garcia), enacted a law that limited the power of church courts—at the time, many countries had already established a separation of church and state by abolishing church courts. But Archbishop Lázaro de la Garza called the move an attack on the church and rallied the clergy to fight back. Further laws allowing the state to confiscate church lands and to tax some parishes angered the clergy even further.

Although much of the military had been angered by Juárez and his laws (not to mention freezing their pay), the first attack came from an unexpected source. Despite being of indigenous ancestry, General Tomás Mejía was a staunch Conservative who considered himself defender of the faith, and launched a rebellion in the central state of Querétaro. Others soon joined him and the Conservatives captured Mexico City, installing their own president—actually, there were eight in four years—while Juárez ran an opposing liberal government from Veracruz. Juárez and the Liberals eventually retook Mexico City and reunited the government, but conservative rebels, including Mejía, continued to operate for many years.

A SECOND EMPEROR

The economy broken by yet another civil war, Juárez suspended interest payments on Mexico's massive debts to the United Kingdom, Spain and France. That angered the Europeans and

Louis-Napoléon Bonaparte (Napoleon III, president and King of France and nephew of Napoleon I) came up with a plan, unknown to Britain and Spain, to invade Mexico and install an emperor who would answer to France.

In January 1862, fleets from France, Spain and Britain landed at Veracruz. The Americans protested vigorously, but with their own Civil War raging, were powerless to do anything. When the Spanish and British realized the French had bigger ambitions than just getting Juárez to restart interest payments, they left. The French invaded and with the help of local Conservatives marched inland. A small but decisive victory by the local army at Puebla on May 5, 1862 is now remembered each year as the Cinco de Mayo holiday.

But the French prevailed and entered Mexico City on June 7, 1863 after months of bitter fighting. They installed a military junta who established a Second Mexican Empire, offering the crown to Archduke Ferdinand Maximilian Joseph of Austria. The 32-year-old navy officer wasn't a Bourbon, but as a Habsburg-Lorraine, at least he was European royalty. Despite never having visited Mexico or being able to speak Spanish, he accepted from his castle, Miramare, in Italy. He took the name Emperor Maxmilian I and his wife, Princess Marie Charlotte Amélie Augustine Victoire Clémentine Léopoldine of Belgium, became Empress Carlota.

Once installed in Mexico City, Maximilian angered Conservatives by re-enacting many of the reforms of the Juárez government. That didn't appease Juárez and the Liberals, however, who opposed him as a foreign dictator. His government was largely ineffective, relying on French military might to get anything accomplished.

The U.S. Civil War ended during his reign, and American protests became more tangible when they started supplying Juárez and his northern commander, General Porfirio Diaz (Mori) with weapons. It was a clever plan that circumvented international diplomacy as the Americans would place arms and ammunition on the banks of the Rio Grande at what is now El Paso, Texas, declare them officially "lost," then repeat the process after Diaz and his men took the loot back to Mexico.

Further angering the U.S., Maximilian started two new communities between Mexico City and Veracruz—the New Virginia Colony and the Carlota Colony—specifically for former Confederate soldiers, though he later opened them up to immigrants from other European and Latin American countries.

Under heavy pressure from the Americans and needing his army for a clearly imminent threat from Bismarck's Prussia, Napoleon III withdrew from Mexico, advising Maximilian to return to Europe. But the emperor decided to stay, instead sending Carlota to other European capitals and even the Pope to seek aid.

None came. Maximilian escaped Mexico City just before it fell and hid in Santiago de Querétaro. The town was surrounded by rebels and one of Maximilian's men betrayed him and told them of his escape plan. Captured, he was tried and sentenced to death. Although many of the crowned heads of Europe and even progressives like Guiseppe Garibaldi and Victor Hugo sent letters asking Juárez to reconsider, he didn't and Maximilian was executed on June 19, 1867 as an object lesson to would-be invaders.

The Liberal Party held sway after that, but became increasingly less liberal as it evolved. By the time Porfirio Díaz took power for the second time on November 29, 1884 his leadership was obviously a dictatorship and he was king in all but name. He brought a great deal of economic prosperity to Mexico, but also a great deal of oppression. His philosophy of government can be summed up in his famous quote: "A dog with a bone in his mouth neither barks nor bites."

But not every dog had a bone. Soon, revolutionary movements of all types began to coalesce under leaders like Francisco I Madero (González), Pancho Villa (a nom de guerre for José Doroteo Arango Arámbula) and Emiliano Zapata (Salazar). Madero, a wealthy young man who was conservative but not in favor of a dictatorship, decided to run in the 1910 national election as a member of the Progressive Constitutionalist Party— PCP, formerly the Anti-reelectionist Party—even though he knew the vote would be rigged in Diaz's favor.

On the day of the election, Diaz jailed Madero and announced he had won another term by a huge landslide. From jail, Madero wrote his *Plan de San Luis Potosí*, a vague proposal for a more democratic government. The "letter from jail," as it came to be known, inspired revolutionaries all over Mexico.

It didn't take long for Madero's army—conveniently but not always willingly allied with socialist, anarchist and indigenous-rights groups—to defeat the national army in what was called the Mexican Revolution and Diaz was soon deposed. Madero installed himself as interim president on November 11, 1911 and called for new elections.

He actually won by a landslide and enjoyed not only the support of his allies in the revolution, but also the United States. However, his government didn't last long, as Madero's centrist approach pleased neither conservatives nor liberals. Many of his former supporters broke from him and formed new revolutionary movements, including the Colorados and Zapatistas. Fearing another revolution, Madero's commander-in-chief, General Victoriano Huerta staged a coup on February 8, 1913.

Madero and his vice-president José María Pino Suárez were held captive until Huerta and his men decided to exile them. Almost as soon as they were freed, both men were assassinated by members of the *rurales*, a mounted paramilitary group loyal to Huerta. Most Mexicans at the time (and now) believe they were acting under Huerta's command.

In a cynical move to give the new regime a sheen of legitimacy, Huerta announced that foreign minister Pedro Lascuráin (Paredes) would be president—even though Attorney General Adolfo Valles (Ibañez) was actually the legitimate successor. But his reign lasted, by some accounts, as little as 15 minutes and his only act would be to step aside for Huerta, who set up a very repressive military state.

Huerta made few friends internationally, and a strong enemy of President Herbert Hoover, who repeatedly asked him to step down. Relations between the two countries worsened in March 1914 when rebels surrounded Huerta's men in the oil refining town of Tampico on the Gulf Coast. Although the American government agreed at least in principle with the Constitutionalist rebels, they rushed navy ships to the port in an effort to protect and potentially evacuate the many American oil workers there. The first American warship to arrive—and the only one that could navigate the shallow harbor—was the USS *Dolphin*, a small gunboat that had seen action in the 1898 Spanish–American War.

When a few American sailors left the ship to get fuel, they were arrested at gunpoint by Huerta's soldiers. None of the Americans could speak Spanish and none of the Mexicans could speak English, so the incident dragged on. When he found out that at least one of the sailors was arrested on board the *Dolphin*—which technically could be seen as an invasion of U.S. sovereign territory—area commander Rear Admiral Henry T. Mayo demanded the men's release and a formal apology. Mexican officials freed the sailors and issued a written apology, but refused to fly the U.S. flag on Mexican soil, which the Americans had demanded.

Using that as a pretext, Hoover asked Congress to invade Mexico in an effort to dislodge Huerta's regime. While he was waiting for their approval, U.S. intelligence learned of an embargo-breaking arms shipment to Veracruz from Germany. That allowed Hoover to mount an invasion without Congressional assent.

The U.S. sent a number of boats and 2,300 men to Veracruz. They landed without opposition—to crowds of curious Americans and Mexicans lining the beach—and quickly took control of the city. Most of the Mexican military retreated, but about 50 remained loyal to the Huerta cause and a few of the cadets at the Naval Academy tried to defend the building. The Americans prevailed and occupied the city for six months. The two countries were on the brink of war until they called upon the ABC Countries—an alliance of Argentina, Brazil and Chile—to mediate at a special summit in Niagara Falls, Ontario.

The situation became complicated in the north of Mexico as well. There were two major armies fighting Huerta's forces—top Constitutional commander Venustiano Carranza (de la Garza) in the south and Pancho Villa in the north. Villa had been very successful in his drive toward the capital when he received word from Carranza instructing him to divert his attack to a coal-mining town because the southern army needed more coal.

Angered by what he saw as Carranza trying to deprive him of the glory of taking the capital, Villa cut ties with him and declared his movement independent. It was a bold move, and one that would cost him dearly. Previously, Villa had been something of a folk hero on both sides of the border, and many of his band of raiders were English-speaking American volunteers attracted by the romance of the lifestyle and the idea of freeing Mexico from a dictatorship. That image began to fade as news of the violence and excesses not only of his men, but Villa himself, became known. A meeting with General John Pershing convinced the Americans that Villa was the wrong horse to back—for years he had enjoyed moral and material support from the U.S., but the U.S. now chose to side with Carranza.

Most of the American volunteers went back home. With great losses in manpower, supplies and ammunition, Villa's men were routed by forces loyal to Carranza—who had taken over as president after defeating Huerta—at the Battle of Agua Prieta. With just 500 followers left, mostly wandering the desert and foraging for food, Villa decided to launch a raid on the small border town of Columbus, New Mexico.

At about 4:00 a.m., Villa launched a terror attack with his horsemen shooting and shouting. They began to loot and burn private homes. One of Villa's scouts had told him that there were only 30 soldiers garrisoned in Columbus, but there were actually 330 with machine guns. The residents of the town were also well-armed, and Villa sounded the retreat after about 90 minutes of bloodshed.

Villa had lost about half of his men and gained nothing but the ire of the Americans. Pershing led a 10,000-man force into northern Mexico to find him, but had to cut the search short when it became obvious the Americans were going to enter World War I. Villa had some contact with the Germans, who may have been hoping to use him in an effort to open a North American front in their European War, but nothing substantial came of it. Friendless, Villa eventually retired.

THE FALL OF THE PRI

Another old ally of Carranza's who had turned foe was Zapata. A *Mestizo* who is said to have spoken Nahuatl fluently, Zapata split with the Constitutional cause and had his own army—

officially the Liberationalist army, but popularly known as the Zapatistas—who rallied under his phrase: "It's better to die on your feet than to live on your knees." Less disciplined even than Villa's men, in the early part of the revolution, Madero asked him to disarm, but he refused and split with his old ally. As he shot and looted his way through village after village, it has been argued that Zapata's men were more like a gang of bandits than revolutionaries.

They were powerful, particularly in the south. While successive governments (and even Villa) tried to defeat Zapata's army, they had failed, so Carranza's Constitutionalists came up with a cunning plan. General Pablo González (Garza) and his second-in-command, Colonel Jesús Guajardo (Martinez), sent word that they wanted to join Zapata. He was suspicious of their motives, and asked them to prove their loyalty before he would meet face to face with them. González then sent Guajardo to ambush an unsuspecting Constitutionalist convoy. When Zapata saw that Guajardo's men had killed 57 government soldiers, he agreed to a meeting. When Zapata arrived in Chinameca on April 10, 1919, Guajardo's men shot him with dozens of bullets.

Without their charismatic leader, the Zapatistas faded away, although many of his followers later became peacefully involved in Mexican governments.

Back in 1917, Carranza had written a socialist-leaning constitution with the primary goal of decentralizing the power of the church and military, while easing out foreign land ownership. He didn't stay in power long enough to put his plans into action, however, as his minister of war, General Álvaro Obregón (Salido), conspiring with fellow officers Plutarco Elías Calles (Campuzano) and Adolfo de la Huerta (Marcor, no relation to the former president), staged a coup, and killed Carranza on May 21, 1920. Obregón's forces later assassinated Villa as well.

With Zapata, Carranza and Villa all out of the picture, there was no obvious opponent for Obregón and his Partido Laborista Mexicano (Mexican Laborers Party or PLM). Unlike previous presidents with a military background, he worked hard for education, labor rights and land reform. In exchange for his agreement not to nationalize U.S. oil interests on Mexican soil, the Americans recognized his government as legitimate, and much of the world followed suit.

After winning a second term as president in 1928, Obregón was assassinated in a Mexico City restaurant by a Cristero, a group of armed rebels who felt he had robbed the church of too much power. His old ally, Calles, who had been president representing the same PLM party from 1924–1928, formed a new party which would eventually be called the Partido Revolucionario Institucional (Institutional Revolutionary Party or PRI).

A decidedly socialist party, the PRI were called communists by many Americans after squabbles over oil rights and the war in Nicaragua, but negotiations eventually softened relations. Throughout much of the 20th century, the PRI would anger the Americans on issues like Fidel Castro and the Sandinistas, but the two countries normally got along well.

While the founders of the PRI may have once had high

ideals, they became increasingly plutocratic and corrupt over the years, staying in power for 80 years and becoming typical of the single-party rulers throughout much of the developing world.

• • •

Other problems have emerged that affect the national economy and peace. Mexico is a very diverse place, both demographically and geographically. The southern states are distinctly different from the rest of the country. Originally covered in thick rain forests, they are now rich in specialized agriculture and hydroelectric power. Indigenous people, mainly Mayans, are the majority in much of the south with the balance of the population *Mestizo*. This has resulted in a cultural and psychological distance between the south and the federal government which often evolves into contempt. Despite its wealth of natural resources, the southern states are far poorer than the rest of Mexico, and many blame the federal government for this, considering racism to be the real issue.

After the North American Free Trade Agreement (NAFTA), which brought Mexico into the free-trade zone between Canada and the United States, became effective in 1994, the southern economy fell even farther behind the rest of Mexico, fueling even more unrest. By 2007, the GDP per capita in Chiapas was just $3,657, as compared to $23,130 in Mexico City. In the south, houses with running water and electricity were in the minority.

Demonstrations, sometimes violent, broke out all over the south in the late part of the 20th century. In 1968, just 10 days before Mexico was to host the Summer Olympics, a demonstration of 10,000 students and others at Plaza de las Tres Culturas (Square of the Three Cultures) in the Tlatelolco neighborhood of Mexico City erupted in violence. The Mexican military claimed they were returning fire from snipers and opened fire on the crowd. In what is now usually referred to as the Tlatelolco Massacre, estimates of as many as 1,000 died (44 have been confirmed).

One man—Mexican authorities say he is Rafael Sebastián Guillén Vicente, the son of Spanish immigrants to Tampico, but his identity is uncertain—was so shocked by the Tlatelolco Massacre that he dedicated his life to bringing down the Mexican government. Despite growing up wealthy—he described his childhood as being from "a family without financial difficulties"—he became a Maoist militant. He took the name Marcos after a friend of that name who was killed by the Mexican military.

Marcos went to the southern state of Chiapas with the intent of starting a proletarian revolution, but the locals didn't take to his traditional communist rhetoric. He believed the problem was that he was a white, university educated, Spanish-speaking child of privilege and in order to succeed, he would have to become more like the Mayans. He immersed himself in their culture and studied the works of Italian communist philosopher Antonio Gramsci, who maintained that cultural hegemony was the only way to maintain a capitalist society.

Marcos became more popular and his enemy list expanded from the Mexican government to the concepts of capitalism and, especially, neoliberalism—the philosophy that encourages private enterprise, free markets and unfettered trade between nations.

His group, Ejército Zapatista de Liberación Nacional (Zapatista Army of National Liberation or EZLN, but commonly known as the Zapatistas), declared war on the Mexican government on January 1, 1994, the day NAFTA—the most obvious sign of neoliberalism—became law. That day, about 3,000 armed Zapatistas stormed and took control of four county seats in Chiapas, freeing prisoners and setting fire to police and military buildings.

The Mexican military responded the next day and the Zapatistas suffered huge losses and were forced to retreat to the rain forests. On January 12, a ceasefire agreement mediated by influential Bishop Samuel Ruiz Garcia put an end to the armed conflict and the Zapatistas switched to non-violent means of spreading their word.

Not everyone chose to abide by the ceasefire, however. On December 22, 1997, a paramilitary group called the Mascara Roja (Red Mask) loyal to the PRI opened fire on a church in the Chiapas town of Acteal. The worshippers were members of Las Abejas (the Bees), a pacifist religious commune of indigenous people who had openly sided with the Zapatistas, and 45 of them (21 of them women and 15 children) were killed and another 25 injured. No arrests were made.

The south and all of Mexico, found hope for an end to official corruption in a presidential candidate named Vicente Fox Queseda. His father's family were of German origin (Fox was originally Fuchs) who emigrated from France to Cincinnati and eventually Mexico; and his mother was a Basque, born in Spain. A Harvard graduate, Fox started working for Coca-Cola in Mexico, eventually becoming its president. Under his leadership, Coke sales increased by 50 percent in Mexico and became the nation's favorite beverage.

He ran twice for governor of the state of Guanajuato for the Partido Acción Nacional (National Action Party or PAN), losing the first time but getting twice as many votes as his PRI opponent in the second election. Fox immediately delivered on promises of financial transparency and developed innovative micro-credit initiatives.

In 2000, he ran for president under a coalition called *Alianza por el Cambio* (Alliance for Change), which combined the conservative-religious PAN with the Greens. After a vigorous campaign, Fox won the election, which was watched by observers from a number of countries and organizations. When outgoing PRI president Ernesto Zedillo signed the documents ratifying Fox as the new president, it was the first time in Mexican history a government had changed hands without bloodshed.

When Fox's election put the PRI out of power, the Zapatistas met with him. He implemented many reforms and projects in the area, but the Zapatistas continue to work outside the government with autonomous communities and education systems.

The six-foot-five Fox was a charismatic and popular president who typically wore jeans and cowboy boots. After serving six years, his popularity helped lead to the election of another PAN president, Felipe Calderón.

And it was his policies that started the Mexican Drug War.

CHAPTER 4
The Rise of the Drug Cartels

Mexico's history has hard-wired its people to be cynical about government. With single-party rule for 80 of the last 90 years and corruption so rampant that it has amounted to a kleptocracy, many Mexicans are prepared to live and work somewhere outside official channels. The fact that Mexico has a legal system based on civil or Napoleonic law, which allows for trials to be conducted in secret and forces the accused to prove his or her innocence rather than benefiting from a presumption of innocence as exists in common-law jurisdictions, added to the enmity and sometimes outright fear many Mexicans had for their own government.

Years of government instability, incompetence and corruption have led to a terribly underdeveloped economy. In 2009, the GDP per capita in Mexico was $9,100, compared to the United States at $46,442 and Canada at $41,016.

Mexicans are very aware of this disparity in wealth, and in recent years, the number of Mexicans legally migrating to the United States has ranged from 165,000 to 180,000 with far more crossing the border illegally, often at risk to their lives. According to the Pew Hispanic Center think tank, there are about 7 million Mexicans living illegally in the United States, with numbers much lower in Canada, but growing rapidly. Interestingly, Mexico has its own illegal immigration problem as people from other Central American countries often pass through Mexico on their way north, straining its resources.

That wealth disparity and a long shared history have led to some cultural friction between Mexico and its North American neighbors. When rank-and-file Mexicans see Americans and Canadians in person, they are almost always tourists. While the retired tourists in Acapulco, the spring breakers partying at Cancun and the high school kids in Tijuana looking to take advantage of more relaxed drinking laws may all mean well, their obvious shows of wealth and frivolity often appear offensive, or at least condescending to the Mexicans living there.

And history is of great importance. Mexicans are very proud of their ability to fight off invaders, including two attempts by the United States. Commodore Manuel Azueta is regarded as one of the nation's most important heroes by the Mexican military for leading the Naval Academy cadets against the American invasion at Veracruz in 1914. The irony is that he was defending the dictatorship of Victoriano Huerta, a man so despised still that some older Mexicans feel a need to spit every time his name is mentioned. While the last overt

American military action in Mexico was almost 100 years ago, many believe that American meddling helped keep the PRI in power for so long. Some point to how President Bill Clinton issued a $50-billion bailout package to the Ernesto Zedillo government after it had devalued the peso, resulting in an unprecedented economic collapse. Canada also got involved, sending about $1 billion in a currency swap.

THE "CORUPTING MENACE"

Rebellious Chiapas is representative of the southern states—which also include Oaxaca, Tlaxcala, Guerrero, Michoacán, Veracruz, Tabasco, Morelos, Yucatán, Quintana Roo and Campeche. These states are generally more agricultural, more populated by indigenous people and poorer than the rest of the country, although Yucatán, Campeche and especially Quintana Roo benefit economically from tourism.

The arable land there is derived from cleared rain forest and is some of the best in the world. In drier areas, corn is grown, but in the more moist regions melons, avocados, citrus fruits and coffee are all harvested. As the 20th century progressed, many people in the southern states realized they could make more money growing another crop—marijuana.

Smoking many different substances, especially tobacco, has been an important social custom among indigenous Americans well into prehistory and its association with religious leaders indicates that it probably originated from the burning of incense. The *conquistadores* reported back to Spain that the

Mayan priests they encountered often became highly intoxicated from their smoking.

Marijuana is native to south and central Asia and made its way to North America—along with opium—with the migrant workers from China starting in 1849. Hired to work on the railroads to connect the developing west with the prosperous east, the Chinese tended to live together and retain their culture, leading to the establishment of "Chinatowns" in many western American cities.

Many Americans, and even more Mexicans, traveled to Chinatowns for opium and discovered marijuana. At about the same time, pharmaceutical companies in the U.S. and Canada were manufacturing home remedies with marijuana, while Spanish and Portuguese traders had introduced it to South and Central America for recreational use. And there was plenty to be had. Cannabis sativa, known as hemp, was introduced to the United States as a crop for its fiber, which has a variety of uses and is especially good for making rope. It became extremely important to the economy of the United States for making textiles during the Civil War because cotton was in very short supply.

Marijuana did not take off with English-speaking Americans at first. Those who took drugs at the time preferred faster acting options like alcohol and opium. It did, however, become very popular with indigenous people and, even more so, Mexicans. Because of a widespread belief that marijuana made workers lazy, a few laws were passed in counties around the western United States and Canada banning its use or at least its use on the job. But where marijuana smoking was popu-lar—especially among miners and railway workers—the laws were mostly ignored. Opium was outlawed in San Francisco in 1875 as many politicians blamed Chinese immigrants there for corrupting the local youth. Many also called for the banning of marijuana.

Throughout the late 19th century and into the 20th cen-tury, marijuana use increased dramatically among non-white and non-English-speaking Americans, and as the Mexican Revolution increased immigration from the south with Mexicans fleeing violence, more marijuana smokers arrived.

Marijuana smoking usually fell under the radar of most Americans—who generally considered it one of many habits particular to minorities—until politicians realized they could make hay of it. In 1914, a violent bar fight broke out in El Paso between a Mexican and a Texan. After police determined that the Mexican, who had started the fight, was under the influence of marijuana, politicians banned it from the city. Other southern cities and towns followed suit, calling marijuana a "corrupting menace." The drug received further bad publicity when it was associated with Pancho Villa and his raiders at Columbus, New Mexico. The popular song "La Cucuracha" was written about his men and their habit of smoking marijuana.

THE WAR ON DRUGS BEGINS

The prohibition of alcohol in North America began in the Canadian Province of Prince Edward Island in 1901 and by

1920 every other province and American state had followed suit. For a brief period, the entire North America north of the Rio Grande—except Quebec, which overturned prohibition almost immediately after passing the legislation—was dry. A few former drinkers turned to marijuana (mainly jazz musicians and other bohemian sorts), but in the national consciousness of the day, marijuana was inexorably associated with Mexicans and Chinese, and believed to have terrifying effects. As late as 1927, *The New York Times* ran an article headlined "Mexican Family Goes Insane" blaming marijuana smoking for one family's eccentric and criminal behavior.

In Canada, however, a well-publicized report of soldiers smoking marijuana led to a backlash against the drug and it was made illegal in 1923 when it was added to the *Opium and Drug Act of 1911*. It could still be prescribed by physicians until 1932.

In 1930, during the Depression, President Herbert Hoover created the Federal Bureau of Narcotics (the forerunner of the Drug Enforcement Agency, or DEA), which oversaw recreational drugs other than tobacco and alcohol. Its first chief, Harry J. Anslinger, called for severe punishment for drug users and for the criminalization of marijuana. He had powerful allies. Newspaper magnate William Randolph Hearst, who published many stories warning against what he claimed were the horrific results of smoking what he and the U.S. government called "marihuana," the original Spanish spelling. People such as financier Andrew Mellon and companies like Du Pont Chemicals lobbied congress against hemp, associating it with marijuana and promoting rival products like Du Pont's own nylon.

In 1937 Anslinger drafted a bill that was introduced by

North Carolina Democrat Robert L. Doughton called the *Marihuana Tax Act*. Against the opposition of Dr. William C. Woodward, head of the American Medical Association, and New York City Mayor Fiorello LaGuardia, both Republicans, the Democrat-led Congress approved the bill and President Franklin D. Roosevelt, a Democrat, signed it into law. It didn't technically criminalize marijuana, but applied a tax on the sale of marijuana and hemp with violators liable to a fine of $2,000 or five years' imprisonment. The only way to legally sell, acquire or even possess marijuana was to buy a Marihuana Tax Stamp from the state government. However, the stamps were extremely difficult to acquire and even just applying for one opened the applicant to investigation.

The first arrest under the *Marihuana Tax Act* came on October 2, 1937, the day after the law took effect. At the Lexington Hotel in Denver, Colorado, police witnessed otherwise unemployed 58-year-old Samuel L. Caldwell sell two marijuana cigarettes to Moses Baca and arrested both men. Judge Foster Symes took a harsh approach, stating:

> I consider marijuana the worst of all narcotics, far worse than the use of morphine or cocaine. Under its influence men become beasts. Marijuana destroys life itself. I have no sympathy with those who sell this weed. The government is going to enforce this new law to the letter.

Caldwell was sentenced to four years' hard labor at Leavenworth Penitentiary, and Baca received 18 months in prison.

Most Americans still considered marijuana a Mexican problem, only affecting them if and when they dealt with Mexicans. That perception changed on September 1, 1948. Unknown to most of their fans, many Hollywood actors and actresses were smoking marijuana regularly. Many acquired the habit during World War II as traditional opium and heroin routes from Asia were cut off while marijuana grown in Mexico was plentiful and accessible. The Los Angeles police mounted a sting operation in Hollywood. Word leaked out and the only well-known celebrities arrested were leading man Robert Mitchum and his girlfriend, promising young actress Lila Leeds, who missed a phone call that would have warned them. He spent 50 days behind bars, she was sentenced to 60.

Although Leeds' career never recovered (she made one anti-drug film in 1949, then left Hollywood and took up heroin), Mitchum's took off. Audiences liked his bad-boy image and his bravado—he told reporters that prison was "like Palm Springs, but without the riffraff." His career reached new heights and so, perhaps not coincidentally, so did marijuana use among non-Hispanic Americans.

Marijuana arrests in the United States increased by 77 percent from 1948 to 1951. After Dr Harris Isbell, director of research at the Public Health Service Hospital in Lexington, Kentucky, testified before Congress that marijuana was not addictive and did not lead to violence or sexual depravity, Anslinger changed course and lobbied that marijuana—even if not dangerous in and of itself—was a "gateway" to harder drugs like heroin and cocaine. The government agreed, passing the

Boggs Act in 1952 that quadrupled mandatory sentencing for marijuana possession and sales, and increased them again with the *Narcotics Control Act of 1956*, also known as the *Daniel Act*.

NIXON'S WAR ON DRUGS

Public, medical and academic attitudes toward drugs, particularly marijuana, changed profoundly in the 1960s. In 1971, the National Commission on Marijuana and Drug Abuse drafted a report that indicated that the laws had not worked to decrease drug addiction or levels of use, and recommended the decriminalization of marijuana. President Richard Nixon refused even to read the report, however, naming drugs to be the nation's top enemy (even though the military was still involved in the southeast Asian conflict) and declaring a "War on Drugs."

His theory was that by using military and paramilitary forces to seal its borders, the U.S. could stem the flow of drugs into the country, reducing use. Billions of dollars and many lives were spent on this controversial policy. Of course, marijuana was just one of many illegal drugs—and one few considered addictive or dangerous any more—but it was included anyway.

In 1986, the RAND Corporation think tank put together a study that concluded that the concept and practice of interdiction did virtually nothing to stem the flow of drugs into the country. Another 1994 study by the same group indicated that the War on Drugs actually helped organized crime by pushing drug prices up.

Still, both the United States and Canada retained it as their policy against illegal drugs, but President Barack Obama decided to retire the phrase "War on Drugs" when he was elected in 2008.

Public attitudes toward marijuana have softened considerably over the years and the individual American states and Canadian provinces have enacted legislation or ruled judiciously to reflect this. In 2007, Ontario ruled that criminal prosecution for small amounts of marijuana was unconstitutional. Justice Norman Edmonson said that, "there is no offence known to law which the accused have committed," meaning that while growing and selling marijuana in Canada is still illegal, purchasing it and possessing it is not. While that may sound like hypocrisy, the theory is that drug dealers are breaking the law, not drug users. After that landmark ruling came a flood of states and provinces changing their attitudes toward the drug. By 2011, although actual decriminalization for small amounts of marijuana for personal use was still rare, law enforcement in all of Canada and the more densely populated parts of the United States stopped charging people for possession of small amounts of marijuana.

As it has been since the Pancho Villa days, most of the marijuana in the United States and Canada comes from Mexico, with a significant amount also from farms on American soil cultivated by Mexican nationals. The DEA also claims that at least 90 percent of the cocaine entering the United States comes through Mexico and that Mexico is also the biggest exporter of methamphetamine.

The most obvious problem with the War on Drugs concept is the border between the United States and Mexico. It is almost 2,000 miles long and much of it passes through wilderness, mountains and desert, making it nearly impossible to defend. Damming and irrigation have reduced much of the Rio Grande to a trickle and, in spots, it is easily forded by foot. There are about 250 million border crossings annually and the U.S. Department of Immigration estimates about 5 million illegal entries into the United States from Mexico each year. There is even a professional class of border-crossing experts called coyotes or *polleros* (chicken farmers).

Illegal crossings are often dangerous. Migrants must face American Border Patrol and Immigration officers, who round up and return as many as they can, as well as dehydration and exposure to the elements. U.S. officials recovered the bodies of 417 illegal crossers in 2009. The Mexican government stopped publishing such figures after finding 499 dead would-be crossers on their side in 2000. In 2007, a purpose-built morgue in Tucson, Arizona had to add refrigerated trucks to handle the overflow of corpses.

But still they keep coming, in rising numbers. The primary reasons for this Mexican diaspora are economic. With wages for even the most menial jobs in the United States far higher than just about any job in Mexico, many younger workers in a wide array of occupations migrate north for work. Compounding this is the fact that many American businesses and individuals routinely hire undocumented workers to save on wages, benefits and paperwork. In fact, large swaths of the American and Canadian economies rely on undocumented workers.

MEXICO JOINS THE COCAINE TRADE

Anslinger may have been wrong about marijuana use being a gateway to harder drugs for users, but if he was talking about traffickers, he was right. Of course, the real money for traffickers isn't in marijuana, but in cocaine. Cocaine is derived from the coca leaf, which is native to the Andes Mountains of South America. Indigenous people in the area chewed the leaves as a stimulant and its use became widespread as the Incas—an indigenous empire not unlike that of the Aztecs—cultivated it as a trade crop. When the Spanish *conquistadores* arrived, they scoffed at coca, but soon came to embrace it, often smoking it with tobacco.

Pharmaceutical cocaine use became widespread as a stimulant and tonic. And, as many people are aware, the iconic American soft drink Coca-Cola actually contained cocaine from 1886 until 1903. Cocaine fell into disrepute for many of the same reasons marijuana did, but the tales of addiction and erratic behavior were far more grounded in fact. It was outlawed in the United States in 1914.

Demand for cocaine rose steadily and it has become the second-most-consumed illegal drug after marijuana for generations. For most of that time, the high price of cocaine meant it was used only by the relatively well off. But in 1984, police in Miami began intercepting a new form of cocaine. Called crack because of the sound it makes when it's cooking, this new type of cocaine offers the same high as traditional powdered cocaine, but at a tiny fraction of the price. For the first time in history, people could get a coke high for as little as $5 a pop.

Crack quickly spread to New York City and then Los Angeles, becoming immensely popular in a very short time. This demand—which still exists today, but generally in smaller cities and towns—fueled a tremendous increase in cocaine importation from South America and violent crime in North American cities, as gangs fought over territory that was suddenly incredibly profitable.

Coca is traditionally cultivated in a number of South American countries—Bolivia and Peru among others—but the biggest producer has traditionally been Colombia, which is also where virtually all cocaine was processed. The coke was then shipped from Colombia's north coast, primarily to Miami, from where it was distributed throughout North America.

The U.S. Drug Enforcement Agency (DEA) and Coast Guard became adept, however, at intercepting the boats and aircraft the Colombian cartels sent across the Caribbean, and cocaine shipments to Florida were slowed considerably from the 1980s to the '90s. The Colombians were forced to look for another route. Because Mexicans had long been funneling marijuana to the United States overland though California, Arizona and Texas, it made sense to hire them to take cocaine along the same route.

At the time, the Colombian cartels—particularly the Cali, Medellin and Norte de Valle—were incredibly powerful within their own country. In an effort to bolster their power, the cartels strove to destabilize the government—which had been fighting a war against a number of rebel groups since the 1960s. They routinely killed or kidnapped police, prosecutors and judges in efforts to intimidate the state into leaving them to conduct their business without interference.

In the middle 1980s, the most visible of these cartels was the Medellin, led by the notorious Pablo Escobar. He supported an opposition party, the Nuevo Liberalismo, and its leader, Senator Luis Carlos Galán. Escobar was hired as a deputy to Congressman Alberto Santofimio, but his notoriety forced Galán to dismiss him, and the Nuevo Liberalismo party later aligned with the War on Drugs.

Rebuffed, Escobar threw his weight behind the *Movimiento 19 de Abril* (19th of April Movement or M19), a guerrilla group supporting the ideals of Simón Bolívar, including national self-sufficiency, pan-Latin American unity and an end to government. With the gradual weakening and eventual collapse of the Soviet Union, rebel groups everywhere lost their primary source of revenue and weapons, and the M19 saw the Medellin Cartel as a suitable financial backer. For their part, Escobar and his group won a great deal of public support and sowed unrest with the government by providing work, healthcare and school supplies for people who could not have otherwise afforded them.

THE FIRST MEXICAN DRUG LORD

At the time that the Colombians turned to the overland route, there were no powerful cartels in Mexico, but there was a Godfather. Born in 1946 in the Pacific coast city of Culiacán, Sinaloa, Miguel Ángel Félix Gallardo sold chicken and sausages from his bicycle as a boy. After school, he became a Federale (officer of the Mexican national police) before being hired as a bodyguard for Sinaloa's PRI governor, Leopoldo Sanchez Celis, in the late 1960s despite carrying just 160 pounds on his six-foot-two frame.

Another of Sanchez Celis' bodyguards was Pedro Avilés Pérez. He is considered by many to be the first true Mexican drug lord, after taking over his old family business which had begun with smuggling alcohol (and some marijuana) into the U.S. during prohibition. He became Félix Gallardo's mentor. Not only did Avilés Pérez control much of the flow of marijuana and heroin into the United States well into the 1970s, he brought innovations to the business like using airplanes to carry drugs and widespread bribery of officials. Félix Gallardo's primary responsibility under Avilés Pérez was to bribe and/or intimidate police and other government officials.

When Avilés Pérez was killed in a shootout with Federales in 1978, Félix Gallardo assumed the reins of his organization and soon controlled virtually all drug trade to the United States through the border city and popular tourist destination Tijuana. He earned the nickname "El Patrino" (the Godfather).

Félix Gallardo had been known by the DEA for years, but they didn't have any idea of the extent of his operations and how much protection he was afforded by the PRI government until 1984. They sent an undercover agent—Enrique Camarena, a former U.S. Marine, police officer and firefighter—to infiltrate the organization. He was quickly very successful, befriending Félix Gallardo and sending information back to the United States. Camarena's nickname was

Kike, a diminutive of Enrique pronounced KEE-kay, but he is often referred to as "Kiki" in mainstream media, although that's a feminine version of the same name.

What he reported allowed the DEA to convince the Mexican Army to launch an operation against Rancho Búfalo, a 2,500-acre marijuana farm with more than 3,000 employees and annual production of $8 billion. With 450 men supported by helicopter gunships, the farm was taken down and the product destroyed.

Félix Gallardo sent word that finding the rat was of utmost importance and Camarena was kidnapped along with his pilot, Alfredo Zavala Avelar, in early February 1985. Their tortured, decomposed bodies were found a month later in the southern state of Michoacán.

The DEA began an investigation and the identity of the kidnappers surprised them. "We determined that the individuals who took Camarena off the street were law enforcement personnel," said then-DEA administrator Jack Lawn. "That was particularly galling to me and to law enforcement agents throughout the nation, because when you send an agent overseas, he has an in-house support mechanism, and that is a fellow law enforcement officer. When the system becomes so corrupt that the law enforcement community in the host country upon which you depend is part of the problem, then nothing is safe."

Shortly afterwards, the Federales informed the DEA that they had five Jalisco state police officers in custody. Under interrogation, they implicated themselves in the kidnapping, giving written statements about their involvement. One of the suspects mysteriously died during interrogation. The Federales arrested 11 more men based on the information from the Jalisco cops, and issued warrants for two of Félix Gallardo's lieutenants, Rafael Caro Quintero, who was already wanted by the DEA for a money-laundering scheme in San Diego, and Ernesto Fonseca Carrillo. Caro Quintero (who many believed paid the Federales to kill Avilés Pérez, facilitating Félix Gallardo's rise to power) was discovered by DEA agents in Costa Rica and extradited to Mexico. Under interrogation, Caro Quintero cracked, admitting to his part in the kidnapping, but said he was unaware of who killed the men and that he was shocked and dismayed to learn that they had been tortured.

Fonseca Carrillo and his right-hand man Samuel Ramirez Razo surrendered after the Mexican Army surrounded Fonseca Carillo's villa in Puerto Vallarta. They both admitted their roles in Camarena's kidnapping, but denied involvement with Zavala Avelar's abduction—which they had already established had happened a few hours after Camarena's—or either death.

After a lengthy investigation, the DEA and FBI located the house in Guadalajara in which the men had been tortured and determined that the Mexican government possessed audio tapes of their interrogation. The Mexicans reluctantly turned over the tapes and the Americans arrested and extradited Caro Quintera's bodyguard Javier Vásquez Velasco, who participated in Camarena's kidnapping and later killed two American tourists believing them to be DEA agents, along with Humberto

Álvarez Machaín, a doctor they alleged kept Camarena alive so that his torture would be prolonged.

The DEA came away from the Camarena investigations with a new understanding of how corrupt the Mexican officials were. "The Mexican government knew what happened, and it became more clear to us that the government of Mexico indeed was covering up the assassination, the killing of Kike Camarena," said Lawn. "When we [asked them about finding the body], they said, 'Well, we have Mexican officers killed all the time. You may never get the body back.' So then, we began to get information. We found a body here, we found a body there, we found another body here. They were finding bodies left and right—none of which were the right bodies. And they said, 'We know that Camarena is at this particular site.' But [it] was not at the site. 'And we found him, he was found by a Mexican peasant in a gully.' The body had not been eaten by insects. We knew it [had been] buried. We were able to have the FBI laboratory tell us about soil samples, where the body had been buried. There was no cooperation. We then asked for the clothing that Kike had on. That was all destroyed. The destruction of evidence was everywhere."

GALLARDO ESTABLISHES THE CARTELS

Because of the massive loss of product and manpower after the Rancho Búfalo raid, Félix Gallardo turned to other sources of revenue. He made friends with Honduran cocaine trafficker Juan Ramón Matta Ballesteros, who had been instrumental in helping his business partner, General Policarpo Paz García, seize control of the country and name himself president in what has since been called the 1978 Cocaine Coup and which supported the anti-Sandanista government Contras in Nicaragua. Matta Ballesteros then introduced Félix Gallardo to Escobar.

Soon, Félix Gallardo was using the effective infrastructure he had put together to move marijuana and heroin into the United States to traffic huge quantities of cocaine. This presented a number of problems for the DEA. The agency's efforts were still aimed primarily at the Colombians and their traditional trafficking routes headed toward Miami over the Caribbean. Overland border crossings are much harder to intercept and control. With 250 million legal border crossings a year (not to mention the illegal ones), determining which vehicle or pedestrian is carrying drugs poses a massive challenge. Making things worse was the fact that relatively tiny amounts of cocaine could be smuggled over the border profitably, while to get the same revenue that a far larger, more conspicuous amount of marijuana would be required.

At first, Félix Gallardo was paid in cash, with literally planeloads of currency landing in Mexico. But as the partnership progressed, he began to demand payment in product. The Colombian cartels—weakened by arrests, including many extraditions to the United States, and infighting—had little choice but to comply, as the DEA's more sophisticated technology and tactics made the Caribbean route increasingly dangerous. This new arrangement allowed Félix Gallardo to become a cocaine baron in his own right, with up to 50 percent of the entire product moving through his channels—instead of being a mere organizer of drug mules, he was a true drug lord like the Colombians.

Aware that he was in the DEA's crosshairs, Félix Gallardo took measures to reduce his profile. In 1987, he moved his family to back Culiacán and set up a summit meeting with all of the area gang leaders who worked for his organization in Guadalajara. This led to the DEA calling his group the Guadalajara Cartel. He told them that he was dividing his territory among them and that, although he was no longer taking an active role in the daily workings of the business, he was still the boss and that they would have to pay him tribute.

He gave his oldest and most lucrative territory, the Tijuana route, to his nephews, the Arellano Félix brothers as the Tijuana Cartel. The second-best route, which links Juárez to El Paso, went to Amado Carrillo Fuentes (who had a fleet of twenty-seven Boeing 727 jetliners ferrying drugs into Mexico and cash out) and his family as the Juárez Cartel. The Sonora crossing south of Arizona was granted to Miguel Caro Quintero, Rafael Caro Quintero's younger brother, as the Sonora Cartel. Juan García Ábrego was given control of the Matamoros crossing to Brownsville and Laredo, Texas, as the Gulf Cartel. The final area, between Tijuana and Sonora was given to Joaquín "El Chapo" (Shorty) Guzmán Loera and Ismael Zambada García as the Sinaloa Cartel because that's where they were based. This is sometimes also referred to as the Pacific Cartel. To maintain control, Félix Gallardo kept the management of relations with the top men in Colombia to himself, naming

Héctor "El Güero" (the Blond) Palma Salazar as his second-in-command and the nominal head of the Guadalajara Cartel, an umbrella group that oversaw the rest.

Back in his hometown of Culiacán, Félix Gallardo did not exactly live quietly. He was a local celebrity and his exploits were often celebrated in local *narcocorridos*. He was known to be a close friend of PRI governor Antonio Toledo Corro, and was photographed with him at various events. It has been alleged that Félix Gallardo stayed at Toledo Corro's residence, but he denies that. For the record, Corro has not been charged with any wrongdoing.

Félix Gallardo's men operated without hindrance from law enforcement and the entire state of Sinaloa saw murder rates skyrocket after he returned. "For years, we have lived under the reign of the machine gun," said Norma Corona Sapien, director of the Human Rights Commission of Sinaloa. "The narcos thought they had protection and could act with impunity, so that's what they did, kidnapping and raping young girls, getting into drunken fights on the street, killing each other and generally acting as if they owned the city."

Late in 1987, Francisco Labastida Ochoa was elected governor of Sinaloa. Despite being a member of the PRI—his great-grandfather had fought in the Mexican Revolution and his grandfather had also been governor—he campaigned on a law-and-order, anti-drug platform. While campaigning he received numerous death threats and two assassination attempts, and after taking office, he worked to rid the state police of corruption. "When the new administration took over in 1987, we found some police commanders to be [traffickers]," Eduardo Aispuro Beltrán, a spokesman for the Sinaloa police told *The New York Times*. "It was the most incredible and intolerable thing to find the police body to be completely infiltrated by narcos."

After a long investigation and at the instigation of the DEA and PRI President Carlos Salinas de Gortari, Labastida Ochoa sent in Mexican Army troops to arrest Félix Gallardo on April 8, 1989. A week later, they interrogated all 300 members of the Culiacán police force. Seven of its commanders were charged with corruption, and as many as 90 officers fled the area after questioning. Toledo Corro was questioned and admitted that he was Félix Gallardo's friend, but had no idea that there were outstanding warrants for his arrest or that he had any connection to crime.

Félix Gallardo would not be extradited to the United States—where he was wanted for the deaths of Caramena and Zavala Avelar—because of Mexico's policy of not extraditing to countries where the accused could potentially face the death penalty. In a Mexican court, he was sentenced to 40 years in prison for kidnapping, murder, drug trafficking, racketeering and other charges. An investigation by American journalists determined that Félix Gallardo was still operating as a key player from inside prison by cell phone until he was transferred to a purpose-built maximum-security prison in 1992. His website (http://www.miguelfelixgallardo.com) is still operational and portrays him as an upstanding citizen and shrewd businessman who was unfairly accused and imprisoned. It provides updates on his failing health and even has a forum where people can ask his advice. They write respectfully and always address him as "Don Miguel."

RIVALRY AMONG THE CARTELS

Without Félix Gallardo's steady hand at the helm, the individual cartels began to operate independently and tensions rose steadily, especially where territories overlapped. This was a particular problem between the Tijuana Cartel and the Sinaloa Cartel. The Sinaloans' original territory was defined as the crossings between Mexico and California other than Tijuana. That region is largely desert and mountain with just two official border crossings—one at the small city of Tecate, Baja California, that abuts an almost unpopulated part of the United States, and the other at the medium-size city Mexicali across the border from the small city of Calexico—neither of which offers a quick or easy route to distribution centers or rich markets like San Diego and Los Angeles. With the strong Sonorans to the east of them, the Sinaloans turned to Tijuana to expand their territories, often resorting to gunfights with those loyal to the Arellano Félix brothers. There was a feeling among many in the Mexican underworld that the Arellano Félix brothers were a weak link in the organization because they had simply inherited their territory, which bred a great deal of resentment among their peers, while other leaders had proven their stripes and were elevated to capos on merit.

But they were more than willing to defend what was theirs. And they were an eccentric bunch, even by the standards of drug lords. Seven brothers born between 1949 and 1969 (along with four sisters, two of whom, Alicia and Enedina, were also involved with the business), the Arellano Félixes divided up their responsibilities based on each brother's skill set.

The leader was the handsome Benjamín "El Min," born in 1952, who was arrested in Downey, California in 1982, but escaped and made it back to Mexico. Carlos, a trained surgeon born in 1955, and Eduardo, who also attended medical school, was born in 1956 and reputed to be the smartest of the brothers, handled money-laundering and other financial matters. At 220 pounds with a mean streak, Ramón "El Commandante Món," born in 1964, was the organization's primary enforcer. He carried a gold-plated handgun and a fake Federale ID and badge with him at all times. The youngest brothers Luis Fernando, born in 1966, and Francisco Javier "El Tigrillo" (the Little Tiger), born in 1969, helped the others and learned the ropes. The oldest, Francisco Rafael, born in 1949, was perhaps the most interesting of them all. A flamboyant cross-dresser who had been arrested in San Diego and in Mexico, Francisco Rafael brokered deals with police and government officials at his disco, Frankie O's, surrounded by his five houses on Avenida Tiburón Ballena in Mazatlán's tourist district. At its peak, the Tijuana Cartel was reported by *Time* magazine to have paid out about $1.5 million in bribes a week.

While most members of crime organizations came from very poor backgrounds or were family members who had been enriched only by crime, the Tijuana Cartel recruited bored, middle-class youth from both Tijuana—many of them former police and military veterans—and San Diego across the border, aligning themselves with existing gangs in both cities. The brothers called these new recruits "narco-juniors" and they represented a drastic departure from traditional Mexican drug traffickers. "Some of those juniors went to school here in the United States," Heidi Landgraff, a group supervisor for a San Diego DEA unit told PBS. "Some spoke English well. They dressed very nicely. They are not tattooed individuals like someone in a gang. So they could be sitting next to you in a restaurant, and you wouldn't know."

Typical of them were the 30th Street Gang from the heavily Mexican Logan Heights neighborhood of San Diego. Originally a car enthusiast club, the members of the 30th Street Gang started selling marijuana and later cocaine to help fund their car customizations, and by the early 1980s were associated with a number of gangland assassinations in San Diego. They often traded heavy weapons—usually unavailable in Mexico—for cocaine.

THE TIJUANA CARTEL PUSHES BOUNDARIES

As long as there has been organized crime in Mexico, murder has been a weapon. Before the Tijuana Cartel rose, however, murder was generally considered a last choice, used only in times of extreme urgency. The Arellano Félix brothers changed that, routinely killing anyone who crossed them, especially dealers from rival cartels. Ramón and his men used terrifying methods like the Colombian necktie (a punishment for informants in which the victim's throat is slit and his tongue pulled through the wound), suffocating victims with clear plastic bags, beheadings, submersion in acid and *carne esada* (roasted meat), in which bound victims would be thrown alive on piles of flaming tires. "Wherever there is danger, that's where you'll find Ramón," a former narco-junior, Alejandro Hodoyán Palacios, told Mexican magazine *Proceso*. "In 1989 or '90, we were at a Tijuana corner without anything to do and he told us, 'Let's go kill someone. Who has a score to settle?' Cars would pass and he'd ask us whom we knew. The person we pointed out would appear dead within a week." Often the narco-juniors would wear Federale uniforms and have sirens in their cars to make abductions easier.

In 1992, when a dealer affiliated with the Sinaloans who had traveled through their territory received a package containing his wife's head packed in dry ice, it looked to many as though the two cartels were on the verge of all-out war.

Sinaloa chief Guzmán Loera called a summit meeting. The Arellano Félix brothers agreed to let Sinaloans through their territory in Tijuana for a considerable cut of their revenues and asked for unfettered access to the Mexicali–Calexico crossing as well. Although the sides appeared to part amicably, on November 8, 1992, Guzmán Loera sent a small army of men dressed as Federales to a disco in Puerto Vallarta owned by a friend of the Arellano Félixes while he knew the brothers were there. Their attack killed 19 people, including eight Tijuana Cartel members, but as soon as the shooting started, the brothers dashed for the men's room and escaped by climbing from a sink to the roof through a skylight. Published reports said that the brothers struggled to get Ramón's sizable gut through the small opening.

Their retaliation was bungled. On May 24, 1993, in the parking lot of Guadalajara International Airport, a number of gunmen ambushed a white Mercury Grand Marquis they were told contained Guzmán Loera. They opened fire and killed both of the car's occupants and five innocent bystanders. The man they believed to be Guzmán Loera was actually Cardinal Juan Jesús Posadas Ocampo.

In such a devoutly Catholic country as Mexico, the gunning down of a cardinal was too much for authorities to sweep under the rug. Francisco Rafael, the most visible and approachable of the brothers, was arrested on weapons charges and linked to the murder. To secure his release, published reports say Benjamín handed over $10 million in cash and two 30th Street Gang members, Juan "Puma" Vasconez and Juan "Spooky" Torres Méndez, to Mexican authorities. He then expelled the Logan Heights men from Mexico, but continued to do business with them across the border. U.S. authorities later arrested nine more 30th Street Gang members in San Diego in connection with the assassination, and when the case was re-opened in Mexico after the PRI lost power, a childhood friend of the cardinal's testified that he had been warned that he was in great danger by high-ranking members of the PRI government. Many Mexicans have told me that they believe that the government intentionally led the Tijuana Cartel to believe that Posadas Ocampo was Guzmán Loera, in effect setting up his assassination.

Business proved more important than revenge to both cartels and they were soon working together again under a rarely broken truce. They were moving so much product that they were overwhelming legal border crossings. Taking a page from the other cartels—particularly the Sonorans—both the Tijuana and Sinaloa Cartels turned the bulk of their trafficking operation to illegal border crossings. Large numbers of Mexicans migrating over the border illegally were then convinced—either by money or threats—to carry drugs with them.

CHAPTER 5
Enemies of the State

The first indication that the Mexican cartels would face difficulty—and perhaps the first move that started the process that became the Mexican Drug War—occurred on March 23, 1994. Crime was rampant, the economy was tanking and discontent with the PRI was growing. The Mexican constitution states that a president may not serve two consecutive terms and tradition states that the outgoing president name his successor. Outgoing president Carlos Salinas de Gortari appointed Social Development Secretary Luis Donaldo Colosio Murrieta as his choice, telling reporters "Don't be confused, the candidate is Colosio."

Colosio Murrieta was unlike any PRI presidential candidate in memory. He campaigned actively all over Mexico—"as though he had a chance of losing," said one Mexican journalist. Handsome and well-spoken, Colosio Murrieta revitalized the party and was a popular candidate. He made a campaign stop in a poor, crime-ridden neighborhood of Tijuana—something unheard of previously—and in the middle of a crowd of thousands, a man lifted a nickel-plated handgun a few inches from his face and shot him through his brain.

The man who killed him was Mario "Alberto" Aburto Martínez, a failed academic from Michoacán who was working in a factory assembling low-quality clock radios for the now-defunct Audiomatic company. Aburto Martinez refused to talk and an official investigation determined he worked alone, killing Colosio Murrieta because he was enraged by his lot in life. Perhaps more important, the legendary muckraking journalist Jesús Blancornelas, a sworn enemy of both PRI corruption and the cartels, conducted his own three-year investigation, including interviewing Aburto Martinez in prison, and concluded that although there were major inconsistencies in the government investigation, Aburto Martinez had indeed worked alone.

But that did not matter to most Mexicans. Rumors abounded. Conspiracy theories like those surrounding the John F. Kennedy assassination surfaced, focusing on a second shot many claim to have heard. So deeply ingrained is mistrust of the government that many academics and journalists have all disagreed, pointing their fingers variously at the PRI, who they claim were afraid Colosio Murrieta was making too many concessions, the opposition PAN party who feared his charisma would make him unbeatable, and Federales anticipating a crackdown on corruption or the cartels for his anti-crime platform.

No matter why Colosio Murrieta was killed, it changed things in Mexico. The PRI scrambled to find a suitable replacement, naming Ernesto Zedillo Ponce de León, a Yale-educated Mexicali native who had been Colosio Murrieta's campaign manager. Zedillo went on to win every state in the 1994 federal election, which was hailed as an improvement over the obviously rigged 1988 vote, but still criticized as intensely corrupt.

Aware that he had to do something to satisfy his critics or face open rebellion, Zedillo made a move that would have been unthinkable even a few years before—he appointed a non-PRI cabinet minister. In an attempt to add legitimacy to his administration and appease his opponents, Zedillo named firebrand PAN prosecutor Fernando Antonio Lozano Gracia as attorney general.

Lozano Gracia's first target was Raul Salinas de Gortari, older brother of the outgoing president, who he arrested on charges ranging from murder to embezzlement. After his arrest, the ex-president fled Mexico and lived in self-imposed exile in Ireland. His wife, Paulina Salinas Castanon, was arrested in Geneva for attempting to withdraw cash from Raul's account, with Mexican officials alleging that the $160 million in the account was drug money. Eventually Raul was acquitted of murder, but not of the other charges. His Swiss accounts were frozen then returned to various Mexican parties with claims against him. Another Salinas de Gortari brother, Enrique, was found tortured and strangled in his car in Mexico City in 2004.

Emboldened, Lozano Gracia's next target was the Federales.

He and his men investigated every one of its 4,400 officers. He fired almost one-third of the national police force for having verifiable links to organized crime: on his first pass, he dismissed 513 of them for having compromised ethics and on his second 737. While his actions shocked Mexico, particularly PRI politicians, he didn't go far enough according to nongovernment observers who estimated that at least 90 percent of all police, prosecutors and judges in northern Mexico were cooperating with the cartels in exchange for cash.

It would be hard to blame them. Not only do police in Mexico make very low wages, but they face great danger if they don't accept bribes. Ramón Arellano Félix—who the *San Diego Union-Tribune* reported seeing frequently at Tijuana's best restaurants, protected by what at least appeared to be Federales—had a saying at the time, that police, prosecutors and judges were to receive their choice of "plata o plomo" (silver or lead). "It's kind of like this," said former chief of International Operations for the DEA Robert Nieves. "You're offered a bribe. If bribery doesn't work, you're offered violence. And that violence will be exacted against you or your family members."

THE POLICE PAY THE PRICE

After a series of shootouts with officers and former officers in Tijuana and the surrounding region, Lozano Gracia was desperate for help. To bolster his weakened police force in the area, he hired Ernesto de Ibarra Santés—who he described as fearless and honest—to take over the local police force. De Ibarra

Santés arrived on August 16, 1996 with 55 of his own men. After a thorough investigation, on September 12 he told *The Los Angeles Times* that "police here have become so corrupted that they aren't just friends of the traffickers, they are their servants" and identified the Arellano Félix brothers as the primary threat to public safety.

On September 14, he and two bodyguards were driving away from the airport in Mexico City, when two other cars blocked their path. Men from the cars opened fire with AK-47s, killing all three. A bag containing $50,000 in U.S. currency was found in the trunk, but a lack of bullet holes in the bag convinced many that it was planted there by the killers or the Federales to discredit de Ibarra Santés.

Less than a week later, Jorge Garcia Vargas, Tijuana chief for the National Institute for Combating Drugs, told reporters that he had compiled enough evidence to arrest at least 15 high-profile traffickers and money-launderers working with the Arellano Félix brothers. Two days later, Garcia Vargas and five of his top men went missing. Their tortured bodies were later recovered in the trunks of cars in a suburb of Mexico City.

Zeta, the magazine published by Blancornelas, became highly critical of the brothers, especially Ramón. The gang's enforcer was particularly enraged when *Zeta* published a letter from a victim's mother that labeled him a coward. First *Zeta*'s co-founder was murdered, then its editor-in-chief. On November 27, 1997, a car stopped in front of Blancornelas on a Tijuana street in broad daylight and its occupants opened fire. Blancornelas was shot four times, but survived. His bodyguard was killed.

Lozano Gracia announced that he was closing in on the cartel, but it wasn't fast enough for Zedillo. After 44 officers were lost, for only eight small-time arrests, Zedillo fired Lozano Gracia and replaced him with Jorge Madrazo Cuellar. One of Madrazo Cuellar's first moves was to appoint General José de Jesús Gutiérrez Rebollo as national drug czar. It was a calculated move because, while the reputations of the police and politicians were tarnished, the military was considered clean.

His tenure and the army's reputation of being above corruption lasted just two weeks. Defense Secretary Enrique Cervantes Aguirre met Gutiérrez Rebollo at home and determined that it was quite lavish for his salary, so he started asking questions. The 62-year-old Gutiérrez Rebollo became nervous and confused and suffered a mild heart attack. Cervantes Aguirre continued questioning him (even within the ambulance that he'd called) and learned that the general had been sharing all of the government's information with Amado Carrillo Fuentes, head of the Juárez Cartel, in exchange for cash, real estate and cars for the previous seven years, essentially protecting him from the law.

Called "El Señor de los Cielos" (The Lord of the Skies) because of the fleet of jetliners he employed to bring product from Colombia, the DEA named Carrillo Fuentes the most powerful drug lord of his era and estimated his personal fortune to be in the neighborhood of $25 billion. He was very different than the wild Arellano Félix brothers. Low-key and well-spoken, Carrillo Fuentes often worked in conjunction with other cartels and organizations without much violence. He'd been on the run from the law since early 1993, and would often fly to places like Russia and Cuba when he felt law enforcement was getting too close.

After his connection with Gutiérrez Rebollo was revealed, Carillo Fuentes decided to change his appearance. While undergoing plastic surgery and liposuction at Santa Mónica Hospital in Mexico City on July 3, 1997, he was killed by an overdose of the anaesthetic Dormicum. Rumors abounded that he was killed by a rival or that it was actually a stand-in who was killed and Carillo Fuentes escaped, but DEA investigators determined it was him by comparing fingerprints to his old U.S. immigration card.

With Carillo Fuentes out of the picture, the Juárez Cartel fell into decline, losing men and territory to the Sinaloans. More important, though, was the loss of his calm diplomacy and his connections with the cops. The cartels became far more violent. With crime absolutely rampant and the economy still in ruins, in the 2000 election, the Mexican people elected Vicente Fox to be their first non-PRI president since 1920. He beat the PRI's Labastida Ochoa, who was also running on an anti-cartel platform.

Early in his administration, the government scored a couple of huge strikes against the Tijuana Cartel. On February 10, 2002, Ramón Arellano Félix was in Mazatlán (allegedly to assassinate Sinaloa's Ismael Zambada García) when he was stopped for a traffic violation by a cop who did not recognize him. The police presence in the city had been increased after two judges were assassinated in less than a week and Mardi Gras was approaching. Ramón got out of his Volkswagen Beetle and shot the cop. In the subsequent shootout, Ramón, his associate and another police officer died. Ramón had been No. 2 on the FBI's Most Wanted List, right behind Osama bin Laden, on the basis that he had killed or ordered the murders of more than 300 people. After his body was stolen from a Tijuana funeral home, rumors that he had faked his death surfaced.

Less than a month later, Benjamín was arrested. The DEA learned through an informant that his oldest daughter had a rare and easily recognizable facial disfigurement and that Benjamín never let her get too far from him. They located her in Puebla, a city between Mexico City and Veracruz. "Once we knew [Benjamín] was with his family, we could keep track of where he was by keeping track of his daughter with the very prominent chin," Mexican Defense Secretary Ricardo Vega Garcia said. By following her, they found Benjamín's otherwise hidden house in the suburbs. A unit of the Mexican Army stormed the house and arrested the drug lord barefoot and in his pajamas. Entire rooms in his house were filled floor to ceiling with cash.

His arrest was followed by that of his lead trafficker, Jesús Manuel "El Tarzan" Herrera Barraza, in Tecate along with Tijuana police chief Carlos Otal Namur and 40 of his officers suspected of helping the cartel. Namur subsequently resigned as police chief, but was never charged.

The arrests were met with cynicism on both sides of the

border. Many Americans, used to the PRI's passiveness in the face of the cartels, thought the arrests were meaningless. "It's going to be very interesting to see if the Mexican judicial system—we're talking about judges—are going to have the capability to try these people, understanding how dangerous they are and what it means to them and their families," said Ana Maria Salazar, former U.S. deputy assistant secretary of defense for drug enforcement and a specialist on Mexican organized crime. "I have my doubts."

While many Mexicans countered that even if Benjamín was put away, there were plenty of other qualified people who would be more than willing to step up to the plate. "You can cut off the heads of an organization, but they will always grow back," said Professor Luis Astorga, who researches drug trafficking at the Institute of Social Research of the National Autonomous University of Mexico. "The business carries on because there are always people from within or outside the cartel that are waiting to take over."

Others believed that the crackdown on the Tijuana Cartel was an indication that Fox and the Americans were conspiring to favor Guzmán Loera and the Sinaloa Cartel. This opinion was summed up in the popular *narcocorrido* "The Ballad of Ramón Arellano Félix" as sung by Los Embajadores del Norte (the Northern Ambassadors).

The Sinaloans had in fact been expanding. In 1996, Guzmán Loera befriended a group called the Colima Cartel—led by the José de Jesús Amezcua Contreras and his brothers Adán and Luis—who manufactured and traded methamphetamine. The major cartels had long tolerated the Colima Cartel because they had their hands full moving cocaine across the border, and most of them considered methamphetamine to be a low-volume, low-profit drug.

THE MOVE INTO METH

Guzmán Loera was the first of the big cartel leaders to see how wrong they all were. When all three Amezcua Contreras were arrested in 1997 and 1998, he took over their immense methamphetamine business. He is said to have loved the idea of meth because it could be manufactured easily in huge amounts with ingredients commonly sold in pharmacies and hardware stores, which meant he owed nothing to the Colombians. He quickly set up a network of meth factories close to the border, earning himself a new nickname, "El Rey de Cristal" (the Crystal King).

And he was expanding the Sinaloa Cartel's territory as well. Four brothers from the Sinaloa town of Badiraguato—Marcos Arturo, Carlos, Alfredo and Héctor Beltrán Leyva—had worked closely with the Sinaloa Cartel, particularly importing large amounts of cocaine from the Cali Cartel in Colombia. With the decline of the Sonora Cartel after the arrests of the Caro Quintera brothers, the Sinaloa Cartel allowed them to set up their own, allied organization called the Beltrán Leyva Cartel to keep pressure against the Tijuana Cartel and to handle the crossings into Arizona.

That move led the Tijuana Cartel to form an alliance

with the Gulf Cartel. To compensate, the Sinaloa and Beltrán Leyva Cartels formed a pact with the Juárez Cartel, effectively creating two opposing groups of drug-trafficking organizations.

By the beginning of 2005, the Sinaloa and Beltrán Leyva Cartels were believed by the DEA to have as many as 40 men working in the city of Nuevo Laredo, across the Rio Grande from Laredo, Texas, which is the heart of the Gulf Cartel's territory. In May, 2005, Guzmán Loera, surrounded by 30 of his men, walked into the posh Paseo Colon restaurant in downtown Nuevo Laredo. His security detail locked the doors, confiscated cell phones from the restaurant's employees and 40 or so patrons "for security purposes," ate a large meal, then paid for it and everybody else's, leaving a substantial tip.

That affront could not be tolerated by the Gulf Cartel, probably the most violent of all the cartels, and may actually have been the spark that ignited the Mexican Drug War. At least, it was seen as a declaration of war between the two cartel alliances.

Original Gulf chief Juan García Ábrego was arrested soon after the creation of the cartel. He was replaced by Oscar Malherbe De León, who was himself arrested almost immediately afterwards. Sergio "El Checko" Gómez Garcia, took over and ruled for two weeks before being murdered by Salvador "Chava" (Chick) Gómez. He was soon killed by Osiel Cárdenas Guillén, who earned the nickname "El Mata Amigos" (the Friend Killer) and undisputed leadership of the organization.

TROUBLE IN NUEVO LAREDO

While he was consolidating his power, Cárdenas Guillén came up with a devilishly clever and effective plan. He was well aware of a group of army special forces officers called *Grupo Aeromóvil de Fuerzas Especiales* (Special Forces Airmobile Group, or GAFE) who went through an intensive, six-month counter-insurgency and urban warfare training course from American, French and Israeli specialists. It was originally formed to provide security for the 1986 World Cup, but had become the government's primary weapon against the cartels.

By bribing and threatening government officials, Cárdenas Guillén managed to gain access to the unit's secret records and approached Lieutenant Arturo Guzmán Decena, who after a healthy bribe and huge salary increase, quit the army and assumed a position as Cárdenas Guillén's bodyguard. But he proved more valuable than that, as Cárdenas Guillén recruited 30 more men from GAFE through him. The men called Guzmán Decena "Zeta," because his old army code name was Z1. Soon the former GAFE men and the men they trained became known as "Los Zetas." Their duties expanded to collecting debts, securing disputed territory and assassinating enemies. Their signature was to make their victims' bodies so grotesque as to add an extra level of terror among those who might think of crossing them. Their tactics and weapons made them a weapon the other cartels, and even the Mexican military, couldn't match.

But Cárdenas Guillén also made a big mistake. In November 1999, a vehicle carrying a Gulf Cartel informant and a number of DEA and FBI agents was stopped and surrounded by Cárdenas Guillén and his men. Despite being apprehended, assaulted and threatened by having an immense number of AK-47s and AR-15s pointed at them, the Americans refused to surrender or hand the man over. Eventually they were allowed to leave as their abductors apparently decided against antagonizing the U.S. government any further.

This made Cárdenas Guillén an enemy of the United States, and on March 14, 2003, a Mexican Army unit acting on American intelligence surrounded his home and arrested him. The Gulf Cartel fell into some disarray after that. Cárdenas Guillén attempted to run things from prison via cell phone, but real leadership fell to his lieutenants, older brother Antonio Ezequiel Cárdenas Guillén and childhood friend Jorge Eduardo Costilla Sánchez. Without Cárdenas Guillén in control—and with Guzmán Decena dead after an assassination at a restaurant in 2002—Los Zetas became less loyal and more militant, often making their own deals without the consent or knowledge of the Gulf Cartel.

With the Sinaloa and Beltrán Leyva Cartels moving in and the Gulf Cartel and Los Zetas protecting their turf, a small war broke out. Automatic gunfire was heard frequently. Locals knew who the bad guys were and stayed as far away as possible. The media started calling Nuevo Laredo "Narco Laredo." Radio journalist Raul S. Llamas told the BBC he stopped reporting on cartel violence after a friend and colleague was murdered for saying the wrong thing. Guzmán Loera upped the ante Colombian-style by paying for the school supplies and healthcare for poor people in the city. José Luis Santiago Vasconcelos, Mexico's drug czar, begged the media to let those people know that everything the cartels were giving people was the result of illegality and violence. "Help me make the people realize that this peso or this dollar that the drug trafficker gives is dripping in blood," he asked.

A Federale chasing a Ford Expedition SUV that was speeding in Nuevo Laredo was killed by passengers firing AR-15 assault rifles. The gunmen then fled on foot. When the truck was searched, it was found to be bulletproof and contained four hand grenades, five more AR-15s, three MP5 submachine guns, two telescopes, 11 cell phones and more than 2,000 rounds of ammunition. In the past, Mexican and U.S. officials said, law enforcement officers probably would not have given chase to an expensive SUV with blacked-out windows, either out of fear or because they were on the drug cartels' payroll. Officials believe Ezequiel "Tony Tormenta (Tony Storm)" Cárdenas Guillén, the brother of jailed cartel boss Osiel Cárdenas Guillén, was a passenger in the SUV.

When the chief of the Nuevo Laredo police abandoned his post, attorney Alejandro Domínguez Coello was the only volunteer for the job. Seven hours after he was sworn into office, the father of three was surrounded by Chevrolet SUVs and shot to death. He was the fiftieth person and fourth police officer to be killed in the Nuevo Laredo war. Three days later, the Federales moved in and were fired upon by the local cops. Nobody was killed, but one Federale was critically injured. When the factions waged a firefight in front of the American consulate using assault rifles, machine guns and rocket-propelled grenades, the consul and his staff packed up and went home. The fact that the consulate left Nuevo Laredo was a shock to many Americans who had no idea how violent their neighbor to the south had become, since the fighting had not yet spilled over the border.

Fox was compelled to move. He sent in 800 army soldiers who detained all 700 members of the Nuevo Laredo police force and sent the 41 involved in the attack on the Federales to Mexico City for interrogation. Fox likened Nuevo Laredo to Chicago in the 1920s. He said it would take years of hard work and millions and millions of dollars to fix the problem.

One of Mexico's most popular singers, Valentin "El Gallo de Oro (the Golden Rooster)" Elizalde Valencia, gave a concert at an open-air festival in Reynosa, just across the Rio Grande from McAllen, Texas, on November 25. At it, he sang a *narcocorrido* about Guzmán Loera and began and ended his show with his song "A Mis Enemigos" (To My Enemies), which had become something of an unofficial anthem for the Sinaloa Cartel. No more than 20 minutes after he left the stage, his Chevrolet Suburban SUV was surrounded and filled with bullets fired from AR-15s and handguns. Elizalde, his manager Mario Mendoza and driver Raymundo Ballesteros were all killed. A fourth person, believed to be a woman, was injured but escaped before authorities arrived.

If there was any doubt who was responsible, it was erased the following week. A series of videos started appearing on YouTube—including Elizalde's official autopsy video—that claimed that Los Zetas were taking responsibility for the hit. The videos received millions of views and hundreds of comments, including unambiguous death threats between Sinaloa and Gulf supporters.

And that's how 2005 ended in Mexico. Millions of people were crossing the border into the United States, a huge number of them with backpacks full of marijuana, cocaine or methamphetamines. They were bringing back immense amounts of cash and heavy weapons. Fox was bragging about the 46,000 drug-related arrests that had happened under his watch, not to mention the destruction of many clandestine airports and poppy fields, but was also begging for patience and funding. The cartels had aligned into two warring factions—the Sinaloa, Beltrán Leyva and Juárez on one side were facing off against the Tijuana and Gulf—who were making billions of dollars, recruiting new staff, appeasing the locals with handouts and bribing or killing opponents at will. Los Zetas were gaining confidence and making their own deals. The DEA, FBI and Border Patrol were spoiling for a fight. And the country was called to vote once again in an election that would determine their very precarious future as a nation.

CHAPTER 6

Trouble in Paradise

The Mexican Drug War did not start in a vacuum. It wasn't simply the case of a federal government cracking down on drug traffickers—nothing in Mexico is ever that simple. Although people in North America have long joked about how corrupt Mexican police and officials were, few realized how entrenched corruption was in the culture until tourists started coming back in body bags.

Few places in the world are as welcoming and as naturally beautiful as the Caribbean coast of Quintana Roo. On the east coast of the Yucatán Peninsula in southeastern Mexico, Quintana Roo offers beaches with warm transparent crystal blue water and fine white sand. Away from the beaches, you can tour Mayan temples and pyramids, try the exquisite Yucatáneco cuisine or buy authentic Mexican handicrafts. Since the 1980s, places like Cozumel and Cancún have become familiar vacation haunts for Americans and Canadians alike. Travel agents refer to it as the Mayan Riviera, and it is where Hernán Cortés landed in 1519.

Most North Americans acknowledge some level of danger when traveling to Mexico, but Quintana Roo has a well-developed tourist culture, as have many other destinations in Latin America and the Caribbean. The best beaches and other hotspots are surrounded by lavish hotels, restaurants and entertainment complexes that cater to North Americans and a few Western Europeans. Everyone speaks English, American dollars are accepted everywhere and on Sundays you can catch NFL games in every bar. They are safe and hospitable, designed to make the visitor feel comfortable, at home, as it were, when thousands of miles from home. The greatest fear for most travelers is "Montezuma's revenge"—diarrhea caused by improperly stored food. Outside of those zones—where few North American tourists venture—lie places we'd call things like "the Other Mexico" where the local population lives. In some tourist destinations—like many in the Dominican Republic—the dividing line is marked with a high fence topped with razor wire; but in most places, tourists rely on visual cues or advice from hotel employees and other locals who rely on tourist dollars.

DEMONS IN EDEN

By 2006, Quintana Roo had made the news as a haven for organized crime. Frequent reports of drug trafficking and subsequent money-laundering made little impact on North Americans—many of whom pay little attention to Mexican news—until a different, more lurid type of organized crime was uncovered. Mexican journalist Lydia Cacho Ribeiro wrote a book called *Los Demonios del Edén* (The Demons of Eden), in which she revealed a massive child pornography and prostitution ring operating in this idyllic setting.

The man she said was responsible for the criminal organization was Jean Succar Kuri, a Lebanese-born Mexican businessman who also has American citizenship. He moved to Cancún in the 1980s—just ahead of the tourist boom—with his 18-year-old second wife and set up a soda stand. Twenty years later, he owned four guest villas and a hotel on the strip and was worth about $30 million.

Using victims' official statements and following Succar Kuri around (often with a hidden camera and microphone) for months, Cacho's book served as compelling evidence that Succar Kuri was indeed the ringleader of a child exploitation ring that was worth millions. It also linked Kuri to politicians like Senator Emilio Gamboa Patrón and national Social Security and Social Services Institute general director Miguel Ángel Yunes, and named another Lebanese-born Mexican businessman, a Puebla-based textile manufacturer and noted high-stakes gambler named Kamel Nacif Borge, as aiding and protecting him. No charges were ever laid against Patrón, Yunes or Borge.

When the book came out, Nacif Borge, also known as the "El Zar de la Mezclilla" (the Czar of Denim), immediately sued

Cacho for defamation. A few days later, Cacho was arrested in Cancún by Puebla state police and taken 900 miles away to the city of Puebla. They did not give her a subpoena or warrant or even a reason for her arrest. She was jailed briefly, paid a fine and was released.

On February 14, Mexico City-based daily *La Jornada* published transcripts of telephone conversations between Nacif Borge and Mario Marín Torres, the governor of Puebla. In them, Nacif Borge asks "mi góber precioso" (my precious guv') if he could arrange to have Cacho arrested and then beaten in jail.

At first, Marín Torres claimed the voice on the recording was not his and that although he knew Nacif Borges, they were not friends. Later, he admitted that it was his voice and they were close friends, but that the conversation was taken out of context.

Cacho sued Marín Torres in Mexico's Supreme Court for bribery, influence trafficking, conspiracy to rape and abuse of authority. She lost the case 6-4, leading *The New York Times* to call the surprise decision "a setback for journalistic freedom in Mexico." The United Nations Human Rights Council advised Cacho to leave the country and offered her protection and a chance to be heard in an international court. She chose, instead, to stay in Mexico and is now researching the Juárez *maquillidora* murders. Succar Kuri was found guilty on a number of charges and was imprisoned first in Chandler, Arizona—where he was attacked by another inmate—then later Mexico.

MURDER ON THE MAYAN RIVIERA

Organized crime, child prostitution, corrupt police and elected officials were part of the Other Mexico, and stories like Cacho's did little to dissuade North Americans from coming to the Mayan Riviera.

In 2006, Liliana "Lily" Ianiero and Marco Facecchia were looking for a place to hold their wedding. They were from Woodbridge, Ontario, a decidedly upscale suburb of Toronto that is populated almost entirely by Italian-Canadians. As is the case with many families of Italian descent, the Ianiero-Facecchia wedding would be a lavish affair with many guests. Lily wanted it to be at an all-inclusive beach resort. Their wedding planner suggested Jamaica, but the couple thought it was too dangerous (Woodbridge is not far from some rough Toronto neighborhoods dominated by Jamaican gangs) so they decided on the Mayan Riviera. To be exact, they chose the 1,000-room Barcelo Maya Beach Resort located between Cancún and Playa del Carmen. And since safety was a concern, they were impressed that the huge complex was accessible only by one gate on one road and patroled by armed security guards 24/7. As is tradition, guests of the wedding had to make their own travel arrangements, but the bride's family paid $45,667 (Canadian) to accommodate the 16-member wedding party.

The wedding party flew down together on February 18, 2006, checked in at about 10:00 p.m. and rested. The next night, they had a party with some of the guests who had also arrived. At about 11:10 p.m., just as the party was moving to a resort nightclub, Captain Morgan's, the bride's parents—

59-year-old realtor Domenico "Domenic" and his 55-year-old wife Annuziatta "Nancy" Ianiero—decided to go to sleep. Nancy said she was still tired from the flight and because they had gotten lost trying to find their room in the massive resort. Domenic joked that gout he had recently developed in his left foot would keep him off the dance floor anyway. He also mentioned that after they were lost the night before, they had flagged down a friendly uniformed security guard who had driven them to their room in an electric golf cart. Before the Ianieros left, they made plans to have breakfast with the groom's parents the next day. The two women agreed to check out the resort's gym before eating.

At 7:30 a.m. on February 22, Dora and Robert Facecchia knocked on the door of Room 4134 where the Ianieros were staying. No answer. Assuming that Domenic and Nancy had overslept, they went back to their own room and returned at 8:00. Again, there was no answer. They tried again and again, shouting through the door and calling them on their cell phone. A crowd of people, some in their group, alerted by the ruckus, gathered around them. Robert Facecchia asked a member of the housekeeping staff to let them in. When she refused, he insisted her manager do so. He complied at 8:20. Later testimony would show that the witnesses were immediately shocked by the colossal amount of blood, far too much for the carpet and the duvet thrown in front of the door to absorb. "The room was full of blood. I don't think there was anything left in them," said a family member who arrived later.

They saw Nancy's body first. She was face down on the

bedroom floor, her throat slashed from ear to ear. She had a Hudson's Bay credit card on top of her and her purse underneath. Domenic was found face up on the bathroom floor. His throat had been sliced open as well.

The family's screams alerted more people in neighboring rooms. Dora sent someone to tell Lily and Marco what had happened. Two women—Thunder Bay, Ontario, residents Cheryl Everall and Kimberly Kim, who were at the resort to attend a different wedding—had emerged from a room across and just down the hall from the Ianieros', and said that they had heard nothing until the commotion that had drawn them out. Other guests who arrived at the scene told the grieving family that they had heard glass breaking, crying and screaming, but didn't think it was anything that serious.

While all of this was happening, hotel housekeepers were hurriedly mopping up blood from the scene under management's orders. Some of the onlookers recorded them doing so on cell phone video cameras. Word spread and curious onlookers crowded the scene. Hotel security told the bewildered family that what they were doing, including cleaning and not sealing the area, was standard policy.

State police arrived at the scene 90 minutes later and acknowledged that some cleaning had been done before they arrived. They found a bloody trail from the Ianieros' room to the one across the hall that Everall and Kim had just checked out of at about 10:00 a.m. The two Canadian women had taken a taxi to the airport and flown back to Thunder Bay without incident. According to the Ianieros' son, the Quintana

Roo coroner refused to examine or even remove the bodies until he was paid $7,000 to cover the costs of embalming and caskets. After he was paid, the Ianieros' remains were taken to Funerales del Caribe—which serves as a funeral home and a morgue—in Playa del Carmen in an unmarked white Chevy Tahoe SUV hearse. Just after a unit of Federales arrived on the scene, someone in hotel security sent an "all clear" message over the staff radios, and the crime scene was again inundated with staff and guests until the Federales could resecure the area. Much to the Canadians' surprise, the Mexican police did not take notes during their initial questioning instead relying on their memories.

For days, the families sat vigil in the hallway, while their room service requests for coffee and water were denied. A clerk handed a family member the Ianieros' personal belongings, which surprised them as they thought they should have been taken as evidence.

Noted Toronto magazine editor Scott Steele left the resort just hours before the bodies were discovered. "This was not the sort of place where you would expect something like this to happen. It seemed pretty safe and secure to me," he said. "It was full of fairly well-heeled North American tourists, and was a compound of sorts. There were not even outsiders on the beach."

He did notice a sizeable gulf between the staff and guests. "If robbery had been the motive, these are the sorts of places that locals might indeed try to target," he said. "Despite the very high security."

Quintana Roo Attorney General Bello Melchor Rodriguez y Carillo told Mexican media that robbery was clearly not a motive for the killing because the Ianieros were still wearing their jewelry and had travelers' checks in their possession. He said that the primary suspects were two Canadians, noting that there was a trail of bloody footprints headed to their room. The Mexican authorities released two names, but due to the language barrier and poor record-keeping at the resort, they were misspelled and it was not clear if the names were of men or women.

• • •

Everall and Kim saw names similar to theirs mentioned in media accounts and reported to police. The Royal Canadian Mounted Police (RCMP) did extensive background checks on both women and found nothing out of the ordinary or remotely incriminating about them. Kim, a psychology student who worked part-time at a hospice, and Everall, a medical student who has since opened a family practice, didn't look like any kind of professional killers. The Thunder Bay police interviewed both of them, and 20 others who attended the wedding. Everall and Kim were not sure if they would be arrested or extradited to Mexico. "We're both mothers of small children," said Everall. "We've been involved in our communities, in all ways, and I think for myself—and Kim can speak for herself— but the thought of being taken away from my children, I can't even imagine it. It's my worst nightmare."

On February 24, Melchor Rodriguez y Carillo announced that he had the names and photos of two suspects and was searching for a third. He did not explain how he had obtained the names or photos—although other tourists at the Barcelo Maya reported that armed security guards were constantly taking pictures of guests—and said that media attention was compromising his investigation. He also said that the murders appeared to be assassinations, that the murderers were likely professionals and that it was likely that the Ianieros had enemies in organized crime in Canada.

The reaction in Canada—particularly in Toronto's fiercely pro-Canadian, often overwrought mainstream media—was huge. Pointing out that the murders were actually sloppy and that if the blood trail was anything more than the footprints of the housekeeper who began to clean up the blood before police arrived, as the family claimed it was, the hit was anything but professional. "Having their throats slashed does not mean it was a professional hit," said Mark Mendelson, a former Toronto homicide detective and now the owner of a private investigation firm. "There are a lot of spontaneous murders and crimes of passion where people have their throats cut. Most professional hits are done with guns. If they're professional, they must be brand new at it, because they haven't covered their tracks very well." The local papers carried lots of personal stories, focusing on what a delightful couple the Ianieros were and how they told each other "I love you" at least once a day.

But while the mainstream media thought the Mexican claim that the Ianieros had powerful enemies in Canada absurd, many others disagreed via social media ranging from Facebook and Twitter to independent blogs, forums and comments on online news stories (virtually all of which were later deleted by the major newspapers and TV stations). They noted that the Ianieros were a well-off family of Italian extraction who lived in Woodbridge, home to many members and alleged members of Canada's Mafia. They also pointed out that during the Quebec Biker War of the 1990s, at least three assassinations were carried out in Mexico because it was easier to get police to cooperate and have evidence "lost" there. No link between the Ianieros and organized crime was ever found, but the idea persists among many Canadians.

On the February 25, Melchor Rodriguez y Carillo backtracked on his earlier comments, telling the Canadian Press wire service that there was no evidence of organized crime involvement in the murders. A spokesman for the Quintana Roo state police promised a news conference in which the investigators would reveal the names and photos of the three Canadian suspects. When it didn't happen, he promised another for the following day. It didn't happen either.

• • •

Dr. Bonita Porter, Ontario's deputy chief coroner, who had been asked by Ottawa to handle the case, had her own doubts about how effectively the Mexicans had conducted their investigation. "We have jurisdiction to issue a warrant to seize the bodies because the information that we have is that the deaths occurred from suspicious circumstances," she said. "Depending on what was done to the bodies in Mexico, what type of autopsy was done, whether the bodies are embalmed—those are the kinds of things that would make some of the testing difficult."

Her colleague, Toronto West regional supervising coroner Dr. David Evans agreed. "'Obviously, if you're looking for trace evidence, whether it's hair, fibers, DNA under the fingernails—all sorts of things—we'd have no idea what their protocol is for doing homicide autopsies," he said.

A significant amount of pressure from Canadian media had put stress on Melchor Rodriguez y Carillo. "There won't be any more press conferences until I finish my investigation; I have made the decision and I don't have to justify anything to you," he angrily told a reporter from Toronto-based *National Post*. "You, the Canadians, are the ones who came to kill other Canadians—that much is clear."

On February 28, Everall and Kim held a news conference with their lawyer, Lee Baig, in which they denied involvement. "They are, at this point, in a controlled panic state," he said. "They are very worried." He blamed their implication in the crime on "poor investigation" and pointed out that his clients did not even know the victims. "I think that the Mexican authorities are concerned about the reputation of Cancún being a safe tourist destination," Baig said. "I'm worried that they are trying to deflect the reality of the situation and simply say it was Canadians—if that is the case, they've surely got the wrong targets."

Despite the inconsistencies in the Mexican authorities' announcements and the doubts of the coroners, on March 2 the RCMP told the Ianieros and the Canadian public to be patient and let the Mexicans do their jobs. "We have full confidence in the Mexican police," said Raf Souccar, assistant commissioner of the RCMP. "I've got no reason to be concerned about the way the investigation is unfolding." When asked by a reporter if he was worried about potential problems arising from the time between the discovery of the bodies and the arrival of police, he responded, "Crime scenes are never uncontaminated." One vital piece of evidence, a cardboard coaster that had some local phone numbers written on its back, was severely compromised. Instead of putting it in an evidence bag, the coaster was glued face-up to the outside of the file folder containing evidence documents. The glue obscured the phone numbers, which were never recovered.

Later that day, Melchor Rodriguez y Carillo told the press that an examination of the bodies indicated that the killer or killers had extensive medical knowledge, something that would back his still vague claim that Everall and/or Kim were involved. At the same news conference, his top deputy, Manuel Sarmiento Silva, announced that all of the hotel employees had been cleared of suspicion. Canadian public security minister Stockwell Day told the media that the Mexicans' story changed "almost by the hour," and that "this thing is taking on bizarre proportions."

On the following day, Luis Ernesto Derbez Bautista, Mexico's secretary of foreign affairs, announced that the

Mexican government had asked the RCMP and York Regional Police through Interpol to take part in the investigation. He said that the move was being taken as a result of a request by Canada's prime minister, Stephen Harper. Two RCMP homicide detectives flew to Cancún.

Twelve days after they had died, more than 700 mourners attended the Ianieros' funeral at St Clare of Assisi in Woodbridge on March 6. The event was closely watched by York police, who videotaped mourners and their license plates. "I have already spoken with the family. They are quite anxious to relay any information they may have that would assist in the investigation," York police inspector Les Young said. "They are very concerned about rumors and innuendoes." The couple's niece, Roseanne Ianiero, delivered a eulogy attendees described as "stirring" and lashed out at the Mexican authorities, who had intimated that Domenic and Nancy had been involved in organized crime.

• • •

On the same day, *Periodico Quequi*, a Quintana Roo newspaper, revealed that police were now hunting four Barcelo Maya employees—two security guards and two housekeepers—as prime suspects. None of the four had shown up for work since February 20, the day the Ianieros were discovered.

In an interview with a Canadian news outlet on March 9, Melchor Rodriguez y Carillo said that Everall and Kim had never been suspects in the case and that he had only wanted to question them. He also said that the Mexican media reports that the four hotel employees were suspects was false, just speculation based on rumor, and that reports that the crime scene had been compromised were "lies." Baig said his clients were happy to hear from Melchor Rodriguez y Carillo that they were no longer suspects, but wouldn't feel any relief until they heard it from Canadian authorities. He also claimed that although the Canadian media had speculated that the Mexicans had botched the investigation, the Canadian authorities did not share that opinion. "The Canadian authorities are happy with us, and have verified all the work we've done," Bello Melchor Rodriguez y Carillo said. "They have said the tests and evidence we've collected will be very useful for the work they need to do in Canada."

Just as the furor was appearing to calm down, Mexico dropped a media bomb on March 29. In an interview with Toronto-based daily *The Globe & Mail* just days before a summit meeting in Cancún at which Prime Minister Stephen Harper and President George W. Bush would be in attendance, Mexican president Vicente Fox said that he believed the killer or killers to have been Canadian because the murders appeared to have been targeted and occurred within the Ianieros' hotel room.

The first, and loudest, to respond was the Ianiero family's lawyer, Edward Greenspan, who accused Fox of tampering. The fact that the family had hired Greenspan lifted many eyebrows in Canada, where he is famous as a defense attorney, having represented several alleged organized crime figures, including the national president of the Hells Angels. "No president of a state should get involved; no president should give marching orders to the police," he said at a news conference held on the March 31. "This investigation has turned into some form of political football—it will be impossible to reach a fair conclusion." Greenspan also said that the Ianiero family had named a Mexican as a likely suspect, but would not disclose his identity beyond saying he was "involved with security" at the resort. He closed by accusing Fox of being more interested in maintaining his country's tourist industry than solving the case.

On that same day, Toronto-based forensic investigators announced that they were analyzing evidence taken from what may have been the murder weapon. A young girl who was vacationing with her family in Cancún, found a backpack near the resort that contained a large knife smeared with blood. She handed it to her father, a police officer in Duluth, Minnesota, who took it back to the U.S. with him because he did not trust Mexican police. When he heard a news broadcast about the Ianiero murders from a Thunder Bay TV station, he gave the knife, which he had treated as evidence, to the Thunder Bay police. They handed it to York police. When the trail of the knife became public, Thunder Bay police said that they received the knife simply because the city is the closest one in Canada to Duluth, not because Everall or Kim had any involvement. York police chief Armand La Barge backed them up. "I do want to make it clear that our seizure of the knife has absolutely nothing to do with these two women from Thunder Bay," he said. It was later determined that the knife was not involved with this particular crime.

The plot thickened once again on April 3, when *Periodico Quequi*'s crosstown rival *Novedades Quintana Roo* announced that it had received an anonymous, typewritten letter stamped March 3 at a post office in Stoney Creek, Ontario, a largely Italian suburb of Hamilton, Canada's most Mafia-friendly city. It read in part, "Will you please ask the police to check out the possibility of Canadians flying from Cuba to Cancún on the week that the murders took place." It went on to describe three suspects, two Canadian (one tall and thin, the other short and heavy) and a third described as a "Latino, possibly Mexican." It concludes with, "Thank you very much, I thought the police will hear you better than myself."

Greenspan then met with Melchor Rodriguez y Carillo on May 19, and announced that the Ianiero family had hired a private investigator to "fill in the gaps" in the evidence collected by the Mexicans. He also alluded once again to the anonymous suspect, whom he now described as a mysterious Mexican who had befriended Domenic and Nancy. He also said comments by the Quintana Roo attorney general were "slanderous, outrageous and completely false," accusing him of "turning a tragic senseless murder into a political three-ring circus." As for the man himself, Greenspan described him as "arrogant, pompous and downright rude."

A little more than a month later, on June 26, Quintana Roo state police announced they had a suspect in the case. Blas Delgado Fajardo was a 35-year-old former Mexican Army paratrooper and bodyguard for former Quintana Roo Governor Joaquín Hendricks Díaz. He had been working at the Barcelo Maya for about six months as an armed security guard. The Canadian private investigator concluded that Delgado Fajardo had befriended the Ianieros and had gained access to their room under the pretence that he had come to tend Domenic's ailing foot. The Ianieros' daughters recalled that a security guard—the same one who had driven them to their room in a golf cart—had said he received medical training in the military, and had massaged Domenic's foot twice the night before. He wore a uniform, but no name tag.

The private investigator also determined that the door to the Ianieros' room had been opened at 7:29 p.m. on February 19 when they were eating dinner at one of the resort's restaurants, and that their safe had been opened 12 times during their stay. It is commonplace for large quantities of cash to be given as gifts at Italian weddings, but the Ianiero family had decided to leave all gifts back in Canada for security reasons.

THE FUGITIVE

Delgado Fajardo had not been seen since February 21, the day after the Ianieros' bodies were discovered. When Canadian authorities requested his employee photo from Barcelo Maya, they were sent a blurry, mostly black square.

The Ianiero case has never been conclusively solved. In October, Melchor Rodriguez y Carillo announced that he was investigating Lily's ex-husband, whom he described as being a member of a Guatemalan paramilitary "hit squad" and involved with drug trafficking. The man in question, who would only go

by the name "Rob" when speaking to the media, denied ever
having set foot in Guatemala and produced employment records that showed he was working in Toronto the day of the
murder. In a slightly comic twist, he was a court officer with
the Toronto Police. Then Greenspan weighed in. "The attorney general, for obvious political and tourism-related reasons
refuses to concede that this crime was committed by a local person," he said. "He would rather blame a fictitious, totally made-
up son-in-law from Guatemala than the local Mexican security
guard toward whom all of the evidence points." After calling
Melchor Rodriguez y Carillo a "bald-faced liar," Greenspan
made it even more personal. "I don't like him much," he said.
"He's a political hack. He's not interested in finding the truth."
He then pointed out that the Mexicans should be working at
finding Delgado Fajardo rather than inventing imaginary suspects in Toronto.

The Ianieros' son, Anthony, who arrived at the resort just
after the bodies were discovered, summed up the family's opinion. "They could have caught the security guard quickly," he said.
"But that a hotel employee at a high-end resort is responsible for
murdering two tourists would devastate the tourism industry. It
was easier to blame the Canadians; it was easier to say my parents were bad people."

On September 17, 2009, three years and seven months
after the murders, Mexican authorities issued a warrant for
Delgado Fajardo's. At publication, despite published pleas
from his mother, Aurora Fajardo Torres, to come out of hiding,
Delgado Fajardo is still at large. She believes he now lives in

the U.S. Everall and Kim were officially cleared as suspects on July 16, 2009.

While the Ianiero case has never been actually linked to drug trafficking, it gave Canadians and Americans a closer look at how criminal investigations are conducted in Mexico. First, the crime scene was profoundly contaminated. Then the police arrived late and used ad hoc, even primitive investigative methods. A great deal of evidence was ruined or ignored. Then the attorney general made wild accusations and he was surprised and angered that the media and the aggrieved dared question them. Even the president—a leader much hailed for his anti-crime and anti-corruption campaigns—joined in and accused nameless Canadians of committing the crime despite absolutely no evidence to support that theory. When a likely suspect was finally pinpointed, nobody could find him. And that man was a former elite soldier in the military who had a connection to a state governor. According to his mother, he is now most likely just another illegal immigrant in the U.S. whose undocumented status allows him to keep his identity secret.

It demonstrated many of the factors that put the Mexican Drug War into play—corruption in government, demands for bribes to get work done, a disregard for established investigative protocols or even getting to the bottom of difficult cases and the relative ease with which Mexicans can get away with murder or even disappear in the unlikely case where a suspect's identity is discovered.

Miguel G, a former Tijuana journalist who now lives in

California, couldn't help but laugh at the credulity with which Canadians greeted the case. "It's always been this way in Mexico," he told me. "In murder cases, the police don't look for *the* killer, they look for *a* killer—if the victims' family hadn't opened their mouths, someone would be behind bars right now. It probably wouldn't be the right guy, but there would be a guy." The part of the whole drama that he thought could best teach North Americans about the mindset of Mexican authorities was how quick they were to blame other Canadians despite no evidence to support the claim. "Your media quickly decided it was all a master plan to make Cancún look safe for tourists," Miguel G said. "That is probably part of it, but there is an old tradition there of blaming someone else for our problems, it's usually the Americans, sometimes the Europeans or Guatemalans or Colombians . . . that time it was Canada."

AN "ACCIDENT" IN ACAPULCO

The Ianiero case was still broiling when another Canadian was killed under suspicious circumstances in Mexico. Adam De Prisco, a 19-year-old from Woodbridge, went to Acapulco with his best friend, Marco Calabro. The boys, who liked to go nightclubbing together in Toronto's entertainment district, were excited because it was their first trip without their parents. De Prisco told his friends on Facebook that he was "so hyped" to be going away. He was thin, but muscular, and liked to dye his short, spiky hair blond. His family described him as a happy, hard-working kid, while his friends said he had a reputation as a big talker who liked to play himself off as a ladies' man, a real player.

On January 7, 2007, the boys' second night in Mexico, De Prisco made a big mistake. At a giant nightclub then called Extravaganza (now called Mandara) on Las Brisas hill over-looking Acapulco Bay, the pair separated. "He wanted to go dancing, he's a dancer," Calabro said. "He likes to pick up girls." Calabro, who didn't like to dance, stayed at the bar, unable to see the dance floor.

De Prisco began to dance with a young woman. Her husband objected, and he and De Prisco got into a loud heated argument. The club's bouncers escorted De Prisco from the building and onto the street.

That much is agreed upon. After that, the Mexican authorities claimed he was a victim of a fatal hit-and-run accident. De Prisco's family said he was beaten to death by the husband's friends. Calabro, who didn't see the actual scuffle or anything that happened outside, only left the bar when another Canadian they had met in Acapulco told him De Prisco had been turfed. "I ran, right away," Calabro said. "I begged and pleaded to know where he was. One bouncer was laughing and pointed me in the direction [of the door]." Once outside, he saw what he thought was a dead body. He didn't realize it was De Prisco and panicked. "My eyes . . . I didn't think it was him," he said. "I wouldn't believe it." He thought about hailing a taxi back to the hotel, but realized he had to find his friend.

He went back to the body and recognized De Prisco, who was badly injured and bleeding from the head. Calabro managed to get a passerby to call 066 (Mexico's 911) for an ambulance and stayed with De Prisco until he died. "It was so bad, I don't even want people to know," he recalled. "The first hour he was awake and he said his last word to me. He looked at me and I [saw] he needed help." He later told media that he was appalled at the treatment he and his friend received in the hospital. "It was a joke," he told them. "Doctors were laughing at us, police were laughing at us; everything to them was a joke because we weren't Mexican." In a pathetic twist, the boys' hotel room was burgled and cleaned out in De Prisco's final hours. Calabro has since said that he believes the robbery was part of a complicated plan that started with the tussle in the nightclub.

After being notified by Mexican police about the accident, De Prisco's uncle, Sandro Bellio, and aunt, Stephanie Pannozzi, rushed to Acapulco and arrived just before he died on the evening of the January 9. When they saw De Prisco, the wounds he had—mainly around his head—did not look to them like they had come from a collision with a car. Pannozzi asked a neurologist who had been working the case what had killed De Prisco. She said that he told her it was likely a metal rod or a rock, not a hit-and-run. Bellio backed her up. "The injuries and the doctors said that it wasn't a car accident," he said. "He had no marks on his body—all the trauma was on his face and head." Bellio also said he spoke with eyewitnesses who said that they saw De Prisco being beaten and of a water truck that washed the blood [and any other evidence] from the scene, but none was willing to talk to police.

After he signed all the papers and made arrangements to transport De Prisco's body, Bellio asked police if there was anything else he needed to do. "Before we left even, this police officer was asking for a tip, for money, for his time," he said. "I looked at him like, you gotta be joking me."

After hearing little from the Mexican police in the days after the murder, the De Prisco family hired Greenspan. As with the Ianieros, rumors immediately circulated online in Canada that linked De Prisco to organized crime and that he was related to the Ianieros. Actually, he was, but very distantly. Bellio told a reporter that one of De Prisco's second cousins married a nephew of the murdered couple. A Canadian autopsy was noncommittal, determining that De Prisco could have died either by being beaten or by being struck by a car. Ironically, Extravaganza's slogan, borrowed from Las Vegas, was "Remember what happens in Acapulco stays in Acapulco."

Since then, at least a dozen Canadian tourists have died in Mexico under suspicious circumstances. In all of the cases, the families of the deceased have refused to accept the explanations offered by Mexican authorities, including three who they claimed fell or jumped off hotel balconies.

Despite such incidents and severely worded warnings from their own government, Canadian tourism to Mexico has actually increased since the Ianieros' murder. Through aggressive marketing and very low prices, travel agents and tour operators have doubled the number of Canadian trips to Mexico between 2005 and 2009, peaking with more than 1.2 million visits per year. Over the same period, American trips to Mexico have declined significantly.

CHAPTER 7
Calderón Versus the Cartels

The federal election of 2006 may have been the most tense in Mexican history. Such a long history of rigged outcomes had put many watchful eyes—both domestic and international—on the campaigns, polling stations and vote counts. Fox's term had achieved some economic success, but many criticized him and his party PAN for not taking a harder line on the drug cartels as organized crime-related murders climbed into the thousands during his tenure.

PAN nominated Felipe de Jesús Calderón Hinojosa as Fox's successor, a career politician from Michoacán whose father had helped create the party. After losing the election, the PRI had since split into two groups. The socialist Partido de la Revolución Democrática (Party of the Democratic Revolution or PRD) had spun off in 1989 and by 2006 appeared to be even more powerful than the traditional PRI. Its candidate was Mexico City's mayor, Andrés Manuel López Obrador.

The PRI in alliance with the Green Party ran Roberto Madrazo Pintado, who was later caught cheating at the Berlin Marathon.

The vote was close enough to force a series of recounts. They eventually determined that Calderón had 15,000,284 votes (35.89 percent) and won 16 states; López Obrador received 14,756,350 votes (35.31 percent) and won 15 states plus the Federal Capital District; while Madrazo took 9,301,441 votes (22.26 percent) and won no states. It looked very much like an even standoff between the Conservative north against the Socialist south.

A tribunal appointed by the Mexican Supreme Court, with the approval of the European Union, named Calderón president over the peaceful protests of López Obrador and the PRD. Calderón's first moves were popular. He worked hard to stabilize corn prices, which had risen sharply with the sudden rise in popularity of ethanol as a fuel, and started an incentive program for first-time job seekers. To help quell government corruption, he put a cap on how much top government officials could earn and announced significant pay raises for the military and the Federales. He announced a War on Drug Trafficking, making it clear that his enemies were not users, but importers and exporters.

He made good on his word almost immediately. On December 12, 2006, less than two weeks after taking office, Calderón ordered a force of 4,000 soldiers and Federales into his home state, to launch Operation Michoacán.

LA FAMILIA MICHOACÁNO

Michoacán had long been seen as something of a safe haven for organized crime. It was known worldwide for growing top-quality marijuana—though the business had become far less profitable in recent years because of competition from growers in the United States and Canada—and as a transit point for cocaine. The people—who had a lot in common with those in Chiapas—had long been aware of the existence of La Familia Michoacáno (The Michoacán Family), which began as a quasi-religious group of vigilantes and activists who served primarily to settle disputes between locals who did not trust the federal or state governments. They financed themselves first by "taxing" local businesses, then turned to trafficking marijuana and later cocaine in close association with the Gulf Cartel. They also distributed bibles and cash to the needy and supported schools and anti-government activists.

Based in Apatzingán, their leader was Nazario "El Mas Loco" (the Craziest) Moreno González. He had published a book of his thoughts, and claimed it was his and the organization's divine right to murder their enemies and anyone else who hindered their path. The DEA described La Familia as having a "Robin Hood mentality," honestly believing they were protecting the people from a corrupt government and the other drug cartels. It also described them as "unusually violent." Like most other cartels, they also took part in other operations, like pirating DVDs, smuggling people across borders and kidnapping, usually while wearing police uniforms.

They announced their independence from the Gulf Cartel in November 25, 2006 in a bizarre and cruel manner. As revelers partied at Apatzingán's Sol y Sombra nightclub, 20 armed men stormed in, firing their weapons in the air. Two of them, who were carrying large bags, walked to the edge of the dance floor and rolled five severed heads in among the horrified dancers and left a note that read: "La Familia doesn't kill for money. It doesn't kill women. It doesn't kill innocent people, only those who deserve to die. Know that this is divine justice." The heads belonged to men affiliated with the Gulf Cartel.

The club's manager, Carlos Alvarez Olmos, leapt to La Familia's defense when questioned by an American reporter. "These men didn't come here to hurt anyone," he said. "They work against bad people; those men whose heads they cut off were like bugs." The reporter described him as "nervous."

After severing ties with the Gulf Cartel, La Familia aligned with the more powerful and geographically closer Sinaloa Cartel. Sinaloa's Guzmán Loera introduced La Familia to the manufacture of methamphetamine, and Apatzingán quickly became the meth-making capital of the entire world with several factories, the DEA claims, each capable of producing 300 pounds of product a day.

THE ARMY MOVES IN

Whether it was because it was his home state, was due to the outrage over the Sol y Sombra incident or because they were the newest and presumably weakest cartel, Calderón struck

La Familia first. The heavily armed soldiers—most of them wearing facemasks so that cartel members would not recognize them and undertake retribution against their families—met little resistance at first patrolling major roads and squares and setting up roadblocks and curfews. There was so little action in the beginning, many critics accused the conservative Calderón government of targeting not the cartels, but the Zapatistas and other activist movements in the south.

He quickly followed Operation Michoacán with Operation Baja California (widely known in the media as Operation Tijuana) on January 2, 2007. With help from the navy, 3,296 soldiers and Federales, using 21 airplanes, nine helicopters, 28 ships, 247 tactical vehicles and 10 drug-sniffing dogs, took control of Tijuana in the middle of a record cold snap that had left a light dusting of snow on the city. If Operation Michoacán—taking place in a largely agrarian, heavily indigenous state—could be compared to the American military taking over New Mexico, the invasion of a large, diverse port city of Tijuana would be like taking over Seattle.

Their first major arrests were police officers. On January 26, video surveillance captured a group of Federales and state police taking a bribe—a $100 bill and a 200-peso note are clearly seen changing hands—to allow a luxury SUV to pass through a checkpoint. As an experiment, the army disarmed all local and state police in Tijuana—on the pretext that they were checking their weapons for fingerprints and other evidence—and, according to *Zeta*, petty crime surged by 50 percent in those two weeks.

MAJOR ARRESTS

On January 20, Calderón delivered on a campaign promise to break with Mexican tradition and extradited convicted Gulf Cartel kingpin Osiel Cárdenas Guillén and 14 other convicted traffickers to the United States on the understanding that prosecutors there would not pursue the death penalty. This was a move that impressed many Mexicans, as Cárdenas Guillén had been taunting Mexican authorities by throwing lavish children's parties in his own honor all over northern Mexico, which he coordinated from his prison cell. Children in the area referred to him as "Abuelo Coca" (Grandpa Coke).

Back in Tijuana, on April 3, 2007, the army made headlines when they arrested Víctor Magno "El Matapolicías" (the Cop Killer) Escobar Luna, a former Baja California state police officer who led a small army of kidnappers and assassins for the Tijuana Cartel. In 2005, the corpse of his brother Ricardo had been dumped at a busy intersection in the Bonita neighborhood, likely the work of assassins from the Sinaloa Cartel.

Two weeks later, the army captured cartel member Teodoro "El Teo" Garcia Simental. He was injured in the raid and taken to Tijuana's General Hospital. On April 18, the cartel led its first offensive against the military when a group of armed, masked men stormed the hospital searching for Garcia Simental, and taking hostages at the same time. In the resulting three-hour firefight, an army private, a Federale and a hospital custodian were killed. After one of the gang's leaders, Ernesto Sánchez Vega, was captured, the raiders abandoned their plan and retreated. Their vehicles were later intercepted by state police who let them pass. Five of the officers were identified by eyewitness accounts and arrested soon after the incident. Their official excuse was that they believed they were too outgunned to apprehend the fleeing suspects.

Mexican authorities extended their targets beyond the obvious, but Calderón's next move was a public relations disaster. Zhen-Li "El Chino" (the Chinaman) Ye Gon was a Shanghai-born businessman who came to Mexico in 2002, becoming a citizen later that year. One of his many businesses was a pharmaceutical firm called Unimed Pharm Chem. With it, he received a license to import huge quantities of pseudoephedrine and its precursor, raw ephedrine, into Mexico from China. Of course, while pseudoephedrine is the basic active ingredient in many over-the-counter decongestants, it is also the primary ingredient for methamphetamine. When Ye Gon allowed his import license to lapse in the summer of 2005, the DEA alleged that he was continuing to import pseudoephedrine for the sole purpose of making methamphetamine and named him as a member of the Sinaloa Cartel.

On March 15, 2007, Federales entered his $2–million house in the posh Las Lomas de Chapultepec neighborhood in northwest Mexico City. Inside, they found $207 million in U.S. currency, 18 million pesos, 200,000 euros, 113,000 Hong Kong dollars and 11 centenarios (Mexican gold coins). The police also uncovered a high-output, medical-quality laboratory. They arrested nine people, including Ye Gon. Four of those arrested were Chinese citizens.

Ye Gon denied being involved in the drug trade or having ties with the cartels. He explained that he did not realize his license had lapsed and that the money was not actually his. Ye Gon claimed that they were illegal contributions to the Calderón presidential campaign and that Secretary of Labor Javier Lozano Alarcón forced him to hide them, by threatening his life, saying "coopera o cuello" (cooperate or it's your neck).

His story became an overnight sensation, with much of the media referring to the story as "coopela o cuello," making fun of Ye Gon's accent. Although Calderón and Lozano Alarcón denied the allegations and were never indicted, many believed Ye Gon's story and there is still a thriving business printing T-shirts, bumper stickers and house signs reading *Creo que el Chino* (I believe the Chinaman). Ye Gon was not indicted and did not appear in court.

THE CARTELS' BRUTAL RETALIATION

National attention returned to the cartels on May 14. In Mexico City, Federal Prosecutor Jose Nemesio Lugo was driving to work in a Pontiac minivan when he was surrounded by gunmen with AR-15s. He was working on a case against the Arellano Félix brothers when he was killed. A few hours later, an army patrol in a crime-ridden neighborhood came across a body. It was that of Jorge Altriste Espinoza, head of the Tijuana's police's special forces. He had been brutally tortured and there were three bullet holes in the back of his head.

In June, the U.S. State Department warned Americans to

exercise extreme caution when visiting Mexico. In response, the Mexican government criticized the Americans for their contributions to the Drug War. Attorney General Eduardo Medina Mora called Washington "cynical" for maintaining that the existence of the cartels was just a Mexican problem, saying that the Americans had done nothing effective to reduce demand for illegal drugs. He also called U.S. gun control laws "absurd" and blamed easy access to high-powered and easily concealed weapons for allowing the cartels to become as well-armed and confident as they had become. This was a break from the Fox government, whom many critics had accused of being subservient to Washington.

Adding to the confusion in Tijuana, a new player stepped into the fray. On August 27, 2007, city workers found three headless corpses in a dump. Investigators later found the men's heads and a note threatening the Tijuana Cartel, specifically mentioning the Arellano Félix brothers. The consensus among the media and public was that the Sinaloa Cartel was taking advantage of the siege, hoping to eliminate the local traffickers and stake the territory for themselves once the army left.

Headless corpses with notes quickly became the calling card for all cartels. "Why do you decapitate people?" Bruce Bagley, a professor at the University of Miami who researches U.S.–Latin American relations, explained to American reporters who were trying to understand the macabre habit. "They are doing this to intimidate authorities, other gangs and the civilian population. The bitterness of the fight has intensified. There's a very unsettled and uncertain set of strategic alliances between these groups that are changing from day to day."

NEW TARGETS: MUSICIANS AND JOURNALISTS

While things were largely calm in the northeast compared to Tijuana, all of Mexico was shocked by what happened there at the beginning of winter. Three days after former Rio Bravo Mayor Juan Gajardo Anzaldua, his brother, two bodyguards and an innocent bystander were mowed down by machine gunfire—an act that forced the army to secure the town—on November 29, a masked man kicked down the door of Room 11 of the Motel Mónaco in nearby Matamoros and opened fire with an AK-47. He hit and critically wounded Zayda Peña Arjona—the popular lead singer of the band Zayda y Los Culpables (Zayda and the Guilty Ones)—and killed her friend Ana Berta Gonzalez and the motel's manager Leonardo Sanchez. The following day, a group of armed men broke into the hospital that was treating her and intercepted her on the way out of emergency surgery. "One can't confront those people, there are more patients around," said a hospital employee who did not want to be named. "What can you do about it?" Seconds after finding her, one of the men put two bullets into Peña Arjona's head. There was no evidence that she was ever linked to the drug trade, and the media postulated that Peña Arjona had angered the cartels by refusing to sing *narcocorridos*.

Born in the Michoacán city of Hidalgo, Paulo Sergio Gómez Sánchez emigrated to a part of Chicago populated mainly by other Mexicans. When the members of the popular band Montez de Durango broke up on Christmas Eve of 2002, many of the members re-formed as a new band called

K-Paz de la Sierra, with Sergio Gómez as their singer. K-Paz, and especially the handsome Gomez, became very popular in Mexico and on Spanish-language radio in the United States. The group's success helped Gómez buy a house in Avon, Indiana, an upscale suburb of Indianapolis. He stayed mainly in the United States, but traveled back to Mexico on occasion to perform.

On December 2, he gave a concert at an open-air festival in the Michoacán city of Morelia. After the show, he and two staff members were driving to their next gig in Puerta Vallarta when their rented Dodge Neon was surrounded by a number of SUVs and forced to stop. The three men were kidnapped and driven away. After two hours of questioning, the two staff members were released.

When the band's publicist, Sergio Gómez Vega (who also went by the name Sergio Gómez), contacted police, he told them that the singer had received death threats before the show in Michoacán, but didn't take them seriously and said he felt he owed his home state a good show. Gómez Vega claimed he had no idea who would want to kill his client or why.

A few hours later, a pair of farm workers found a body by the side of the road. They could not identify his face but said they feared it was Sergio Gómez because of a recognizable tattoo he had on his left bicep. The Michoacán assistant attorney general later told the media that it was indeed Gómez and that he had been severely beaten and burned by acid before being choked to death. His body was returned to his family in Indiana.

On the same day, popular trumpeter Jose Luis Aquino went missing. Three days later, his body was found on a rural Oaxaca roadside with his hands and feet bound and a plastic bag tied over his head.

The killing of three popular musicians in less than a week shocked the nation. Neither Peña nor Gómez sang *narcocorridos* nor had either had any been known to use drugs let alone have connection to the cartels. Peña's father was a deputy prosecutor, but had not been involved in any cases involving the cartels. Aquino's father maintained that although his group, Los Condes (The Counts), did sing *narcocorridos*, he had no connection to the cartels and that his death was likely the result of a car theft. He could not explain why his son was brutally tortured before being put to death, though.

The deaths of the popular musicians not related to the drug trade indicated that nobody was safe—you no longer had to actively oppose (or favor) a cartel to be murdered, you just had to be in Mexico.

A few days later, on December 9, another brazen killing shocked Mexico. Gerardo Israel García Pimentel had just finished his shift at *La Opinión de Michoacán*, a daily newspaper with about 6,500 readers. He was riding his motorcycle to his Uruapan apartment when an SUV tried to force him off the road. He raced home as fast as his little 125cc bike could go, and was followed by the truck. He got to his apartment building, jumped off his bike and ran to his door. Just as he reached the stairwell, the men in the truck fired 45 shells from a pair of AR-15s and three from a Super .38

handgun. At least 28 of those rounds went into or through García Pimentel.

Journalists had certainly been targeted by the cartels before—look at the staff of *Zeta*—but García Pimentel was no investigative reporter causing trouble for the cartels or the police. He worked on *La Opinión*'s farm beat, occasionally writing a low-ball crime story when all of the paper's more senior reporters were too busy, but nothing that would appear to endanger his life. His killing struck many Mexicans as senseless, as though the cartels were picking their targets almost at random.

Faith in local authorities took another big hit near the end of the year. On December 28, the entire 65-strong police force of Playas de Rosarito—a popular vacation spot for young Americans just outside Tijuana—was disarmed and interrogated. "We recognize that the enemy is inside our house and for this reason we are purging the ranks," said Baja California state police chief Daniel de la Rosa Anaya. "We need to have confidence in our police."

As 2007 drew to a close, many in Mexico openly questioned whether the army's presence in Nuevo Laredo, Michoacán and Tijuana was actually helping the overall national situation. Murders and kidnappings were down slightly, but police corruption was still rampant. Critics, like the editors of *Zeta*, pointed out one particularly chilling statistic—that arrests among minors had quadrupled since the invasion. The cartels were outsourcing their criminal tasks, including assassination, to youngsters who were much less likely to arouse suspicion and would, by constitutional law, not face stiff prison terms if caught.

Calderón stressed that the Mexican people had to be patient. He told them that the official corruption ran too deep and that the crime organizations were too powerful for his administration to fix everything right away, and warned them that the results of his actions might not begin to be seen until after his six-year term as president.

CHAPTER 8
Battling the Beltrán Leyva Cartel

While the forces fighting against cartels and corruption had little to celebrate at the end of 2007, they started 2008 with a bang. On January 21, the army announced that it had captured Alfredo "El Mochomo" (the Little Ant) Beltrán Leyva. Tipped off by an informant, a mixed squad of army soldiers and Federales arrested Beltrán Leyva and two associates on their way to Beltrán Leyva's home in Culiacán. He was carrying an AK-47 and two suitcases containing just over $900,000 in U.S. currency, along with a number of luxury watches valued at close to $100,000.

One of the founders of the Beltrán Leyva Cartel, Alfredo Beltrán Leyva was its undisputed leader and was second only to Sinaloa chief Joaquín Guzmán Loera himself in their cartels' alliance. According to Mexican authorities, Alfredo was in charge of transporting drugs over the Mexicali–Calexico crossing, was also involved in money laundering and even commanded a number of *sicarios*, a Mexican slang word for assassins, derived from classical Roman times. His arrest was a huge boost to the president's plan, and was praised by the Americans as well. "Today was a significant victory for Mexican armed forces," said Tony Garza, American ambassador to Mexico. "This arrest demonstrates once again the ongoing commitment of President Calderón and his administration to hit the criminal organizations where it hurts."

Alfredo's brother Arturo (the cartel's new boss) was so enraged by the arrest that he ordered the assassinations of the acting chief of the Federales, Édgar Eusebio Millán Gómez, and other top officials. On May 8, his team cornered Millán Gómez and two bodyguards at 2:30 a.m., just after he exited his white Chevrolet Trailblazer SUV outside of the high red fence in front of his home at 132 Calle Camelia in the Guerrero neighborhood of Mexico City and opened fire. Millán Gómez was hit eight times in the chest and once in the hand. He died the following day in Metropolitan Hospital. He was the tenth member of the Federale management team killed that month.

Somehow, one of Millán Gómez's seriously wounded bodyguards, Warrant Officer Daniel de la Vega Hernández, managed to wrestle one of the assailants to the ground and arrest him. The man, 34-year-old Alejandro Ramírez Báez, was wearing latex gloves, had a pistol with a silencer and appeared to be drunk or high. Although he had been convicted for a couple of car thefts in the past, he was not known to be a cartel member.

Under questioning, he revealed that he had been sent by the Sinaloa Cartel to exact revenge for the arrest of Alfredo Beltrán Leyva. His information led to the arrest of low-level cartel members José Antonio Martín Garfias, Virginia Juana González Bravo, María Teresa Villanueva Aguirre, Jose and Jorge Ortega Lugo and Alejandro Ramírez Báez Gallegos. A search of a nearby house used as a staging area for the attack revealed dozens of assault rifles (both AK-47s and AR-15s), pistols, grenade launchers, 30 hand grenades and bulletproof vests marked with the letters "FEDA"—which the Federales claimed stood for Fuerzas Especiales de Arturo "Special Forces of Arturo." All of the suspects were later implicated in the assassination of Roberto Velasco Bravo, senior director of the Federales' organized crime unit, and the possession of illegal radio equipment and listening devices.

While the murder of Millán Gómez was the most prominent in Mexico that week—his funeral was attended by Calderón and most of the top military brass—it was just one of more than 100 assassinations kicked off by that of Velasco Bravo.

And while Millán Gómez was still clinging to life, another hit squad was at work. Just as the chief of Mexico City's investigative police force, Esteban Robles Espinosa, was getting into his Ford Fiesta at 8:30 a.m. on his way to work, his way was blocked by a gray Nissan Quest minivan. When the side door slid open, masked gunmen jumped out and shot 13 handgun bullets at Robles Espinosa. Eight hit him, including two in the head and another two in the chest. He was unarmed because a girlfriend had left with his gun after an argument the night before.

Although most media sources believed the police assassinations were a sign of goodwill from the Sinaloa Cartel to the Beltrán Leyva brothers, they did not improve relations between the two groups. In fact, Arturo Beltrán Leyva believed that Guzmán Loera had actually tipped off the Federales and was responsible for Alfredo's arrest. And he wanted revenge.

REALIGNING ALLIANCES IN THE CARTELS

At 8:30 in the evening of the day after Millán Gómez was shot, three SUVs roared into the parking lot of the City Club supermarket on Boulevard Universitarios in the north end of Culiacán. As soon as they stopped, some 15 masked men opened fire with pistols and assault rifles. The three targeted men were too surprised to draw their weapons or flee. Two of them were killed at the scene and one was critically injured. One of the dead men was Edgar Guzmán Lopez, Guzmán Loera's 22-year-old son. He was in his second year at Sinaloa Autonomous University, studying business administration and had a two-year-old daughter with his girlfriend, Frida Muñoz Roman. More than 500 cartridges were recovered by investigators and 20 vehicles were damaged beyond repair.

It was clear that the Beltrán Leyvas could no longer work with the Sinaloa Cartel. Instead, they aligned with (but did not join) the Gulf Cartel, dealing particularly with Los Zetas. This shift in the balance of power also affected relations between the Sinaloa and the Juárez Cartels. Although weakened by the loss of the Beltrán Leyva Cartel's support, the Sinaloa Cartel had since absorbed the Colima Cartel, Sonora Cartel, Milenio Cartel and what remained of the original Guadalajara Cartel. Now it was the Juárez Cartel who appeared to be the weakest and most vulnerable of all the major gangs, despite controlling some of the most lucrative crossings into Texas.

But the Juárez Cartel was willing to fight. Back in January, someone had taped a poster to the police memorial in Juárez that showed the names and pictures of 12 high-ranking police officers and described them as "executable." It was addressed to "those who still don't believe." For much of that year, someone hacked into the police radio frequency and threatened individual cops over their two-way radios. The day after Guzmán Lopez was killed, Juan Antonio Roman Garcia, the second-in-command of the Juárez police force, was headed to a family party when his official car was intercepted by two trucks. Without getting out of their vehicles, the gunmen pumped 50 rounds into Roman Garcia and his car. He was the eighth victim of the 12 officers on the executables list. Hours after Roman Garcia was killed, his boss, police chief Guillermo Prieto Quintana quit and moved to El Paso, Texas. He didn't make any elaborate excuses; he was just scared.

On a giant billboard that read "Juárez Needs You! Join up and become part of the city police," someone had painted "Los Zetas want you—we offer good salaries to soldiers." Less than a week later, a banner was stretched across Nuevo Laredo's Avenida Reforma reading: "Los Zetas operations group wants you, soldier or ex-soldier. We offer you a good salary, food and attention for your family. Don't suffer hunger and abuse anymore." In smaller text there was note that pointed out Los Zetas did not serve their men instant ramen noodles, a jab at the military's rations. Not to be outdone, the Gulf Cartel put one up in Tampico that read: "Join the ranks of the Gulf Cartel. We offer benefits: life insurance, a house for your family and children. Stop living in the slums and riding the bus. A new car or truck, your choice."

News of more violence—some of it against U.S. nationals—from that weekend emerged. Three men driving a gray Ford Crown Victoria home from a horseracing track stopped at a red light on Avenida Vicente Guerrero in downtown Nuevo Laredo and were showered by more than 70 shots from assault rifles from a white van. Lorenzo Juárez Aguayo and Agustin Damian Navarrete died, while backseat passenger Juan Verdugo was critically wounded. It is believed they were shot because their Crown Victoria looked like an undercover police or DEA vehicle. And four more Americans from El Paso—Juan Manuel Contreras Machado, Luz Elena Velazquez, Jorge Jimenez and Alejandro Vazquez—were shot as they exited the Arriba Chihuahua nightclub in Juárez. They were not known to be connected to the drug trade.

The U.S. government increased its warnings to Americans about traveling to Mexico, especially to border cities like Juárez, Tijuana and Nuevo Laredo where the violence had been most frequent. "It's almost like a military fight," said Jayson Ahern, the deputy commissioner of U.S. Customs and Border Protection. "I don't think that generally the American public has any sense of the level of violence that occurs on the border."

But at the same time, they indicated that people should not be worried about the violence if they stayed north of the Rio Grande. "We just trust and believe that it will not come across to our side of the border," acting El Paso county sheriff Jimmy Apodaca said. "If it does, we are ready."

Later that month, the cartels set a new and disturbing precedent. Previously, when the army and/or Federales surrounded one of their houses or clubs, the men inside would surrender. But on May 28 that changed. A raid on a house containing suspected Sinaloa Cartel members took place that evening, but this time, the men inside decided to fight their way out. Seven Federales were killed in the ensuing melée. Two men were arrested, but they were just foot soldiers, the important cartel members having escaped. It had been abundantly clear that the cartels were as well armed as the police (if not better) and were now willing to fight to stay out of custody.

THE WEAPON OF CHOICE—THE AK-47

One of the guns confiscated in the raid was a Romanian-made copy of an AK-47. The AK-47—arguably the world's favorite weapon—is an assault rifle developed by Soviet general Mikhail Kalashnikov just after World War II. It is capable of firing ten 7.62 mm cartridges a second at 1,600 miles per hour for an effective range of about 330 feet. Its simple, rugged construction makes it a reliable weapon in any climate and under strenuous conditions, and keeps its price down. The AK-47, variants and copies, have been produced in more than two dozen countries and have been used by countless armies, both official and rebels, around the world. It has even appeared on national flags.

What was interesting about this particular AK-47, though, was the fact that it could be traced by the FBI. Four months earlier, a 21-year-old American named Cameron Scott Galloway walked into X Caliber Guns, a weapons shop in a sleepy strip mall next to the Little Shoppe of Hair in north-western Phoenix, not far from the Phoenix National Forest. He paid $3,000 for six AK-47s, getting an impressive deal. The FBI tracked him down, arrested him, but reduced the charges after he became a cooperative witness. He told them that all he knew was that a co-worker's brother had offered him $3,600 for the guns and all he had to do was sign for them. He knew they were going to Mexico, but claimed he did not know that they were to be used by people in organized crime.

Digging further, the FBI traced the gun back to the factory, getting a clear indication of how these dangerous weapons get into the hands of cartels, despite being illegal not just in Mexico, but also in the U.S. The gun was manufactured at the Regia Autonomă pentru producţia de Tehnică Militară (RATMIL) factory in Cugir, a small town in the Transylvanian district of Romania. RATMIL makes both military and civil-ian versions of the rifle. The civilian models are heavily modi-fied, with features such as automatic fire removed.

These reduced-specification rifles are imported legally to Century International, a Delray, Florida-based company that specializes in surplus military and military-style weapons. The stripped-down AK-47s are marketed to gun shops—Century International sells only to registered retailers—as the WASR-10 hunting rifle which is legal in all American states, except New Jersey and California. Despite its power and wow appeal, the WASR-10 can be had in many parts of the U.S. for as little as $500 brand new.

Of course, the modifications made by RATMIL are easily reversed by a skilled gunsmith, and kits are sold online to change the WASR-10s back to full-featured AK-47s. The kits are strictly illegal, but companies get around the loophole by selling half the kit, while another company sells the other half. The finished AK-47s are then smuggled to Mexico, where they fetch prices of about $2,000. This was big business—of the 62 AK-47s confiscated by police in Mexico in the first half of 2008, more than half of them could eventually be traced back to X Caliber.

GUNS ACROSS BORDERS

The other commonly seen assault rifle in Mexico, the AR-15, follows a similar trajectory. A civilian version of the U.S. military's M-16, the AR-15 is widely available as a hunting rifle and is also easy to modify back to military specifications. Although it is lighter, has a higher rate of fire, higher muzzle velocity and is much more accurate than the AK-47, it's not as popular with the cartels because it is not nearly as reliable and its 5.56 mm ammunition is harder to acquire.

Mexican officials frequently blame the U.S. for the massive importation of weapons into Mexico, pointing out that the

U.S. has 54,000 legal firearms dealers (Canada has about 520), while Mexico has just one, and it is strictly controlled by the army. American critics, meanwhile, have pointed out that only a tiny fraction of the weapons seized by the Mexican government have been tracked at all and only some of those originated in the U.S. They also noted that many of the AK-47s seized were made by Norinco, a Chinese firm long banned from importing to the U.S. for supplying weapons to Iran and other hostile groups, and that the cartels' heavy weapons like rocket-propelled grenades are hardly legal on the streets of Texas. While acknowledging that some weapons come from north of the border, those critics remind the Mexicans that at least 160,000 soldiers defected from their military in the period between 2003 and 2009—many of them with their weapons— and that cartels and rebel groups from Guatemala to Colombia regularly trade in heavy weapons for drugs.

Two days after the raid that killed seven Federales, President George W. Bush set his own precedent. He imposed sanctions on a number of groups he considered to be dangerous to the United States because they trafficked illegal drugs. They included the Kurdistan People's Party, the 'Ndrangheta (which had usurped the Costa Nostra as the dominant Italian mafia organization), as well as the Sinaloa and Beltrán Leyva Cartels. This allowed the Americans to arrest anyone caught doing business with them. "This action underscores the president's determination to do everything possible to pursue drug traffickers, undermine their operations and end the suffering that trade in illicit drugs inflicts on Americans and other people around the world, as well as prevent drug traffickers from supporting terrorists," said White House spokeswoman Dana Perino.

It was still open season on police commanders in Mexico. Igor Labastida Calderón was one of the few surviving officers remaining from the "executables" list. The chief of the Federales, Igor Labastida Calderón, agents Humberto Torices Morales and Alvaro Perez Mendoza, and Yezel Heidi Cruz Osorio, director of material resources for the Federales, sat down for lunch on June 26 at the popular Buenos Aires soup restaurant in the "Little Argentina" neighborhood of Mexico City. They were approached by two young men. One pulled out an Uzi and began firing, while the other had a video camera. When they were satisfied Labastida was dead (the other two were wounded, but survived), they continued filming for a few moments, then fled. Portions of the video showed up later on YouTube. The next day, national Interior Minister Juan Camilo Mourino said that the assassinations "have a clear objective to intimidate, frighten, paralyze society and, with that, force the federal government to retreat." The day after that, four more Federales were killed after their car was forced off the road in Culiacán and gunmen emerged with AK-47s.

THE MÉRIDA INITIATIVE IN THE WAR ON TRAFFICKING

For months, the Bush and Calderón governments had been working on an arrangement to coordinate their offensives against drug traffickers and allow aid from the U.S. to get to

Mexico. The Mexicans wanted the Americans to acknowledge that the problem was largely due to American demand and the relative abundance of firearms, while the Americans wanted the Mexicans to be more transparent in their financial dealings and to be more aggressive in investigating human rights abuses by its police and military.

After much negotiation, the $1.6 billion Mérida Initiative was signed into law on June 30. It began with $400 million in aid to Mexico, $65 million to neighboring Central American countries to fight the trafficking of drugs into the United States and $74 million to American agencies to try to stem the flow of weapons into Mexico. The deal included:

- Non-intrusive inspection equipment including ion scanners, gamma-ray scanners, X-ray scanners and drug-sniffing dogs
- Software that improved telecommunications for Mexican investigators
- Training for investigators and prosecutors
- The establishment of offices for citizen complaints and professional responsibility and the introduction of witness protection programs
- Thirteen Bell 412 EP utility helicopters and eight much larger UH-60 Black Hawk transport helicopters
- Four Spanish-built CASA CN-235 military transport airplanes
- Anti-gang equipment, training and community action programs for the Central American countries.

There was a great deal of criticism of the deal on both sides. Many Americans thought the money could be better spent on drug education and rehabilitation rather than more interdiction, while many around the world found the concept of further militarization of Mexican society to be frightening. That criticism reached a crescendo on August 2, when a videotape from the city of León in Guanajuato was leaked to the media of police training methods that included torture techniques like forcing trainees to roll in their own vomit or blasting carbonated water into their nostrils. One of the instructors was an American, speaking in English, but he was later determined to have been a non-government contractor hired before the Mérida Initiative came into effect.

As the video was broadcast over and over again on Mexican TV, it sparked outrage. "This is troubling," said Sergio Aguayo Quezada, founder of the nonprofit Mexican Academy for Human Rights. "In the past, torture was usually hidden; now they don't even bother."

Some Mexican officials, however, defended the videos and the methods, explaining that a different kind of war demanded different tactics. "Perhaps it looks inhumane to us," León Mayor Vicente Guerrero Reynosa told *El Heraldo de León*, the newspaper that broke the story. "But it is part of a preparation method that is used all over the world."

That didn't inspire much faith in the Mexican government among human rights observers around the world. "The only thing that I thought when I saw those videos was: 'Thank God the U.S. Congress attached some human rights conditions,'" said José Miguel Vivanco, director of the Americas for Human Rights Watch.

THE KILLING MOVES TO CIVILIANS

For the most part, the people who had been killed or injured in Mexico were cartel members, informants, police officers, military personnel or politicians. There were a few targeted celebrities and journalists, some mistaken identities and some collateral damage (an infant and his four-year-old brother had been killed by stray bullets in an assassination attempt in Chihuahua in August), but ordinary civilians had never been in the crosshairs until Mexican Independence Day.

At about 11:00 p.m. on September 15, 2008 in the Plaza Melchor Ocampo in the center of the Michoacán city of Morelia, Governor Leonel Godoy Rangel was introducing his speech with the traditional *vivas* to Mexican revolutionary heroes in preparation for a reenactment of Hidalgo's "Grito de Dolores" when somebody threw a hand grenade into the crowd. The resulting panic sent townspeople stampeding down a side street, where an assailant threw another grenade among them. Later that night two more explosions were heard on a road out of town. A local journalist described people "falling like dominoes." When the dust settled, eight people—including a 13-year-old boy—were dead and more than 100 were injured.

Godoy toured local hospitals and blamed the unprecedented and terrifying attack on "organized crime," but no group claimed responsibility for it. In fact, La Familia vehemently denied it would ever attack women and children, going as far as to distribute pamphlets and hang up banners to that effect, as well as text messaging reporters denying they would ever stoop so low. "Coward is the word for those who attack the country's peace and tranquility," said one typical message.

Most people blamed the other cartels, particularly Los Zetas, who were well known as the most aggressive and most likely to use terroristic tactics. But since the blast occurred in President Calderón's hometown on Independence Day, some blamed the attack on paramilitary groups affiliated with the PRI or even the Zapatistas.

In an interview with *The New York Times*, Calderón expressed sympathy for the victims of violence all over Mexico, but said that the upsurge in terror tactics indicated that the cartels were feeling the heat from his offensives and were fighting among themselves for a diminishing market. He defended his long-range plan. "What are the alternatives?" he said. "Is the alternative to allow organized crime to take over the country?"

Two days after the Morelia grenade attack, the DEA—in conjunction with the FBI and Italian police—launched what U.S. attorney general Michael Mukasey called a "massive raid," arresting 200 people in New York City and the southern Italian state of Calabria. The culmination of a 15-month investigation of the 'Ndrangheta, Operation Solare (also known as Operation Reckoning) also implicated some allies of the 'Ndrangheta that surprised few at the DEA. Among those were Gulf Cartel chief Ezequiel "Tony Tormenta" (Tony Storm)

Cárdenas Guillén, his second-in-command Jorge Eduardo "El Coss" Costilla Sánchez and Heriberto "El Verdugo" (the Executioner) Lazcano Lazcano, the leader of Los Zetas. The Mexican government issued 30-million peso bounties for each of them and the DEA added another $5 million for the head of Lazcano Lazcano.

Although the arrests put away many of the most important members of the Aquino-Coluccio clan of the 'Ndrangheta, Calabrian deputy prosecutor Nicola Gratteri said that the drug trade between the Mexicans and the Italians (who imported cocaine and heroin throughout Europe, the U.S. and Canada) would go on because there was just too much money to be made, and because the Mexicans charged much less than the Colombians while being more reliable.

On September 28, three men—Juan Carlos Castro Galeana, Julio Cesar Mondragon Mendoza and Alfredo Rosas Elicea—were arrested for the Morelia grenade incident. Under heavy interrogation, they admitted to the attack and revealed that they were paid to do it by Los Zetas in an effort to "provoke" the government. "I was hiding it in my hands, and it made me shudder," Castro Galeana said of the first grenade in a videotaped confession. "I was desperate to get rid of it."

Mexico was not the only government the cartels wanted to provoke. Just after sundown on October 12, two masked men got out of a car in front of the U.S. consulate in Monterrey and opened fire with handguns. One of them threw a fragmentation grenade over the fence, but it failed to explode. Nobody was hurt and the overall damage was negligible, but the message was clear. The U.S. government was a target because of its support of the Calderón war on drug trafficking.

Law enforcement scored a huge hit on October 22, coinciding with a visit to Puerta Vallarta by American secretary of state Condoleezza Rice. Acting on a tip from an informant, the army and Federales stormed a mansion in the Desierto de los Leones neighborhood of Mexico City. After a prolonged firefight, they made 16 arrests, the most important being Jesus "El Rey" (the King) Zambada García, one of the four regional bosses of the Sinaloa Cartel. He handled the Central Mexico/ Capital region, answering only to Guzmán Loera. Also arrested were his son, 21-year-old Jesus Zambada Reyes, and nephew, 23-year-old Jorge Zambada Niebla, both accused of being cartel bigwigs.

The arrested men were shown on nationwide TV and, for the first time, so were some of the incredible luxury items they owned. By showing gaudy and expensive goods like customized Bentleys and gold-plated AK-47s, the government was stressing the point that the men who ran the cartels were hardly fitting the mold of Robin Hood.

The day after the arrest, children in the central city of Cuautitlán found a human head in a black plastic garbage bag. It was later identified to have belonged to a state police officer. Later that day, a courier dropped off a cooler at the police station of Ascensión, a small town about 20 miles south of the border with New Mexico. It sat there most of the day until a curious cop opened it to find four severed heads inside and a note from the Gulf Cartel warning them not to cross them.

The following day, Assistant Attorney General for the State of Morelos Andres Dimitriadis Juárez was driving his Ford Focus in the Diana Delicias neighborhood of Cuernevaca when his way was blocked by two small cars, one white and one red. As he honked his horn for them to move on, gunmen emerged and pumped more that 100 shells into his car no more than 100 yards away from the Federales local headquarters. He and two assistants riding with him died. Dimitriadis Juárez was new to the job when he was killed, having taken over when his boss, Victor Enrique Payan, was found in the trunk of a car in May. Just as news of his assassination was being broadcast, another severed head with a warning note to La Familia from the Gulf Cartel was found in a cooler in the central square of the Michoacán port city of Lázaro Ramirez.

The forces against the cartels got a much-needed shot in the arm on October 26, when, for the second time, the daughter of a drug lord made his arrest possible. An 11-year-old girl in the upscale Chapultepec neighborhood of Tijuana known as Alicia Bracamontes let it slip that this was not her real name. Investigators soon determined that her father, Samuel Bracamontes, was none other than Eduardo "El Doctor" Arellano Félix, chief financial officer for the Tijuana Cartel.

Their house was surrounded by 100 Federales, the special forces of the army's 28th Infantry Battalion and the Second Motorized Cavalry Regiment. When asked to surrender, Arellano Félix and his men answered with gunfire. After a three-hour firefight, Arellano Félix was arrested, along with 28-year-old Luis "El Güero Camarón" (the Blond Shrimp)

Ramirez Vázquez, a known cartel operative who was badly injured in the gunfight, and 21-year-old Benitez Villa Ester, a native of Culiacán. Alicia was found unharmed. Police confiscated $1.2 million in $100 bills, two AK-47s, a submachine gun, two fragmentation grenades, three bulletproof vests, eight vehicles, 12 cell phones and 15 radios.

The incident was hailed as a huge arrest, as the Arellano Félix brothers were being taken down one by one. Federal Undersecretary of Public Security Facundo Rosas Rosas warned that although the original generation of the Arellano Félix brothers was being neutralized, they had since passed on the day-to-day operations of the cartel to nephew Luis Fernando "El Ingeniero" (The Engineer) Sánchez Arellano, who is a known fugitive named as head of a gang by the Mexican government. Many believed he was assisted by his aunt, Enedina Arellano Félix, who is also a fugitive.

Rosas Rosas acknowledged men loyal to Teodoro García Simental and the Sinaloa Cartel were fighting their own war on the city's streets, recalling the five bodies (four decapitated) a month earlier. One of the bodies had his head placed on his lower back with "we are the people of the weakened engineer" scrawled in blood between his shoulder blades, a reference to new Tijuana capo Sánchez Arellano.

CORRUPTION IN THE RANKS

Before law enforcement could make an effective push against the cartels, it had to win the war inside its own ranks. In the month after the capture of Eduardo Arellano Félix, there was a series of high-profile arrests as part of Operación Limpiar (Operation Clean Up) within the police that revealed how widespread corruption was at the top. It kicked off on November 2 when Victor Gerardo Garay Cadena, chief of the Federales, resigned to pursue other career options. It had long been rumored that he had been taking bribes. "I am resigning because in the bloody fight against organized crime, it is our duty to strengthen institutions, which means it is essential to eliminate any shadows of doubt regarding me," he said. Garay Cadena was arrested a month later after testimony from a number of captured traffickers revealed that he had received cash, jewels and even gold bricks in exchange for co-operating with the Beltrán Leyva Cartel, including calling off at least two different offensives against them and allowing them to escape police manhunts on several occasions. The investigation into his behavior began when three Colombian women who attended a party testified that Garay Cadena—who was sitting in a hot tub with four prostitutes at the time—ordered his men to rob them of nearly $500,000 worth of cash and jewelry.

Two weeks after Garay Cadena stepped down, the attorney general's office announced the arrest of Ricardo Gutiérrez Vargas, a former chief of Mexico's Federal Investigative Agency who had since become Interpol's top officer in Mexico, and his No. 2 man, Rodolfo de la Guardia García. They were accused of leaking police information to the Sinaloa Cartel.

And two days later, Noé Ramírez Mandujano, who had stepped down as the chief of Subprocuraduría de Investigación

Especializada en Delincuencia Organizada (Specialized Investigation of Organized Crime or SIEDO, an investigative organization that answered to the attorney general) earlier in the year, was arrested after an investigation revealed that he had received $450,000 from the Sinaloa Cartel in exchange for inside information.

The mass arrests greatly weakened the upper echelons of law enforcement in Mexico, but they also rid it of a significant amount of corruption. Calderón again asked the Mexican people to stand firm with his war against traffickers: "The Mexican government is firmly committed to the fight against organized crime and not just organized crime but corruption." The government was desperate to replace these high-ranking officers and had to hope that the new appointees were not only competent, but above corruption.

The arrests did not stop the government from launching its own offensives. On November 7, in the midst of Operation Clean Up, the attorney general's office announced the arrest of an original member of Los Zetas, Jaime "El Hummer" González Durán. He surrendered without violence, but police uncovered a huge cache of weapons at his residence. He was charged with a laundry list of drug-related charges and revealed that he orchestrated the violent rescue of Gulf Cartel member Daniel "El Mejilla" (the Cheek) Perez Rojas from police custody four months earlier. González Durán was also widely believed to be responsible for the murder of singer Valentin Elizalde Valencia.

But there was little for Calderón and his allies to celebrate at the end of the year, as news that the war was spilling over Mexico's northern and southern borders. A story broke in *The Houston Chronicle* that cartel members were fraudulently purchasing massive numbers of firearms in Texas and smuggling them south. "Our investigations show Houston is the top source for firearms going into Mexico, top source in the country," said J. Dewey Webb, special agent in charge of the U.S. Bureau of Alcohol, Tobacco, Firearms and Explosives Houston division. He pointed out that many of the weapons were purchased for the cartels by American citizens or had been sold to the cartels by unscrupulous gun dealers. "They are just as responsible for the killing of that person in Mexico, that police officer or innocent bystander as if they had pulled the trigger themselves," he said. "They have blood on their hands, just like that person who pulled the trigger in Mexico."

Then on December 5, a firefight broke out in La Libertad, Guatemala, just over the border from Mexico. When it was over, 18 bodies were recovered. Some of the vehicles abandoned at the scene had license plates from the northern state of Tamaulipas, the heart of Gulf Cartel territory.

Guatemalan officials were quick to accuse rival Mexican cartels of bringing their war into their country. "The hypothesis we have is clear, and it is that several cartels here that are operating in Guatemalan territory already have certain alliances with Mexican cartels, specifically the alliances that have been made for the trafficking of drugs," said the chief of Guatemala's National Civil Police, Marlene Blanco Lapola. "We are studying the arrival of many Mexicans, specifically members of Los Zetas, who have wanted to come to take advantage of the Guatemalan territory, a situation that we, as authorities, will not allow."

Nor did the cartels want to let Mexicans forget that the war was in their own front yard as well. On December 22, a woman who did not want to be named and her mother drove their beat-up blue Dodge pickup truck into the parking lot at the giant Sam's Club department store in the medium-sized Guerrero city of Chilpancingo for a little late Christmas shopping. They chanced upon a large black plastic garbage bag. Inside were nine severed heads, some still with duct tape over their mouths. Three had their military identification badges stuffed into their mouths.

Later that day, their bodies were found at two separate locations on opposite ends of town. Each had a cardboard sign attached which read "For every one of mine that you kill, I will kill 10." Eight of the dead were soldiers and the other was a former Chilpancingo chief of police.

It was a sobering reminder that the government was at war with a well-armed, well-disciplined and dedicated enemy. In 2006, when the cartels were mainly fighting each other and President Fox had sent the first government troops into Nuevo Laredo, there were 62 deaths—about one every six days—associated with the War Against Drug Trafficking. In 2007, after President Calderón kicked off the New Year by deploying huge numbers of soldiers throughout the country, that number rose to 2,837. And as the cartels reorganized and went on the offensive in 2008, the death toll increased to 6,844 or about 19 per day.

CHAPTER 9
Carnage in 2009

The Mexican government decided to wait until after New Year's Day 2009 to announce two huge arrests that had been made the previous week. The first was the latest corrupt official caught up in Operation Clean Up: SIEDO determined that army major Arturo González Rodríguez, who had once been part of President Calderón's personal security detail, had been receiving $100,000 a month for providing weapons to and coordinating military-style training for Los Zetas.

His arrest, and the admission by Secretary of Defense Guillermo Galván Galván that at least 100,000 Mexican soldiers had switched sides and gone to work for the cartels for higher pay, led many to criticize the military and its role in the war on drug trafficking. Even the most ardent critics had to admit, however, that the war had reached a scale at which intervention by the military was inevitable. "The participation by [the military] is necessary because there is a threat and harm to national security," said Guillermo Velasco Arzac, spokesperson for Mejor Sociedad, Mejor Gobierno (Better Society, Better Government), a citizen's rights advocacy group that had been highly critical of Calderón in the past. "It's known that many of the successes have come from the work done by military intelligence and investigation."

The other major arrest was that of Alberto "La Fresa" (the Strawberry) Espinoza Barrón, a high-ranking lieutenant in La Familia. Acting on an anonymous tip (many Mexicans believe it was a former La Familia member who had switched sides to Los Zetas), a special forces unit of the army surrounded his home on December 29, 2008, and he surrendered without a shot fired. Despite La Familia's vehement denials of involvement in the grenade attack in Morelia, it was among the many charges leveled at Espinoza Barrón. From his home and vehicles, police confiscated three AR-15s, an AK-47, 37 ammunition clips, six pistols, five fragmentation grenades and four plastic bags containing marijuana and crack cocaine. They also found a list of 150 "workers" he was to have paid that day.

NATIONAL JOURNALISTS ARE TARGETS AGAIN

The news, literally, took a turn for the worse on January 7, 2009. The cast and crew at the Televisa's Monterrey affiliate were getting ready for their Tuesday night newscast when they heard shots and then a loud explosion. Nobody was hurt, but the gunfire and grenade thrown at the front entrance damaged the building and 16 nearby vehicles. When the smoke cleared, a note was discovered tied to the front door. It read: "Stop broadcasting only about us, broadcast about narco-political leaders too; this is a warning."

That the cartels were attempting to bully the national media into reporting only what they would allow was a huge blow to the collective Mexican psyche. At least 11 journalists were killed in Mexico in 2008 alone (second only to Iraq's 15), but none were noteworthy on a national scale. For years, reporters in hot areas like Juárez, Nuevo Laredo, Tijuana, Culiacán and Morelia routinely refused to cover drug-related stories or reported under assumed names.

But Televisa—Mexico's biggest broadcaster and a trusted national institution—was another matter entirely. "We face a huge risk of becoming a blind and deaf country, because the messengers are not telling us what they are observing out of sheer fear," said Gerardo Priego Tapia, a PAN congressman who many consider a future presidential candidate. "We think that this case, against the most important TV company in Mexico in one of the most important business capitals in Latin America, is not an accident. It's a symbol and a warning of how this year is going to be."

THE STEWMAKER

Mexicans, now inured to news of shootings, bombings and even beheadings, were shocked again later that month. On January 22, police and army troops stormed a beach house near Tijuana owned by Tijuana Cartel boss Teodoro García Simental. He managed yet another narrow escape, but the authorities arrested a man named Santiago Meza López as he was attempting to get into his car. Under interrogation, Meza López revealed that he was paid about $600 a week by García Simental to dissolve the bodies of the cartel's victims in drums of sodium hydroxide, also known as lye or caustic soda. After he "cooked" them for eight hours, all that remained were teeth and nails. He disposed of those final pieces by burning them with gasoline in a nearby landfill. He was known in the cartel as "El Pozolero" (the Stewmaker), because his mixtures of bodies and lye reminded them of *pozole*, a local delicacy. Interestingly, in the days before the *conquistadores*, *pozole* was actually made with human meat, the remains of prisoners sacrificed by the Aztecs.

Meza López claimed to have disposed of more than 300 corpses that way. "They brought me the bodies and I just got rid of them," he told reporters. "I didn't feel anything." The next story on Televisa's newscast that night was about a cooler containing two severed heads and a note threatening La Familia that showed up on the doorstep of a Guanajuato police station. The contents of the note were not made public, but police acknowledged that it was signed by Los Zetas.

NEW AUTHORITIES IN QUINTANA ROO

On February 2, retired army General Mauro Enrique Tello Quiñonez was sworn in as special drug investigator for the

Benito Juárez municipality in Quintana Roo, which includes the popular tourist destination of Cancún. A former leader of the nation's infantry, Tello Quiñonez left the military after reaching the mandatory retirement age of 63. Less than 24 hours after assuming his new post, his body, along with those of his aide, Lieutenant Julio Cesar Roman Zuniga, and his civilian driver, Juan Ramirez Sanchez, were found in a white four-door pickup truck in a roadside ditch just outside Cancún. All three had been tortured before they were killed. "The general was the most mistreated," said Quintana Roo State Prosecutor Bello Melchor Rodriguez y Carillo. "He had burns on his skin and the bones in his hands and wrists were broken." An autopsy showed Tello Quiñonez had also had both his knees broken before he died and was shot 11 times. Only the last shot was fatal.

Before Tello Quiñonez was killed, Quintano Roo—despite its desirable location on the route from Colombia to Mexico and the notoriety it gained after the Ianiero murders—had been relatively tranquil, with an average of just 12 murders a year since the Drug War began. That image was changing rapidly. "The reality is that Cancún, like the rest of Mexico, is at war," said Cesar Muñoz Sola, editor-in-chief of *Novedades Quintana Roo*, Cancún's leading daily newspaper. "It's at war with the drug cartels."

And that war came back to resort town a week later when an army special forces unit stormed the Cancún central police headquarters, disarming and interrogating every one of its officers on February 10. Cancún mayor Gregorio Sanchez

Martinez said the show of force was necessary "to facilitate all types of investigations into the triple murder that happened last week."

The army arrested Francisco "El Vikingo" Velasco Delgado, the chief of police, on suspicion that he aided and protected the 11 men accused of kidnapping, torturing and killing Tello Quiñonez and his men. Velasco Delgado, witnesses testified, had a habit of frequenting Cancún's vibrant beach strip in a Nissan Armada SUV with police markings. Investigators determined that the vehicle had been stolen in Mexico City and had been provided to Velasco Delgado as a gift from the Gulf Cartel. Inside the vehicle, they found CDs with *narcocorridos* celebrating the exploits of Los Zetas. He was later convicted.

The war didn't take a break in the rest of the country, either. On February 5, Federales arrested Jerónimo "El Barba" (the Beard) Gámez Garcia—cousin of Arturo Beltrán Leyva, and head of the Beltrán Leyva Cartel's logistics and finances—Pablo Emilio "El Chapiritto" (Little Shorty) Robles Hoyos—a representative of the Colombian Valle del Norte Cartel—and seven other men as they met in a restaurant in Naulcalpan, a small city just northwest of Mexico City. They seized $1 million in U.S. currency and some weapons, but no drugs.

Two months later, Gámez Garcia was being transported in secret from the airport at Tepic, not far from Guadalajara, to a nearby prison when the convoy containing the nine prisoners from the Naulcalpan raid was intercepted by a group of SUVs and pickups loaded with gunmen. Six Federales and two prison guards died in the firefight, but the attempt to free the prisoners was unsuccessful.

Brazen attacks on law enforcement continued. Ramón Jasso Rodríguez, chief of homicide investigation for the Nuevo León state police, was getting into his dark blue Chevy Malibu in front of his home at the corner of Avenida Ciudad de Pamplona and Calle Pedro Infante in the upscale Cumbres Oro neighborhood of Monterrey on February 12 when a white Nissan Sentra and a silver Chevy Equinox slowly pulled up beside him. Men burst out of the compact car and the SUV and rained 58 shells from AK-47s into Jasso Rodríguez's car. Eleven of the bullets embedded in his body. He died at the scene.

Three days later, a U.S. Coast Guard cutter was patrolling international waters about 800 miles offshore of Puerta Chiapas when it came upon a Mexican-flagged fishing vessel named *Polares 1*. Although it was a popular spot for commercial fishing, the *Polares 1* aroused the Americans' suspicions because of the poor weather conditions and the fact that the ship seemed much lower than would be considered safe, as though it was carrying too heavy a load.

Rather than intercept, the captain of the cutter alerted the Mexican Navy, which sent in a special forces team. After boarding, they found nearly eight tons of cocaine in 299 individually wrapped packages. The five men aboard—Mexican nationals José Martín Oleas Solís, Mario Partida Chiquette, Juan Martín Martínez, Joaquín Moreno Díaz and Juan José García Mexta—were arrested.

With a wholesale value of over $300 million, the cocaine taken from the *Polares 1* interception angered the cartels in much the same way the Rancho Búfalo raid had years before, and they reacted in an unprecedented way.

MARCHING IN THE STREETS

Throughout Mexico, but mostly in three big cities on the U.S. border—Juárez, Nuevo Laredo and Reynosa—masses of people began to protest the military presence in their cities and the Calderón government in general. Thousands of people marched through the streets—Monterrey joined a few days later—disrupting commerce and blocking traffic. Eventually, the mobs—carrying placards accusing the soldiers as being "crooks," "kidnappers" and "terrorists"—closed the borders to the U.S., crippling legitimate businesses in their cities. The mainstream Mexican media began to call them "narco-protests," claiming that the demonstrators were protesting not so much against the government, as for the cartels.

There is a long history of paying people to protest in Mexico—depending on a person's status, the cause and the sponsors, the fee for a protest can range from a free lunch to a new car—and that's what the government claimed was happening in the border cities. José Natividad González Parás, governor of Nuevo León (Monterrey's state), accused Los Zetas, then still part of the Gulf Cartel, of orchestrating the demonstrations. "There are reasons to believe that the Gulf Cartel is behind the protests," he said. General Edgar Luis

Villegas Meléndez, commander of the Eighth Military Zone in Reynosa, went further, claiming he had actually seen cash change hands between masked men and the protest leaders. At least two protestors (who refused to be named) told a British reporter that they had been paid to march.

Human rights activists around the world called for an investigation into the military's conduct in Mexico, but even non-government officials within the country itself openly questioned the ethics and goals of the protestors, and whether they were simply a peasant army recruited by the traffickers. "It's a hypothesis you have to consider," said Jorge Chabat, a security expert at Mexico City's Centro de Investigación y Docencia Económicas (Center for Research and Teaching in Economics). "Someone is organizing these protests. They don't seem spontaneous. Whoever the organizer happens to be, is not showing their face."

The tension erupted into violence on the morning of February 17. Police stopped a black Jeep Grand Cherokee at a routine checkpoint in an upscale neighborhood of Reynosa, across the Rio Grande from Hidalgo, Texas, and not far from the much larger city of McAllen. Despite being right in front of the playground at Felipe Carrillo Puerto middle school and across from the busy Plaza Real shopping mall, the men in the Jeep opened fired with assault rifles as did the occupants of the silver Chevy Suburban behind them. Inside the school, children ducked for cover. "We were hearing the gunfire," said the school's assistant director, Enrique Marquez Perez, who used its public address system to tell "everyone to stay calm, to exit (on the other side of the building) calmly." None of the children was hurt, but the school remained closed until February 19.

As the gunmen fled, some of them forced drivers to block intersections to delay police pursuit. When it was over, there were four people (two civilians and two gunmen) dead and one of the gunmen from the Suburban was severely injured. The suspect was taken to a nearby hospital under heavy guard and died later that day. Although Mexican authorities never revealed his identity, U.S. officials announced he was Hector Manuel "El Karis" Sauceda Gamboa, head of the Reynosa branch of the Gulf Cartel.

Although Reynosa Mayor Oscar Luebbert Gutiérrez repeatedly called for people to stay calm and get back to business as usual, the city changed. Few people were seen on the streets after 6:00 p.m., restaurants and nightclubs were empty and those parents who didn't keep their children home from school began to pick them up and drop them off as quickly as possible.

JUÁREZ: A HOTBED OF VIOLENCE

It was Juárez, though, that has taken the crown of most violent city in Mexico from Tijuana. The least protected but one of most traveled of major border crossings, the Juárez–El Paso corridor attracted the attention of the Sinaloa and Gulf Cartels, who were fighting with the traditional Juárez Cartel for the territory. The U.S. State Department issued a warning about traveling to the city of 1.5 million, which it said suffered 1,800 murders (including 71 police officers), 1,650 carjackings and 17,000 auto thefts in 2008. That gave it a murder rate far higher even that Baghdad, Khandahar or Beirut. On the day after the Reynosa gunfight, second-in-command of the Juárez police force, retired army captain Sacramento Perez Serrano and three other officers were ambushed and sprayed with assault rifle fire when their four-door Ford pickup stopped at a red light in the upscale Zona Dorado neighborhood. Perez Serrano and two others died at the scene, while the other officer was severely injured.

Later that day, signs appeared all over the city threatening that one police officer would be killed every 48 hours until the chief of police resigned. The chief, retired army major Roberto Orduña Cruz, had taken over in May after his predecessor, Guillermo Prieto Quintana, fled to El Paso. He was tough, firing and replacing half of the city's 1,600-member police force. Initially he stood firm against the threats, but when the bodies of a police officer and a jail guard were found a few hundred feet from his office with another note threatening him on February 19, he stepped down. "Respect for the life that these brave officers risk every day on the streets for Juárez residents obliges me to offer my permanent resignation," Orduña Cruz said.

Juárez's PRI mayor Jose Reyes Ferriz tried to put a positive spin on it, saying that Orduña Cruz "didn't blink" in the staredown with the cartels, but had decided to fight them in other ways. His tough talk sounded somewhat hollow a day later when the El Paso police force revealed that Reyes Ferriz had fled north of the border and was guiding Juárez's government business from the basement of a friend's house. "We received information that the Juárez mayor lives in El Paso, and that possibly (the cartels) were going to come to El Paso to get him," El Paso Detective Carlos Carrillo said. "He has not asked us for our help, but it's our duty to protect any resident of our city who may be under threat." With the violence just yards from the border and a frequently threatened official in its midst, Texas took action, activating "Operation Border Star Contingency Plan," which put local, state and federal officials on high alert. "The most significant threat Texas faces is spillover violence from Mexico's drug cartels," Steve McCraw, the state's homeland security director, said at a presentation to the state senate. "You can never be too prepared."

On February 28, Calderón sent 1,800 more soldiers to Juarez to bolster the 5,000 soldiers and Federales already there.

Perhaps emboldened by how they had terrorized the government of Juárez, the cartels continued to pursue official targets, including some big game. On February 22, the three-car motorcade of Chihuahua's PRI Governor José Reyes Baeza Terrazas stopped at a red light in the capital city, also named Chihuahua, when they were ambushed and fired upon by masked men. In what was probably a case of mistaken identity, the would-be assassins fired only at the trailing car, killing a bodyguard (Alejandro Chaparro Morales) and injuring two others, while the governor's car, in the lead, was untouched.

Two days later, on Mexican Flag Day, Calderón delivered

a firebrand speech about how he would never give up the war against the cartels. An hour after that, at 5:20 p.m., Octavio Manuel Carrillo Castellanos, mayor of Vista Hermosa, a suburb of Calderón's hometown of Morelia, was assassinated by two masked gunmen as he got out of his car in front of his house.

• • •

It was also in February 2009 when American consciousness (outside of El Paso) of the Mexican Drug War intensified. Miguel Angel Caro Quintero—former head of the Sonora Cartel and younger brother of Rafael Caro Quintaro, who was involved in the Camarena incident—had been in a Mexican prison since his arrest in 2001. At the time, he claimed to be an innocent rancher and said, "If I had a cartel, I'd have a lot of money and my brother wouldn't be in prison." But in February 2009, he was extradited to the U.S. where he pleaded guilty to a number of charges, admitting to personally sending at least $100 million from the U.S. to Mexico, and was sentenced to 17 years in an American maximum-security facility.

On the same day he was extradited, February 24, the DEA announced that it had arrested 755 people in California, Maryland and Minnesota under Operation XCellerator. At least 50 of them, U.S. attorney general Eric Holder said, were members of the Sinaloa Cartel. Conducted with data from Mexican and Canadian police forces, the raid also allowed the DEA to seize $59.1 million in U.S. currency, over 26,000 pounds of cocaine, 16,000 pounds of marijuana, 1,200 pounds of methamphetamine, 18 pounds of heroin, 1.3 million ecstasy pills, 149 vehicles, three airplanes, three seaworthy boats and 169 firearms. Michele Leonhart, acting administrator of the DEA, also said that her forces uncovered a "super meth lab" capable of manufacturing 12,000 hits of methamphetamine a day.

On the same day as it was reporting on Operation XCellerator, *The New York Times* published an investigative piece that alleged that over 90 percent of all firearms seized in the Mexican Drug War originated as legal purchases in the U.S. This re-ignited a decade-old debate in the U.S. about the legality of stripped-down versions of military assault rifles like the AR-15 and the WASR-10.

Citing a study that Mexican cartels had dealings with contacts in at least 230 American cities and that kidnappings and murders had significantly increased in Phoenix, Atlanta and Birmingham, Alabama, where the Mexican cartels were very significant players in the drug trade, Director of Homeland Security Roger Rufe outlined a plan to use the U.S. National Guard as a threat to prevent the Drug War from spilling northward. He suggested that the two countries were nearing a "tipping point," after which sending in U.S. military forces to protect Texas would be inevitable. While he admitted that the Mexican cartels were the greatest organized crime threat to American security, President Barack Obama said he did not see a "tipping point" in the future and reiterated his intention not to militarize the border.

That month, Calderón secretly purchased six Eurocopter EC 725 heavy transport helicopters from the French military and U.S. Secretary of State Hillary Clinton announced that the U.S. was delivering eight more Black Hawks to Mexico.

ARRESTS AT A QUINCEAÑERA

As winter turned to spring in 2009, Calderón's forces made a series of stunning arrests. While the news on the morning of March 19 mostly centered around the discovery of five severed heads and notes threatening the Sinaloa Cartel in the small Jalisco town of Ixtlahuacán del Río, Federales and soldiers in Tijuana were quietly surrounding the massive ornate Mezzanine banquet hall. It was the setting of a *quinceañera*, the traditional 15th birthday celebration thrown for girls throughout Latin America.

But this particular girl had some notable relatives. The army stormed the party and detained 58 guests, including the band and several members of staff. After questioning, 26 people were arrested. The real prize, though, was Ángel Jácome Gamboa—his nickname "El Kaibil" is a reference to the Mayan rebel Kay'bil B'alam who evaded capture by the *conquistadores*; it is also a name he shares with the Guatemalan military's special forces, which have recently been linked to Los Zetas. A former state police officer, Jácome Gamboa was said to be second-in-command of the Tijuana Cartel and his primary responsibility was to manage a staff of *sicarios*. He was charged with ordering the murders of 12 police officers in Rosarita Beach, along with trafficking and gangsterism.

At the scene, police seized Jácome Gamboa's gold-plated 9mm handgun. On it, were two revealing carvings. Embossed on the left side of the handle was an illustration of *Santa Muerte* (Saint Death). A mixture of Catholic and indigenous beliefs symbolized by a Grim Reaper-like character, *Santa Muerte* is a cult of sorts that is condemned by the Catholic Church, but adhered to by millions in Mexico, particularly people of lower social and financial classes, including prostitutes, thieves and drug traffickers. It is often linked with folklore hero Jesús Malverde, a mythical Robin Hood-like character from Sinaloa who is revered by many in Mexico and believed to grant miracles to true believers. He is known as *El Rey Guei de Sinaloa* (the People's King of Sinaloa) and is considered the patron saint of drug traffickers.

On the other side of the gun's handle was an inscription reading "EL TEO," the nickname of Tijuana Cartel boss Teodoro García Simental, whom police alleged gave Jácome Gamboa the weapon as a gift.

Also arrested were Jácome Gamboa's 18-year-old brother Bartolo and eight police officers, two of whom had been employed as bodyguards for Baja California's PAN governor José Guadalupe Osuna Millán.

Acting on information from accomplices arrested at a Sinaloa hub in Chicago as part of Operation XCellerator, Mexican Army officers surrounded a luxurious mansion in the exclusive Jardines de Pedregal neighborhood of Mexico City on the morning of March 19. They arrested its owner, 34-year-old Jesus Vicente "El Mayito" Zambada Niebla, son of Ismael "El Mayo" Zambada García, second-in-command of the

Sinaloa Cartel. Zambada Niebla was alleged to be responsible for the cartel's logistics and to have the authority to order assassinations, and was wanted in the U.S. for importing at least $50 million in drugs. He was arrested with four bodyguards and police seized three AR-15s, three .38-caliber handguns, three bulletproof luxury cars and $67,480,866 in U.S. currency. Zambada is a known fugative.

On March 25, two days after the Mexican government published a wanted poster of their 37 highest targets in the cartels, and the same day Secretary of State Hillary Clinton arrived in Mexico City for a summit meeting with Calderón, the military surrounded a luxury car dealership in San Pedro Garza García, a suburb of Monterrey. They arrested its owner, Héctor "El Burra" (the She-Donkey) Huerta Ríos, one of the 37 faces on the poster. Four of his bodyguards—Gilberto Treviño Herrera, Jorge Barrera Lozano, José Donato Moreno Bustos and Manuel Ruperto Martínez—were arrested with him and two AK-47s, an AR-15, a submachine gun, four handguns and four fragmentation grenades were confiscated, along with 18 luxury cars and cash.

Huerta Ríos was arrested in connection with the murder of a police officer, as well as trafficking. "We have information that as the representative of the Beltrán Leyva Cartel, he held meetings with members of the Gulf Cartel with the aim of agreeing on drug distribution zones, in order to avoid clashes between the rival gangs," said Marisela Morales Ibañez, deputy federal attorney general for organized crime.

His odd nickname came from the fact that low-level drug

exporters, the people who actually carry the drugs with them over the fence or the Rio Grande, are called Burros (Donkeys), and as the local boss, he was considered mother of the donkeys.

On the morning of April 2, a wealthy businessman known as Alejandro Peralta Alvarez put on his snappy new, bright white Abercrombie & Fitch tracksuit and went for his daily jog in Bosque de Chapultepec park in Mexico City's exclusive Las Lomas neighborhood. As he entered the park, he was arrested by dozens of cops. Although he had official identification indicating his name, Peralta Alvarez was an alias for Vicente Carrillo Leyva, son of Juárez Cartel kingpin Amado Carrillo Fuentes and No. 2 in the organization now led by his uncle, Vicente Carrillo Fuentes, a fugitive from justice although not charged as of the writing of this book. Federales tracked him down because his wife, Celia Karina Quevedo Gastelum, had refused to change her name.

On the same day, Guatemalan police arrested Juan Policarpo, who in November 2008 had led a gang that ambushed a bus in that country. Believing the passengers to be members of a rival gang, he had them all shot and then burned their bodies. The bus actually contained 15 Nicaraguan farm laborers and a Dutch tourist. Guatemalan authorities blamed the Mexican cartels, which they claimed had spilled into their country.

INSIDE LA FAMILIA

In Michoacán, an informant told police that members of La Familia would be attending the christening of a baby boy born to one of the cartel's members. He also told them how La Familia works. Cartel member travel the state, visiting rehab centers, hospitals, employment offices and anywhere else they can find people who are desperate or at least needy. They take them in, feed and clothe them, give them a place to stay in exchange for abstention from drugs and alcohol and regular attendance at prayer meetings. After a while, the person becomes a cartel employee, doing whatever they can to further the cause. "La Familia uses religion as a way of forcing cohesion among its members," said Raúl Benítez Manaut, a researcher for the Humanities Centro de Investigaciones Interdisciplinarias en Ciencias y Humanidades (Center for Interdisciplinary Research in Science) and the Smithsonian Institution. "They are building a new kind of disciplined army that we have never seen here before. It makes them more dangerous." The informant said he had been expelled because he had strayed from the drug-free path.

And police had noticed a change in La Familia as well. Their victims were always found with cardboard notes attached to them, often poorly spelled. At first, most of the notes had anti-drug messages, pointing out that the victim had been killed for manufacturing or selling drugs in Michoacán. But in 2009, the notes turned more sinister with messages like: "I was victim of a kidnapping by those who call themselves La Familia Michoacána; thus, I am carrying out justice by my own hand."

At least 400 police and soldiers surrounded a church in Morelia on April 19. After a tense standoff, they arrested 44 people, including Rafael Cedeño Hernández, who was said to be second-in-command of La Familia. Along with the detainees, police discovered three AR-15s, an AK-47, six handguns, five grenades and four bags of marijuana and cocaine.

CHAPTER 10
The Roll Call of Death

But all these arrests came at a steep price. On March 22, Édgar Garcia Dimas, commander in charge of kidnapping and extortion for the Michoacán state police who had been decorated by the FBI for finding and returning an American fugitive who was hiding out in Morelia, was stopped at a red light in the town of Chapingo when two cars stopped on either side of his. Gunmen pumped 50 shells into him. A nearby patrol car heard the noise and its driver shot at the fleeing cars. Somehow, he managed to shoot one of the drivers in the head, killing him. The car careened out of control and slammed into a university building. The passenger, clearly hurt and perhaps shot, staggered a few feet before the other car picked him up. The police officer was also shot in the exchange. Later that day, unknown gunmen took a few pot shots at a police squad car on the other side of town.

On March 26, news broke that the body of an agent of the U.S. Marshals El Paso office had been found in Juárez. Vincent Bustamante had indeed been killed execution-style with four bullet wounds to the back of his head, but he was in Juárez because he was on the run from American authorities. When he tried to pawn a Glock pistol in El Paso, the shop's owner called the ATF. The subsequent investigation concluded that Bustamente had stolen and pawned a number of Glock and Ruger handguns, a shotgun and a pair of binoculars from the marshal's office. He was wanted after failing to appear at a court date a week before his discovery. The reasons for his execution are still unclear.

On April 21, two days after the failed attempt to free Gámez Garcia that cost the lives of six Federales and two prison guards, the Archbishop of Durango, Héctor González Martínez, called a press conference to discuss the fact that more than 200 priests had fallen victim to extortion plots by the cartels. Frustrated, González Martínez revealed what he claimed was the whereabouts of Mexico's most wanted man, Sinaloa Cartel chief Joaquín "El Chapo" Guzmán Loera. "He lives in Guanaceví," he said. "Everybody knows it except the authorities." Guanaceví is a small, pleasant town tucked away in the coniferous forests of the Sierra Madre mountains.

After the press conference, the Archbishop's spokesman, Victor Manuel Solis, went into damage control, saying that his comments were "reckless, dangerous and to a certain degree, irresponsible." He added that "we have had to take some precautionary measures for the lives of our priests." Officials in

Guanaceví immediately denied El Chapo was in or around their town.

The following day, Guzmán Loera, who had recently been named by *Forbes* magazine on its list of billionaires, sent González Martínez a reply. Police came upon a Ford Fiesta on a road just north of Guanaceví. Inside were two plain clothes Federales. Their hands and feet were bound with duct tape, and there were obvious signs of torture. Their bodies had been riddled with fire from numerous AK-47s. Attached to one them was a note that read: "You'll never get to El Chapo—not the government, not the priests."

And on May 17, fifteen people were murdered in Chihuahua in seven separate incidents. The first victim was 18-year-old Victor Manuel Felix Soto, who was hanging out at the corner of Avenidas Arturo Gámiz and Francisco Villa in Chihuahua. He was shot 10 times by a 9mm handgun from inside a car that sped off at 1:30 a.m. A few hours later, at 5:40, a man in the Dr Porfirio Parra neighborhood of Juárez discovered two decapitated bodies in his front yard. One was identified as 25-year-old neighbor David Olivos Aguilera, the other was never claimed. At 7:25 a.m., the body of a middle-aged man bound and gagged with duct tape was found at the old Honduras Raceway in southern Juárez, which was being converted into luxury housing. He had two bullet holes in the back of his head. At 11:50 a.m., an unidentified man walking through the Barrio Alto neighborhood of Juárez was shot in the head by a masked gunman, who became lost in the crowd. At 2:48 p.m., the bullet-riddled body of Jose

Alfredo Gallegos Torres, a young father and owner of a small trucking firm, was found in the middle of a Juárez intersection. At 3:05 p.m., witnesses in the Salvarcar Sauzal Plains neighborhood Juárez saw masked men slit known drug dealer Grade Jorge Lopez's throat then shoot him three times in the face. At 7:58 p.m., an unidentified man was gunned down in a drive-by in the San Angel districts of Juárez. And, at about 11:00 p.m., a white Jeep Grand Cherokee stopped in front of the trendy Bar San Martin in Juárez, let out two gunmen who killed Roberto Acosta and his friend, Juan Holguin Rascon, before fleeing. Nearby officers from the attorney general's office heard the shots and came running, but could not pursue the SUV.

On May 18, the cartels showed that they were capable of large-scale military-style operations. On federal highway No. 23, between the central cities of Zacatecas and Jerez de García Salinas, there is a sleepy road that goes for two miles and leads to nothing except a prison called the El centro regional de readaptación social de Cieneguillas (The Cieneguillas Regional Center for Social Rehabilitation). At 4:45 a.m., a helicopter landed outside the prison. It was soon joined by about 17 vehicles, some bearing Federales logos. At least 80 armed men assembled and 30 of them in Federales uniforms approached the prison and were allowed entry. The helicopter then took off and circled above the prison.

Once inside, the men in Federales uniforms forced the prison's guards at gunpoint to free 53 men from their cells, most of them were associated with Los Zetas and at least 11 of whom had been convicted of murder. All the men were taken to the trucks, which drove off without incident.

After watching the prison's surveillance tapes, authorities became convinced it was an inside job. Noting that the whole operation took just a few minutes, not a shot was fired and that it looked like it was staged beforehand, 42 prison employees, including its director, were arrested. "It is clear to us that this was perfectly planned," said Zacatecas PRD Governor Amalia García Medina. Six of the men were recaptured in Zacatecas on tips from informants, but state authorities later determined that they had been decoys and that the "informants" were actually associates of Los Zetas, who were keeping the police busy chasing the six while the perpetrators and their friends escaped.

Later that day, three severed heads were found by a roadside in the resort town of Zihuatanejo de Azueta, just three miles from Ixtapa in the state of Guerrero. Their matching bodies were found in a taxi about a mile away. There was a note, but authorities would not release what it said. It was later determined that all three of the dead men were police officers who had participated in a raid on a chili-drying facility in the Zacatecas city of Fresnillo the previous January that had netted about 12 tons of marijuana.

About a week later, on the morning of May 26, in a series of raids all over Michoacán, Federales arrested the mayors of 10 cities and towns (Apatzingan, Uruapan, Buenavista Tomatlan, Coalcoman, Nuevo Urecho, Arteaga, Tepalcatepec, Aguililla, Tumbiscatio and Ciudad Hidalgo) on various corruption charges. They represented all three major parties. Also arrested were 17 other officials including Citlali Fernandez Gonzalez, Michoacán's former secretary of state for public safety and by then an advisor to Governor Leonel Godoy Rangel; Mario Bautista Ramirez, the head of the state police academy and formerly the state's public security minister; and Carlos Vega Saldana, Michoacán's deputy secretary for public security. "They didn't inform us of the operation," Godoy Rangel told reporters. "Initially we didn't know if the officials and former officials had been kidnapped or were detained." Charges were eventually dropped against Gonzalez, Ramirez and Saldana.

Information leading to the arrests came from informants after a raid in the state uncovered 22 high-volume methamphetamine labs, and was seen as a major move by the government. "This is a huge blow to the cartel. These ties are indispensable for the operation of these organizations," said Victor Clark Alfaro, head of the Binational center for Human Rights in Tijuana. "Until now the government has never dared to touch the political classes tied to drug trafficking . . . this is an important step."

SIEGE TACTICS

The next major confrontation between the government and the cartels took place in Acapulco, which was the center of so much trafficking that Mexican media had been referring to it as Narcopulco, and introduced a new weapon, the rocket-propelled grenade. The Caleta neighborhood had once been a prime tourist destination with hotels visited and even owned by people like John Wayne, Elizabeth Taylor and Johnny Weissmuller, but has since attracted a lower-budget crowd mainly from Canada and the rest of Mexico.

The ignition point for what happened on June 6 is up for debate. The official word is that a mixed force of soldiers and Federales were acting on an informant's tip and stormed a building known to contain members of the Beltrán Leyva Cartel. But eyewitnesses told local media that the shooting began when a white Chevy Suburban smashed through a Federale checkpoint. The ensuing battle—in which both sides exchanged automatic gunfire and the occupants of the building shot grenades at the invaders—went on for at least two hours and left 13 cartel members, two Federales and two innocent civilians dead.

Early in the struggle, some Federales who had broken into the building discovered four shirtless, handcuffed men who identified themselves as Guerrero state police officers. They were taken for questioning to determine if they had been kidnapped or were collaborating with the cartel members. Some men from inside the house tried to make an escape, but their black Mercedes-Benz M350 ran into a wall when soldiers shot out the tires. They were killed. Another group of armed men came from another part of Acapulco in an effort to surround the government forces, but they fled after two of them were killed by .50-caliber machine gun shells from an army Humvee that arrived just after them.

After the siege, reporters were given a tour of the house by the army colonel who led the assault. He wore a mask to protect his anonymity. He showed them the 13 handguns, 36 assault rifles and two rocket-propelled grenade launchers seized in the building. One Federale told a Mexican newspaper that their weapons and communications equipment looked like "toys" compared to those of the cartels. They arrested the five surviving men within the building. The dead and arrested men were identified as *sicarios*. One of the dead was a much-feared assassin the government would only identify as "El Comandante Magaña," an important member of the Beltrán Leyva Cartel.

Less than 48 hours later, gunmen emerged from two SUVs in front of a Tijuana police station. They raked the building with automatic weapons and threw grenades, managing to kill two officers who were in a car parked in front of the station. At about the same time, another police station, about two miles away, was shot up the same way. Two officers who were outside the building were hit and wounded. One died later that day. The message was clear.

At another resort, the government apprehended another big prize. Since the investigation of the murder of Tello Quiñonez led to the mass arrest of the Cancún police force, the army had been acting in their place. Acting on an informant's tip, on June 15 the army stormed a luxury beachside estate and arrested Juan Manuel "El Puma" Jurado Zarzoza, Luis Aguirre "Martin" Rafael Muñoz, Cristina "La Flaca" (Skinny) Marquez Alcala and Estanislao "El Gordo" (Fatso) Alejandro Sanchez. According to the attorney general's office, Juardo Zarzoza had been sent to prison for robbing a jewelry store in 2003, had become involved with drug traffickers while incarcerated and worked for the Gulf Cartel in Cancún, eventually becoming their top man there. Inside the house, the army confiscated nine assault rifles, 10 handguns, 35 pounds of cocaine and 100 pounds of marijuana. Interrogation of the suspects and records found within the home led officials to believe that two men—Octavio Almanza Morales and Napoleón de Jesús Mendoza Aguirre—were responsible for the assassination of Tello Quiñonez, and issued warrants for their arrests.

On the same day, the Chihuahua state police received an anonymous citizen's complaint about some "funny business" going on at a ranch just outside the mountain town of Madera. When soldiers from the 35th Infantry Battalion arrived, they were met by men in army uniforms wearing ski masks and were told "we're on your side; we have authorization to work in this town." But when the commander of the battalion noticed that the men were carrying AK-47s—the Mexican Army issues only German Heckler & Koch, Belgian FN, American Colt or domestic FX assault rifles—he ordered their arrest. All 25 men at the ranch were rounded up without a shot being fired. It was a chilling new wrinkle in the drug war. Although cartel members and associates had long posed as police to commit crimes more easily, this was the first time that men had been caught in counterfeit army uniforms. Since the army was held in much higher esteem than police by the public when it came to honesty and integrity, this was a significant find.

The incident followed just two days after Mexican human rights watchdogs appealed to the American media to reveal abuses by the military in Mexico, particularly in Juárez. A coalition of non-government organizations accused them of using abusive tactics to obtain information about suspects, particularly kidnapping potential witnesses off the street, blindfolding them and beating them during interrogation. They called for a thorough investigation of the military's role in four unsolved murders and eight missing people. "The guarantee of public security has been totally broken," said Gustavo de la Rosa Hickerson, president of the Chihuahua Human Rights Commission. "Juárez was better off without the soldiers."

That night the national newscasts led with the story of a Michoacán ambulance that was attacked with grenades and assault rifle fire allowing gunmen to kill the patient inside (who had already been wounded in a firefight in Morelia) and set the vehicle ablaze and the family whose 1972 Chevy van was shot up in Juárez, leaving all four—including a 14-year-old boy and 12-year-old girl—dead. The girl, Priscilla Ibarra Alfaro, was a U.S. citizen from San Elizario, Texas, who was riding with her uncle, aunt and cousin to their home in the Barreales neighborhood.

As the long hot summer of 2009 went on, government forces suffered many setbacks. Ernesto Cornejo Valenzuela was a firebrand PAN politician who was actually in jail serving a sentence for his part in an anti-PRI riot when he was elected mayor of the Sonora town of Benito Juárez. On June 26, he was campaigning to become a congressman for the district when he and some campaign workers stopped at a taco stand in downtown Benito Juárez. When gunmen from an SUV opened fire, Cornejo Valenzuela managed to get safely to the ground, but two of his volunteers were killed. Many of his followers blamed PRI governor Eduardo Bours Castelo for the attack, who was never charged, but the mainstream media accused the Sinaloa Cartel, which had absorbed the Sonora Cartel, and considered pro-Calderón candidates to be their enemies.

Later that day, the normally tranquil Guanajuato city of Apaseo el Alto exploded as state police investigating a routine complaint of the sighting of an armed man at a nondescript house were shot at and had grenades thrown at them. Reinforced by the army (and .50 caliber machine guns), the police returned and the ensuing firefight left the twelve occupants of the house dead and one officer seriously wounded. Police linked the dead men to Los Zetas.

A NEW REVENUE STREAM: KIDNAPPING

It had become routine for the cartels to kidnap individuals who were not involved with the drug trade or law enforcement for no reason other than to raise money through ransoms. Communities who were out of the mainstream were particularly hard hit, especially if they were thought to have money. One such community lived just outside the Chihuahua town of Galeana. A group of Mormons left Utah in the early 20th century after the American government cracked down on polygamy and settled in the dry foothills of the Sierra Madre, founding Colonia LeBaron near Galeana. They made a good living growing pecans. Few, if any, of their descendants still practise polygamy and not all of them are even Mormons any more, but the 1,600-member community has retained its identity. All members speak English and Spanish fluently, and they live in a level of luxury in stark contrast to the farmers and laborers around them.

The group made headlines in 1974 when one of its leaders—Ervil LeBaron, son of the colony's founder, Alma Dayer LeBaron—was accused of ordering a series of revenge-motivated murders that included that of his brother Joel. His series of trials in Mexico ended in acquittals on technicalities (which many attributed to bribes), but he died in a Utah prison after he was extradited to the U.S. in 1980 when it was determined that one of his victims had retained U.S. citizenship.

In the summer of 2009, Colonia LeBaron was shocked by two kidnappings. The first was 72-year-old Meredith Romney, president of the area's Mormon organization, the Colonia Juárez Chihuahua México Temple, and a relative of U.S. presidential candidate Mitt Romney. After having the tires of his pickup truck shot out while he was driving, Romney was secured by three gunmen who hustled him into their car. He was held in a cave under armed guard. Concerned about his need for insulin, his family came up with a substantial ransom and he was released unharmed.

The second victim was 16-year-old Eric LeBaron, Joel's grandson. He and a younger brother were bringing fence posts to their father's farm from a Galeana lumberyard when their truck was surrounded by gunmen. The masked men forced Eric into their own truck and told the other boy to go home and tell their father, Julian, to wait for the phone to ring. When it did, the men demanded a $1-million ransom for Eric.

Julian refused to pay. "We knew the last thing we could do was give them the money, or we would be invaded by this scum," he said later. Explaining the family's hard line, Julian's brother Craig told American reporters: "If you give them a cookie, they'll want a glass of milk. If we don't make a stand here, it's only a matter of time before it's my kid." To show they were serious, the kidnappers put an empty coffin in the bed of a pickup owned by Galeana mayor Vern Ariel Ray Angel, a distant relative of the LeBarons.

The day after Eric was taken, about 150 community leaders met in a church to discuss strategy. Many wanted to form an armed posse, while others recommended hiring bounty hunters or even mercenaries. Eric's 32-year-old brother Benjamin (better known as Benji) had formed SOS (Sociedad Organizada Segura or Secure Organized Society) a group that trained local people in crime prevention, and lobbied the government for stiffer penalties for offenders and more transparent investigations.

The lobbying paid off when an army unit was sent into the area to find Eric. Eight days after his capture, Eric was simply told to go home. He walked for four hours until he found a pay phone and called home for a ride. Many in the LeBaron community attributed his safe return to prayer, but the army dragnet certainly didn't hurt.

On the night of July 7, between 15 and 20 masked, armed men broke into Benji LeBaron's home. He was bound, dragged out to the front yard and beaten. His brother-in-law, Luis

Carlos Widmar, heard the commotion from his own house two doors away and rushed to his aid, but he too was captured, tied up and beaten. The gunmen threatened to rape LeBaron's wife, Miriam, in front of her children if she did not reveal where LeBaron kept his weapons, but she told them he had none. The gunmen then fled with the two captives. Their bodies, both with multiple bullet wounds to the head, were found the next day on a roadside just outside of town. A banner hung between two trees accused Benji LeBaron of being responsible for the 25 arrests at the ranch in Madera.

Chihuahua Attorney General Patricia González Rodríguez gave a press conference in which she accused La Linea (The Line), a secret society of former police officers who act as enforcers for the Juárez Cartel of the killings. Later that day, a banner was hung in a public square in Juárez that read: *La Sra. Fiscal, evitar problemas por ti mismo, y no culpar a La Línea* (Mrs. Prosecutor, avoid problems for yourself, and don't blame La Linea). Another one appeared on a Juárez overpass that accused LeBaron of being a gangster and implored people to *Pregúntate a ti mismo, De dónde provienen sus propiedades?* (Ask yourself, where did all his properties come from?)

The residents of Colonia LeBaron then formed a volunteer police force and González Rodríguez granted their request to arm themselves.

The week after LeBaron was killed, the cartels showed their boldness once again, this time in Morelia. Federales arrested Arnoldo "La Minsa" (the Tortilla Maker) Rueda Medina and a 17-year-old associate they referred to as "Francisco N" in

Morelia. Authorities alleged that Rueda Media was third in command of La Familia in charge of their logistics and communications and that Francisco N. was responsible for organizing La Familia's safe houses.

The convoy carrying the prisoners was followed and as the police were transferring Rueda Medina from an armored car to a detention center, they were fired upon by gunmen. The gunmen were fought off by army troops and Federales, and the attempt to free Rueda Medina was unsuccessful. A police spokesman said that it appeared that the attackers were prepared to kill Rueda Medina in an effort to keep him from talking.

A few hours later, gunmen opened fire on police stations in six Michoacán cities—Morelia, Zitacuaro, Zamora, Lazaro Cardenas, Apatzingan, La Piedad and Huetamo—at virtually the same time. The attacks killed five Federales and two soldiers and wounded 10 more Federales. A search of the area yielded no suspects, but police did uncover a safe house with weapons and tables they said had been used for torture.

Later that day, a pedestrian in nearby Uruapan discovered three bodies—bound, tortured and shot in the head—under a blanket at the side of a road. In Tecate, across the border from southeastern California, police found three more bodies of men killed by assault rifles. And in the evening, soldiers, Federales and local police stormed the luxurious house of Eduardo Morquecho Hernandez, a U.S. citizen wanted by authorities for a domestic violence incident in Orange County back in 2003. Inside the residence, police seized 32 guns of various types, 1,500 pounds of marijuana and drums of sodium hydroxide, the same chemical "El Pozolero" Meza López admitted he used to dissolve corpses of the Tijuana Cartel's enemies.

The violence against police continued in Michoacán. Twelve state investigators on a bus to a crime scene were ambushed on a country road by La Familia gunmen. All of them—11 men and one woman—were tortured and executed. A note was found tied to one of the bodies that warned police officers that if they did not "line up" with La Familia, they would be killed.

THE CYCLE OF CORRUPTION

On the same day, the Michoacán attorney general's office issued arrest warrants for two politicians—Governor Godoy Rangel's half-brother Julio César Godoy Toscano, a PRD congressman and former mayor of Lázaro Cárdena, and Saul "El Lince" (the Lynx) Solis Solis, a PRD candidate who lost his bid for a congressional seat in the same election—who they alleged were working for La Familia's Servando Gomez Martinez. Gomez Martinez had recently admitted on a radio call-in show that he was part of the cartel's management team and that they were at war with police and the military.

And the government took another huge hit at the start of August. Patrick Leahy, a Democrat senator from Vermont and head of the U.S. Foreign Operations Subcommittee of the Appropriations Committee, determined that the U.S. must withhold at least 15 percent (about $100 million) of its Mérida

Initiative aid program because the Mexican government had not done enough to guarantee its military and police had improved their human rights violations records.

The arrests in Michoacán represented another profound blow to Mexico. Since the war began it had confirmed long-held suspicions that state and local police were often in league with the traffickers. Then the Federales, who were held to a higher standard, were shown to be just as vulnerable to bribery and threats, followed by the military, who had been considered untouchable. By the end of the summer of 2009, it was clear that even elected officials were part of the immense drug trade. Mexicans who hoped for law and order were seriously disheartened. They didn't know who to trust.

And even if the people within the government forces could be trusted to be honest and not intimidated by threats and violence, it was looking very much as though they were seriously outgunned. No longer were the cartels hiding in the countryside. They were masquerading as cops and soldiers, ambushing the real authorities and even brazenly attacking police stations and other places of government power with sophisticated and powerful weapons, including rocket-propelled grenades.

By the middle of 2009, nobody doubted Mexico was at war. But for the first time, many people were openly wondering if the government could survive long enough to win it.

CHAPTER 11
The War Expands

The illusion that the violence in the Drug War was limited to the border or big cities was shattered on August 6, 2009. Pachuca is a small city in the state of Hidalgo that was settled primarily by English, particularly Cornish, immigrants. They brought with them tennis, golf and soccer, as well as an architectural style and a local cuisine not found elsewhere in Mexico. Pachuca is considered one of Mexico's most orderly, prosperous and safe cities.

That's why it was such a shock when news leaked of a prolonged gun battle there. Police had been tipped off about traffickers in the area and stopped four trucks at a routine checkpoint. Immediately men inside the trucks opened fire and fled. Three state police officers were killed at the scene and nine alleged cartel members were killed in a battle that destroyed all four of their vehicles. Along with weapons and cash, the police recovered almost seven pounds of cocaine.

Nobody, however, was surprised by the 13 bodies, including one of a police investigator, that were found on the streets of Juárez that day.

Two days later, Saturday August 8, the Federales announced that they had arrested Manuel Invanovich "El Jimmy" Zambrano Flores, a high-ranking lieutenant in the Tijuana Cartel. When a state police cruiser attempted to pull over his black VW Touareg SUV on Tijuana's Calle Coahuila, he stepped on the gas, but quickly collided with other vehicles, stopping his progress. He emerged from the SUV with a gun, but dropped it when he was surrounded. Inside the car, police seized seven AK-47s, three AR-15s, seven handguns and fake state police identification. Zambrano Flores' job, they said, was to coordinate shipments over the border.

The government scored an even bigger media sensation the following day. Just as Calderón was about to open a summit meeting in Guadalajara with President Obama and Prime Minister Stephen Harper, the Federales announced that they had discovered and broken up a plot to assassinate Calderón at the summit. At a Sinaloa Cartel safe house in Culiacán, Federales arrested Dimas "El Dimas" Diaz Ramos, Miguel Angel Bagglieto Meraz, Joel "El Raspu" (Rasputin) Gonzalez Esparza, Benni "El Brother" Jassiel Ramirez and Jesus Aaron "El Tarraya" (the Fishnet) Acosta Montero. The attorney general's office said that the plot had been planned for months and was revenge for the huge coke bust aboard the *Polares 1*. Diaz Ramos was the ringleader of the group and his primary job for the cartel had been moving marijuana and methamphetamine up the coast from Michoacán to the border.

THE CHICAGO CONNECTION

Another investigation that began two years earlier in the heavily Mexican neighborhood of Pilsen in Chicago yielded huge results. It started in 2007 when a cop arrested a man on suspicion of selling cocaine on a street corner. He had a bag of corn chips, but inside the bag was a hidden compartment that was used to smuggle cocaine. The suspect began to cooperate with police, leading them to another man who he claimed to be working for. Police stopped that man and found an unregistered gun in his car. He also cooperated with police, claiming the gun was for self-defense because another drug dealer, "Fat Mike," had promised to kill him, producing a Hallmark greeting card with a threatening message as evidence. The police then recorded a call between Fat Mike, who also cooperated with the investigation and his connection, "Slow Poke," who he assured the police was "cool" and "had lots of money." It was Slow Poke who eventually led them to a prize bigger than they could have imagined.

A man named Guillermo Flores had come to Chicago from Sinaloa in the 1970s and supplemented his income with some small-time drug dealing. His twin sons, Pedro and Margarito, joined and expanded the family business to a ridiculous degree. Through a barbershop in Pilsen and a restaurant in nearby Little Village called Mama's Kitchen, the twins ran a drug distribution business making deals primarily with the Sinaloa Cartel and, astonishingly, the Beltrán Leyva Cartel as well.

The drugs were smuggled in shipments of fruit, vegetables or electronics to a warehouse outside Los Angeles where they were loaded into tractor trailers and driven to a set of Chicago warehouses and condominiums where they would be distributed among the twins' street-level dealers. Cash was then shrink-wrapped and sent back to Mexico.

When undercover American police officers infiltrated the Flores Crew (as their gang was called), they discovered that the gang had been receiving threats of violence from both the Sinaloa and Beltrán Leyva Cartel who each wanted an exclusive arrangement, though neither cut off or even reduced their shipments.

When the indictments came down, the authorities seized $20.6 million in cash, almost 7,000 pounds of cocaine and 140 pounds of heroin. Half of the 46 suspects were arrested in Chicago, Atlanta and Brooklyn, while the rest—including the twins—were fugitives. The DEA said that the 28-year-old twins' business generated about $700 million a year and sued for the forfeiture of two houses, three cars, a tractor trailer and $1.8 billion. They also claimed that the Flores brothers had street-level dealers as far away as Washington DC, and Vancouver, B.C.

While the DEA and other agencies were ecstatic about dismantling the Flores Crew, the DEA's chief of intelligence, Anthony Placido, warned that the success of such a slapdash, unsophisticated organization prone to taking ridiculous risks like the Flores Crew was an indication that the drug traffickers were becoming more reckless and violent. "There have always been gatekeepers—people who use their familial relationships to facilitate the movement of drugs across the border," he explained. "Those people used to be gods, and they would control an area for years. Now they often last months before they are arrested or assassinated. What that creates is opportunities for a 28-year-old who . . . isn't worried about dying."

DECRIMINALIZATION OF DRUGS IN MEXICO

The day after the Flores Crew was taken down, Calderón enacted a controversial law that had been under negotiation since 2006. On August 21, Mexico decriminalized the possession of small amounts of drugs. Under the legislation, Mexicans were allowed to carry five grams of marijuana, a half gram of cocaine, 50 milligrams of heroin, 40 milligrams of methamphetamine or 0.015 milligrams of LSD. If police found an individual with these new amounts of drugs, they were compelled to advise the individual to seek counseling. If an individual was caught a third time, the law stated that drug counseling would be mandatory, but it didn't mention any definite penalties if the individual did not seek counseling. Originally, Calderón had lobbied for first-time offenders to agree to voluntary counseling or face imprisonment, but he was voted down.

The Calderón government played down the move, saying that it only put on paper what was already happening in practice, reminding the public that their opponents were drug traffickers, not drug users. "The Mexican authorities were not [targeting] small-scale drug users before, so this law just legalizes the status quo," said Juan Carlos Hidalgo, Latin-American project coordinator at the Washington DC-based Cato Institute. "But certainly it is a signal that Mexico is sending to the world that [going after] small-scale drug users is counter-productive."

Another tacit effect of the law was that it reduced the ability of police officers to extort Mexicans caught with small amounts of drugs. Previously, it had been commonplace for police to accept bribes in such cases because they had the threat of jail time for the offender.

The North American reaction was mixed. By that time, possession of small amounts marijuana was illegal but not enforced in Canada and many U.S. states, and had actually been decriminalized in a dozen states. U.S. drug czar Gil Kerlikowske did not immediately criticize the law, instead saying he would adopt a "wait-and-see attitude." He actually said he would not be very concerned unless Mexico removed possession limits altogether. "If the sanction becomes completely nonexistent I think that would be a concern," he said. "But I actually didn't read quite that level of de facto [decriminalization] in the law."

Significantly, more criticism of the law came from within Mexico itself, largely because it seemed hypocritical on the part of the Calderón government, whose Drug War had cost so many lives and billions of dollars. "If they decriminalize drugs it could lead the army, which has been given the task of combating this, to say 'What are we doing?'" said Javier Oliva Posada, a political science researcher at Mexico City's Autonomous University.

Many critics also pointed out that while allowing personal possession of drugs shifted criminality from the user to the trafficker, it did little to reduce the amount of trafficking or the violence involved with it. "As long as drug production remains illegal, we are going to see the drug traffickers running a black market," said Hidalgo. "I don't see how the new measure will help calm down the drug violence in Mexico."

It didn't. At about 5:15 p.m. on September 3, Michoacán's deputy public safety secretary, José Manuel Revuelta Lopez, was being driven home from work in Morelia when his car was intercepted about 200 yards from his office and forced to stop. As was becoming routine, gunmen burst out of the trucks and showered his vehicle with gunfire. Revuelta Lopez, who had been on the job just two weeks, two bodyguards and an innocent bystander were killed.

A NEW TARGET: DRUG REHAB CENTERS

Later that day, in Juárez, a new terror tactic emerged. Members of cartels had long hung out in and around Mexican drug rehab centers. Not only were sales easy—although La Familia forbade selling drugs within Mexico, the other cartels did not—but so was recruitment. Nobody, they quickly discovered, is more willing to take on a risky, illegal assignment that a desperate addict.

About a dozen masked gunmen arrived at El Aviane rehab clinic and forced all 23 people inside to line up against a wall. Then they opened fire. Seventeen people died immediately and one other hung on until that evening; the other five were seriously injured. The belief at the time was that one cartel believed that the patients inside the clinic were actually traffickers posing at addicts. "At the very least, it was one organized crime group thinking that another group was operating in that place," Juárez mayor Jose Reyes Ferriz told reporters from his office in El Paso. Another 21 bodies were found throughout northern Mexico that day, one of them beheaded.

On the morning of September 6, José Francisco Fuentes Esperón—a former university rector who had declared his candidacy as a PRI member for a congressional seat in the southern state of Tabasco two days earlier—was late for a campaign meeting. When he wouldn't answer his phone, an aide was sent to retrieve him. When she arrived at his home in Villahermosa, the state capital, she was surprised to find his front door was open. Inside, she found the bodies of Fuentes Esperón and his wife, Lilian Arguelles Beltran, both shot in the head, and those of his two sons, eight and ten, both asphyxiated. "There are no words to express these events," said Rafael Gonzalez Lastra, Tabasco's attorney general. "We are deeply moved and at the same time indignant." All candidates took two days off campaigning, and Gonzalez Lastra offered them all bodyguards.

A few hours later, the military announced the arrest of Jose Rodolfo "El Riquin" (the Hindu) Escajeda Escajeda. Acting on an anonymous tip, they arrested him and three other armed men who were driving a bulletproof Mercedes-Benz ML350 SUV in Nuevo Casas Grandes, Chihuahua, not far from Colonia LeBaron. He was wanted in connection with an incident back in January 23, 2006—before the Drug War began in earnest—in which 10 men dressed as Mexican soldiers in three green Humvee-style SUVs were spotted by Texas Rangers driving north on a dirt road surrounded by forest about 50 miles down the Rio Grande from El Paso. On the Mexican side, the road ends literally in the river at a spot known as Neely's Crossing because, for most of the year, the Rio Grande is shallow enough to wade across. The three vehicles drove through the river to the American side, but when they spotted the Rangers with weapons drawn, they U-turned and drove back into Mexico, escaping arrest.

Initially Hudspeth County sherriff Arvin West called the incident "a military incursion" and accused the Mexican Army of "escorting drug dealers" across the border, but an investigation by the U.S. Border Patrol and DEA absolved the military and fingered Escajeda Escajeda. After his arrest more than three years later, evidence emerged that Escajeda Escajeda was the most prolific assassin for the Juárez Cartel and was behind the El Aviane massacre—he suspected the patients were actually working for the Sinaloa Cartel, which was still attempting to use the Juárez–El Paso crossing—and was also probably responsible for the murders of LeBaron and Widmar on July 7.

Putting Escajeda Escajeda behind bars did little to stop the violence in Juárez. The murders kept coming, with gunmen taking out victims in hardware stores, car washes and out on the streets. And, at 10:30 p.m. on September 16, a dozen masked, armed men stormed the Anexo de Vida drug rehab clinic. It was lights-out time for the patients who were compelled to pray before going to bed. The *sicarios* lined up the 10 patients and shot them, leaving the staff unharmed. Pools of blood spilled out into the dirt road, which had been made almost impassable for vehicles because of heavy rains.

Relatives of the dead insisted that they were innocent people seeking help, not cartel members. "Why? Why them?" said Pilar Macias, whose brother, 39-year-old Juan Carlos Macias, was one of the victims. "He was recovering, he wanted to get back on the right track and they didn't let him, they didn't give him a chance. This is going to kill my mother." Maria Hernandez, whose 25-year-old son Carlos was also killed said: "He was good, he didn't hang out with gangs, he didn't have narco friends. He just began with marijuana, and then they killed him."

At about the same time in Tijuana, police came across a burning car. Once doused, they found four bodies in the car's seats and two more in the trunk. All had been bound, tortured and shot in the back of the head.

A new form of reprisal

Military intelligence received a tip that Arturo Beltrán Leyva, leader of the Beltrán Leyva Cartel and the third most-wanted man in Mexico, was staying at a friend's condo in Altitude Punta Vista Hermosa, the tallest and most exclusive building in the Lomas de la Selva neighborhood of Cuernavaca, the capital of the state of Morelos. When he was spotted there on December 16, 2009, while Calderón was at the UN Climate Conference in Copenhagen, the building was surrounded by Naval Infantry (analogous to the U.S. Marine Corps).

In the ensuing battle, Beltrán Leyva and five of his gunmen were killed and another shot himself in the head just before he was to be apprehended. The losses did not cripple the organization, but it was a severe blow. Three of the special-forces soldiers were severely wounded when one of the cartel gunmen threw a fragmentation grenade at them, and one of them—30-year-old Petty Officer Melquisedet Angulo Córdova—later died from his wounds.

Angulo Córdova's grieving family was shown on national television, and he was regarded as a hero in the Drug War. The same news programs also aired pictures and video footage of Arturo Beltrán Leyva's bloodied corpse with his pants around his thighs.

Angulo Córdova's funeral, on December 21, was attended by Secretary of the Navy Mariano Francisco Saynez Mendoza, who presented the victim's mother, Irma Córdova Palma, with a ceremonial flag.

A few hours later, just after midnight, masked men invaded Córdova Palma's house in Villahermosa and shot everyone inside with AR-15s. She and her 22-year-old daughter Yolidabey died at the scene, and her sister Josefa Angulo Flores and 28-year-old son Angel Benito died later that night. Another daughter, 24-year-old Miraldelly, died the next day.

The attack horrified Mexico. The pointlessness of murdering the innocent family of an already dead soldier rocked the nation. It was yet another brutal new twist in a war that was raging out of control. The family had no official protection because that kind of attack was unprecedented. Authorities were harshly criticized for making the soldier's family so prominent on TV and for publishing their names. And experts warned that it would not be the end of this sort of deferred violence. "There will be more reprisals, both symbolic ones and strategic ones," said Guillermo Zepeda Lecuona, a founding partner of the Mexico City-based Centro de Investigación para el Desarrollo (Center of Research for Development) think tank. "They will take revenge against not only the top people, but anybody who participates."

And that's how 2009 ended for Mexico. It was a terrifying and depressing time. The fact that many well-known cartel leaders were being caught or killed seemed to have little to no effect on the volume of drugs being moved or levels of violence being meted out. The cartels were fighting each other, the police and the military. Their targets were getting farther and farther from the expected victims: they were drug users looking for help in rehab clinics, they were the families of soldiers, they were people standing on a street corner when a group of *sicarios* opened fire on a government official. The death rate in 2009 jumped more than 40 percent over 2008. According to authorities, 9,635 people were killed in Mexico as a direct result of the Drug War in 2009, more than 26 per day. Of those victims, 79 were Americans and one was Canadian. By comparison, the U.S. military, fighting two wars, lost 149 people in Iraq and 317 in Afghanistan over the same period.

The real fear—both inside and outside of Mexico—was that the government could actually lose the war, that it could either be pushed aside by the cartels or step aside after realizing the fight was futile. This situation is far from unprecedented, and countries like Somalia, Chad and Sudan, in which governments have been over-run and made redundant by armed non-government groups are collectively known as "failed states."

As early as the middle of 2008, George Friedman, an American political scientist, author and CEO of STRATFOR, a private intelligence corporation, published a paper indicating that Mexico was well on its way to failed state status. By the middle of 2009, the phrase was commonly used in mainstream media describing what seemed like the nation's inevitable future.

And at the end of 2009, the transition of Mexico to failed state status looked like it began in the Michoacán town of Tancítaro. A week after seven bound bodies were found on the town's main street, town clerk Gonzalo Paz Torres was taken from his house by masked gunmen, tortured and shot five times in the head by AR-15s. His death, along with a constant barrage of anonymous threats, were cited on December 4, when the mayor, Jose Trinidad Meza Sánchez, and the entire city council tendered their resignations. One of them told a BBC reporter that being on council was like "having a rope around your neck." Three days later, every one of Tancítaro's 60 police officers quit. The local government had—out of fear—essentially handed the town over to the cartels.

Rather than let that happen unopposed, Michoacán Governor Leonel Godoy Rangel, stepped in and appointed a new council to oversee the town and moved 100 state police in to take over for Tancítaro's defunct police force. "Unfortunately, these terrible incidents not only occur in Michoacán, but also in other parts of the country, and they demonstrate the degree of power of organized crime," he said. "But it also shows the authorities' determination to fight it, while creating opportunities for education, health and employment—it's how we can ultimately defeat this terrible cancer that has invaded Mexico."

It was Calderón's plan in a nutshell—when there's trouble, move in progressively higher levels of authority. But there's a problem with that theory. As those organizations are eroded by defections due to fear, better offers from the cartels, arrests or assassinations, their numbers dwindle. And the number of people fighting on the other side gets bigger.

On April 21, 2009, Americans were shocked to see that cartel violence had hit in a place few would have expected. Hoover, Alabama, is a quaint suburb of Birmingham more than 1,000 miles from the Mexican border. That morning, Shelby County Sheriff Chris Curry responded to a call for help from one of his officers investigating a disturbance call at the low-rent cahaba lakes apartment building not far from downtown. He drove up from Columbiana, a half hour's drive away. As soon as he arrived at the crime scene, Curry started calling for more help. He first called the state troopers, then the FBI and finally the DEA. "I don't know what I've got," he told them. "But I'm gonna need help."

Inside the apartment were the bodies of five men, all illegal immigrants from Mexico. They had duct tape binding their hands and feet and covering their mouths. There were burn marks on their ears from the clamps of booster cables that had been used to torture them by electrocution. All five had their throats slashed. Autopsies indicated that the men were all dead before their throats were cut.

Investigators determined that the apartment was a drug stash, and that the men were involved with the Gulf Cartel. Shelby County, a quiet suburb with good schools and lots of retailers, was one of the fastest growing communities in the U.S. Latin Americans had been a rare sight in the area until 2005 or so, when Mexican day laborers started lining up on County Road 35 looking for work. Since then, investigators revealed that Pelham had become something of an area hub for drug trafficking.

On the other side of the country, the DEA and local police forces began a painstaking 19-month investigation on the meth trade in the state of Washington. The investigation just kept getting bigger and bigger until the operation was launched on October 22 and 23, 2009, as Project Coronado. Three hundred and three people were arrested in 19 states. Items seized on those first two days included 140 pounds of cocaine, 740 pounds of methamphetamine, 970 pounds of marijuana, 144 firearms, 109 vehicles and two complete meth labs. By early 2011, information from Project Coronado had led to a total of 1,186 arrests and had added much more evidence, including 29 pounds of black-tar heroin (a type particular to Mexico), 4,400 pounds of cocaine, 2,700 pounds of meth, 16,400 pounds of marijuana, $32,795,000 in U.S. currency and two maritime vessels.

Most of those arrested were Mexican nationals who had crossed the border illegally, and U.S. authorities named them as members and associates of La Familia, working in coordination with the Sinaloa Cartel. "This operation has dealt a significant blow to La Familia's supply chain of illegal drugs, weapons, and cash flowing between Mexico and the United States," U.S. attorney general Eric Holder said. "The cartels should know that we here in the United States are not going to allow them to operate unfettered in our country." American authorities had long considered La Familia among the most violent of the Mexican drug cartels, and with its quasi-religious shadow-state mentality, among the most dangerous. "The sheer level of depravity of violence that this cartel has exhibited far exceeds what we unfortunately have become accustomed to from other cartels," said Holder.

Despite the number of arrests and huge amounts of product confiscated, many observers countered that it was just a token effort when compared to the overall cartel picture in the U.S. "These raids indicate that the U.S. is beginning to roll up at least one of its sleeves in the war with the cartels," said George Grayson, a Mexico specialist at the College of William and Mary. "Most of the arrests in this week's raids are probably of low-level dealers, couriers and look-outs."

While Mexican gangs had long been established in the southwestern U.S. and Florida, it surprised many to see how powerful they had become in places like Seattle, Boston, Syracuse, New York and St. Paul, Minnesota. And one other fact the case revealed opened many eyes in the U.S.—much of the marijuana seized was not from Mexico, nor even California, but was the legendary BC Bud.

BC "BUD"

In the 1960s and 70s, much of Canada's self-identified hippie population moved to its westernmost province, British Columbia. Large areas of B.C. are warmer and wetter than the rest of Canada, and the Gulf Islands (between the mainland and Vancouver Island) and the Kootenay Plateau in the province's southeast proved very suitable for marijuana cultivation.

Since then, marijuana farming in B.C. has become a huge industry. A 2006 study by Burnaby, B.C.-based Simon Fraser

University indicated that the people of BC not only have a much more relaxed attitude toward marijuana than other Canadians do, they are also much bigger consumers. The province itself estimated the value of the rapidly growing crop in 2006 at $6.3 billion, and Larry Campbell, a senator and former mayor of Vancouver, has made repeated calls for marijuana not simply to be decriminalized in the province, but legalized.

The farming of BC Bud has become incredibly sophisticated. While there are still thousands of amateur marijuana farmers in British Columbia, the BC Bud brand name refers to a specific type of super-potent pot grown using specific methods. The process begins with shipping containers which are taken to isolated rural or wild areas. They are then fitted with halogen lights that are computer-timed to provide an optimum amount of artificial daylight. These are supplemented by sprayers that provide a constant cloud of mist, keeping the plants moist and heaters to maintain a constant temperature. Since the primary method of detecting marijuana farms in Canada—where they are usually called "grow-ops"—is to investigate residences that use much higher than normal levels of electricity, BC Bud growers often use their own electricity from diesel generators, solar panels and/or wind turbines.

The resulting product is so potent, that it is considered the gold standard of marijuana. And its high quality guarantees it a high price. The price it demands tends to rise the farther away it gets and many published reports have stated that in places like Miami, BC Bud is sometimes traded ounce for ounce for cocaine, a transaction that would be unthinkable with any other type of marijuana.

So high are the profits in dealing with BC Bud that police have arrested traffickers transporting it by kayak, through tunnels under the border, by airplane and helicopter and even in the backpacks of teenagers on a school bus taking Canadian kids to study in Port Roberts, Washington.

ENTER THE HELLS ANGELS

And, of course, wherever that kind of money is being made illegally, there will be violence. For generations, British Columbia's drug trade had been in the hands of the Hells Angels, who left the work of dealing and distributing to support groups, or what police call "puppet gangs." The most notable of them—the United Nations—was actually formed in opposition to the Hells Angels, whose puppet gangs would often target teens of Asian descent for abuse. Despite engaging in a number of brawls with Hells Angels supporters, the management of the United Nations could not resist the rewards of trafficking and became the Hells Angels' primary puppet gang in mainland British Columbia. Because the United Nations was a multiethnic gang, they could more easily make deals with communities the Hells Angels and their supporters could not reach. "We have a completely new infrastructure that supports the movement of cocaine, ecstasy, marijuana, you name it," said Pat Fogarty, RCMP superintendent with the combined forces special enforcement unit.

The United Nations had been fighting a bloody turf war in Vancouver and the nearby Fraser Valley with another multiethnic gang, the Red Scorpions. After dozens of shootings and stabbings of young people associated with those and other gangs, and the seizure of items like AK-47s and bulletproof vests, the police acknowledged that drug trafficking violence had created a gang war in British Columbia. "As police, we've always been told by media experts to never say or admit that there is a gang war," said Vancouver chief constable Jim Chu. "Well, let's get serious. There is a gang war, and it's brutal."

On the morning of September 27, 2009, residents of a Puerto Vallarta condominium community heard gun shots. Witnesses say that a masked man with an AR-15 shot two men in the pool area from a distance, and that another man with a handgun shot them again at close range. The local paper *Noticias Puerta Vallarta* ran pictures of the two bodies. One was shirtless, the other was wearing a souvenir T-shirt from Toronto's Hockey Hall of Fame.

The victims were identified as B.C. natives and former construction workers Gordon Douglas Kendall and Jeffrey Ronald Ivan, who had moved to Puerta Vallarta a year earlier. When the names were released, Canadian reporters phoned their friends and family but nobody would describe what the two did for a living. The Canadian consulate in Puerta Vallarta issued a press release stating that the murders looked like they were done to "settle a score." Then the police made it a little clearer. "Both the organized crime team and the gang task force have been aware of these two males for a while," said Sergeant Bill Whalen of the RCMP's Combined Forces Special Enforcement Unit. "We've been aware that these two males have been involved with the drug trade for a while. We've been aware of . . . some of their activities recently in Mexico." And a friend of theirs eventually came forward. "He went down there to do some stuff for the Hells Angels, as far as I know," the man, who refused to be identified, told reporters. "I tried to talk him out of it. I knew this was going to happen. He was involved in a nefarious venture, to say the least." The Hells Angels denied the two men were members of their organization—but they always do.

And Kendall and Ivan were hardly the first shooting victims in Mexico from B.C. and not the first connected to organized crime, either. On July 12, 2008, two Vancouver-area residents—Guatemala-born Elliott "Taco" Casteneda, a 28-year-old Abbotsford, B.C., realtor, and Lebanon-born Ahmet "Lou" Kaawach, a 26-year-old car customizer from Vancouver—were sitting down to lunch at a restaurant in the Santa Teresita neighborhood of Guadalupe when they were shot and killed. Both men were high-ranking members of the United Nations gang and were said to be "close friends" with its leader, Clayton Roueche. Kaawach had fled to Mexico after he was deported from Canada due to a weapons charge.

Six months later, two other men from British Columbia—28-year-old Brendhan Stowe and 26-year-old Nguyen Minh Trung Do—were shot by a lone gunman with an automatic weapon as they were enjoying the show at Mermaids, a topless bar in Cabo San Lucas, at about 1:30 a.m. Stowe was hit in the leg, while Trung Do took a serious hit to the neck and is now in a wheelchair. Though neither man had extensive criminal records, or was ever charged, the RCMP said they "were well known to police."

MEXICAN REFUGEE CLAIMS IN CANADA

As the Drug War in Mexico intensified, the number of Mexicans applying for refugee status in Canada jumped from a steady 1,000 a year to a peak of 9,309 in 2008. Almost all of them came through British Columbia. Far more Mexicans traveled to Canada as tourists, and simply stayed in the country without documentation. The RCMP and other organizations said that many of the immigrants came to traffic BC Bud. Since the Mexican military and the U.S. Border Patrol had clamped down on the Mexico–U.S. border, it made sense for traffickers to target the U.S. from the comparatively relaxed Canadian border. And they were not, police allege, all low-level cartel mules. Some came to purchase large amounts of BC Bud, and since large amounts of cash are difficult to smuggle into Canada, they were bartering cocaine for BC Bud. Suddenly, even small towns in British Columbia had communities of Mexican immigrants, mostly undocumented. And at the same time, those places started seeing rapid increases in cocaine and methamphetamine arrests, as well as gunfire. "The Mexican cartels are a factor that has contributed to the violence," said Fogarty. "The situation is quite serious insofar as historically there have not been shootouts in public places here, so the people are concerned for their safety."

The skyrocketing number of refugee claims led many Canadians to question their validity. "My concern is we're going to be swarmed by Mexicans [from] the U.S. who don't have status there and can come to the border because they don't need a visa to come to Canada," said Francisco Rico-Martinez, a refugee who came from El Salvador in 1990 and who is now codirector of the Toronto-based Faith Companions of Jesus Centre, a resource center for Latin American refugees. "We're starting to get calls from Mexicans in the States—five to six a week—hoping to file refugee [claims] in Canada. But we may not even know half of the Mexicans here who are without status, because they don't need visas to come."

The number rose so quickly that the Canadian government felt compelled to act. As of July 14, 2009, Mexican nationals would need to apply for visas to visit Canada. "In addition to creating significant delays and spiralling new costs in our refugee program, the sheer volume of these claims is undermining our ability to help people fleeing real persecution," said Citizenship, Immigration and Multiculturalism Minister Jason Kenney. "All too often, people who really need Canada's protection find themselves in a long line, waiting for months and sometimes years to have their claims heard. This is unacceptable."

That made things hard for legitimate Mexicans refugees who now had to apply for visas in advance, meet the requirements and wait to hear for an answer. The concept angered people like Juan Escobedo, who fled to Toronto after finding his life threatened repeatedly in Mexico. His struggles began with a June 2008 incident in which men who said they were members of Los Zetas kidnapped him and his wife, nearly drowned him, beat him and then told him he was going to work for them and that they would use his house for trafficking. "They said, 'We want a place from which to make sales and you are going to work for us, you understand?'" Escobedo told reporters. "My wife was sick [with cancer], and even so. They made her sell drugs from our house." The Escobedos' four children also lived in the house with them.

Escobedo could not refuse—he said Los Zetas paid his neighbors to watch him—and could not leave because his wife, an Oaxaca state employee who worked as a cleaner at the Social Security Institute, only qualified for free chemotherapy in their home state. Escobedo said he openly dealt drugs on the private bus he drove, while passengers and police routinely ignored the transactions.

On one occasion, the couple were kidnapped and blindfolded. When the blindfolds were taken off, he said, they were in a room with other bound people, some he knew. Then two masked, armed men walked in with another bound man. They beheaded the third man in front of the crowd and warned everyone in the room that they would receive the same treatment if they tried to escape.

In September, Escobedo's wife died and he refused to work for the cartel any longer. He received a visit from a man he knew to be a state police officer. "He said, 'You'll keep on working for us because you work for us,'" Escobedo told reporters. "I really didn't want to, so he said, 'Here it's not whether you want to or not,' and he pulled out a knife. I didn't know if he wanted to kill me or what his intentions were, but he stabbed me twice in the leg."

Unable to take it anymore, Escobedo sent his kids to live with relatives and used his life savings to buy a ticket to Toronto. When he arrived, he applied for refugee status. He had five dollars in his pocket. Fortunately for him, it was granted.

Canadians were sharply divided on the issue, with advocates on both sides of the visa requirement argument. Rico-Martinez, whose profession is to help refugees, said while there is a need for safe countries like Canada to take in authentic refuges, it had been all too easy in the past for Mexicans who were not actually in danger to abuse the system. "We can't have a blank-check solution that discriminates [between] people who need to come for protection [and] those with resources to come," he said. "To address the issue, Canadian officials need to reach out to the Mexican public and educate them about our immigration and refugee system."

While the Canadian mainstream media continued to stress the refugee angle (perhaps because it's a hot-button issue with two clearly defined sides), the bulk of arrests of Mexican nationals in Canada were not those who had made refugee claims. On September 22, 2010, a Sinaloan named Victor Perez Rodrigues was arrested along with Canadians Clifford Roger Montgomery, Barry Michael Ready and Tariq Mohammed Aslam when they attempted to import a fruit-grinding machine from Argentina to Kelowna, British Columbia. Inside the machine were a little more than 213 pounds of cocaine. On October 5, a raid on the Colour & Culture Trading Corporation, an import-export firm based in a downtown Vancouver office tower, netted the RCMP 600 pounds of meth, cocaine and marijuana. Arrested were Tijuana native Eduardo Sierra Gonzalez, as well as Jason Quinn Lawrence and Francisco Javier Gomez, owner of Colour & Culture, both of Vancouver. Neither Perez Rodrigues nor Sierra Gonzalez were asylum seekers, both having entered Canada as tourists and not having left. The RCMP linked both to established Mexican cartels.

While the police and prosecutors acknowledge that there are Mexican cartel members (or at least associates) operating within the Canadian drug trafficking system, the consensus opinion is that they are not, at present, major players within the country. Instead, the overwhelming majority of cocaine in the country comes from people like Kendall and Ivan (if not specifically them) who travel to Mexican resorts like Acapulco and Mazatlán or American cities with strong Mexican gangs like San Diego, Los Angeles and Las Vegas to make deals for cocaine from the major cartels, especially the Sinaloa.

"Anywhere there are narcotics to be sold, [the Mexican cartels] want to be in on that action. They are consistently and constantly looking to expand," said Robert Gordon, director of Simon Fraser University's School of Criminology. "So we're going to start seeing these organized criminal elements in places we've never seen them before."

And law enforcement is seeing them in Canada. "I've dealt with Mexican cartel types up here [in British Columbia]; they do exist," said Fogarty. "You have to see this as a north-south trade . . . marijuana comes down and cocaine heads up."

CHAPTER 13
The Violence Escalates

After the brutality of 2009, the nation breathed a tiny sigh of relief (or at least closure) when authorities arrested suspects for the killing of the Angulo Córdova family early in 2010.

Chiapas state police, reinforced by army soldiers, stopped a luxury car at a routine checkpoint in Tuxtla Gutiérrez, the state's capital and largest city, on January 2. The men inside seemed nervous, so the police asked to search their vehicle. At that point, the group's leader admitted that they were *narcomenudistas* (street-level drug retailers) and offered the police a bribe to let them go. When the police refused, the man who appeared to be the group's ringleader changed his story. He told the cops that they were members of Los Zetas and it would be very dangerous for the officers if they were not allowed to continue.

Police arrested the three men—Gudiel Iván Sánchez

Valdez, Dorilian López Alatorre and Elías León López—and seized their car, their weapons and an ounce of cocaine. The boss was Sánchez Valdez—a member of Los Zetas known as "El Chito" (the Cool) and "El Poblano" (the Guy from Puebla)—who later admitted to leading the group that assassinated the Angulo Córdova family. He said that the hit was ordered as retribution for the death of Arturo Beltrán Leyva and that he was paid $12,000.

This incident was followed by a stunning series of arrests. With intelligence gathered by sources they would not reveal, the Federales surrounded a car in Culiacán. The lone man inside presented a driver's license that indicated he was Carlos Gámez Orpineda. Police searched the car, finding a .45-caliber handgun and 31 small packages of what they believed was cocaine. Lab tests proved that the powder was indeed cocaine and that the driver's license was a fake. Interrogation led to the man admitting that he was actually Carlos Beltrán Leyva, brother of recently killed Arturo, the "*jefe de jefes*" (boss of bosses) of the Beltrán Leyva Cartel. Carlos' role in the gang was not made clear, but it was apparent that he had not taken over as boss.

At about the same time, the DEA informed Mexican authorities that their intelligence revealed a plot to break another brother, Alfredo Beltrán Leyva (who had taken over the reins of the gang for the period that began when Arturo was killed and ended when Alfredo was arrested), out of prison. The Mexicans beefed up security, but the assault never came.

Still, revenge for the arrest of Carlos Beltrán Leyva was swift and public. A man named Hugo Hernandez Robles was kidnapped in the Sinaloa city of Los Mochis the day Beltrán Leyva was arrested. His link to the drug trade or law enforcement is unclear. Hours after police announced who they had in custody on national television, Hernandez Robles turned up: pedestrians found his arms, legs and skull in a cardboard box on one side of town; his torso was dropped off in front of a police station in a plastic cooler; and the skin from his face was sewn over a soccer ball found in the town square in a clear plastic bag. It had a note with it that read "Happy New Year; it will be your last."

Later that day, two more bodies were spotted hanging by their necks from a highway overpass in Culiacán. Spanning them was a banner that read, "This place already has an owner."

These novel ways of sending messages were indicative of the war being played out by the cartels. Theirs was a terror campaign designed not just to frighten the public and intimidate the government, but also to show the other cartels that they were willing to go the extra mile to defend their territories. "Criminals earn respect and credibility with creative killing methods," a high-ranking Mexican law enforcement official, who preferred not to have his name published, told *The Los Angeles Times*. "Your status is based on your capacity to commit the most sadistic acts. Burning corpses, using acid, beheading victims . . . this generation is setting a new standard for savagery."

THE END OF THE SIMENTAL GANG

The Carlos Beltrán Leyva arrest paled in comparison to what happened January 12. At 6:00 a.m. on a calm Tuesday morning, residents of and visitors to the well-heeled resort town of La Paz on the southern end of the Baja Peninsula were awakened by what sounded like an explosion followed by the roar of two military helicopters. Five busloads of soldiers had been deployed at the corner of Avenida del Paz Vela and Calle Sardina, in the heart of Fidepaz, the town's ritziest neighborhood.

Onlookers watched as soldiers knocked down the front door and emerged with two men, one fat and one thin. The fat one was Teodoro "El Teo" García Simental, who had once been one of the most important men in the Tijuana Cartel until a downtown, broad daylight standoff in April 2008 between men loyal to him and those loyal to the Arellano Félix left 15 men dead and García Simental in charge of his own, smaller gang. The thin one was Diego Raymundo Guerrero García, one of his lieutenants.

Using equipment and methods obtained from the DEA, Mexican military intelligence managed to track death threats made to Baja California attorney general Rommel Moreno Manjarrez and Julian Leyzaola Perez back to García Simental and his La Paz residence. "Today another Mexican cartel leader was taken off the street and is no longer able to carry out his bloody turf war," said Michele Leonhart, acting administrator of the DEA. "This was not an isolated event; it exemplifies the growing effectiveness of our information-sharing with the [Calderón] administration, and our continued commitment to defeat the drug traffickers who have plagued both our nations."

Information gathered from that arrest—two laptops and 16 cell phones were seized—led to another massive blow against the Simental gang about three weeks later. In the same Fidepaz neighborhood on February 9, soldiers and Federales arrested José Manuel "El Chiquilín" (the Kid) García Simental and Raydel "El Muletas" (the Crutches) López Uriarte. El Chiquilín was El Teo's younger brother and second-in-command, while López Uriarte was the gang's enforcer. Although he was linked to about 250 murders, he was better known for torture, and his signature was to leave his victims using crutches for the rest of their lives. In fact, authorities seized uniforms with an insignia that featured a skull with crossed crutches underneath it and the name "Fuerzas Especiales de Muletas" (Crutches' Special Forces).

Acting on information obtained through the arrests, soldiers and police raided a home in Tijuana. Inside, they found five police officers, six members of the García Simental gang and two rival members of the Tijuana Cartel who were being held captive.

It was the end of the García Simental gang. Those members who were still alive and at large either fled or joined other groups. Although the demise of the gang would have little net effect on the levels of drug trafficking—other, even bigger gangs had been dissolved or absorbed before with only temporary results—it did make Tijuana a somewhat safer place. Shootouts between the followers of García Simental and those loyal to Arellano Félix (essentially two factions of the same cartel) had been common-place. Police in the city had warned residents and visitors to steer clear of any collection of Cadillac Escalade SUVs or Ford F-250 pickups (especially if they were customized) because those were the vehicles favored by traffickers.

LOS ZETAS VERSUS THE GULF CARTEL

But as things were getting less violent in northwest Mexico, northeast Mexico erupted into another separate war. The Gulf Cartel had been working in conjunction with the Beltrán Leyva Cartel since the Gulf Cartel and Sinaloa Cartel declared a truce in 2008, which limited their need for Los Zetas to fight on their behalf. With less enforcement work to do, Los Zetas had become more independent of the Gulf Cartel and started making their own import and export deals. They had, in effect, become a de facto cartel in their own right—and declared independence from the Gulf Cartel in February 2010.

It began when a high-ranking member of Los Zetas, Victor Mendoza Perez, was killed by a gang from the Gulf Cartel in January. When the Gulf Cartel refused a request by the leadership of Los Zetas to hand over the killers, war was declared. A mass e-mail warning of brutal violence circulated to a set of teenagers on February 17 spread rapidly around the region and set off the war. People all over Tamaulipas, Nuevo León and some of Coahuila panicked. Many businesses closed, few parents sent their children to school and the streets of most cities and towns were deserted. Violence broke out on the February

18 when a suspected Zetas safe house in Villahermosa, not far from Reynosa, was shot up in the afternoon. Later that night, a Petroleos Mexicanos (the state-owned petroleum company, better known as Pemex) filling station employee reported that armed men were forcing the station's staff to leave. It had been well-established that Pemex stations were often used as transfer and retailing spots for marijuana. A navy helicopter was sent in to investigate, but it had to withdraw due to heavy ground fire.

Rumors abounded of massive gun fights and helicopters downed. There was no coverage of the event in the local media, though residents could hear the shooting. "Before, if there was a shootout, the scene would be full of journalists," a Mexican reporter who admitted that he stopped covering cartel-related stories out of fear, told *The New York Times*. "Now, sometimes there will not be a single journalist. Everyone stays away." On the following day, a Pemex truck carrying four tons of seismic booster pentolite, a powerful explosive, was hijacked.

Because the media refused to cover the violence, a few brave people took it into their own hands. Among the boldest of them was CiudadanoReynosa100 (Reynosa Citizen 100), a woman in her early forties who took videos of the carnage and posted them on YouTube. She shot one video "Ciudadana graba evidencias de balaceras en Tamaulipas (Citizen's evidence of the shootings at Tamaulipas)" from the front passenger seat of a car. The six-minute video begins on a largely deserted highway. As they pass by the Pemex station, they come across at least 10 shot-up SUVs. She sees a lone boot surrounded by hundreds of spent cartridges from what she calls a "cuerno de chivo" (goat's horn), Mexican slang for an AK-47, and remarks "they must've taken that guy away in pieces." As they pass the military checkpoint, there are two Escalades (one white, one black) about three feet away from each other, each riddled with literally hundreds of holes. In an instant, she notices a dead body in between them. At the end of the video, she complains about what the war has done to the local economy and points out, "Look, even the traffic lights don't work anymore."

Shootouts in the area became routine and, by February 24, officials admitted that 16 people had been killed in and around Reynosa, and the U.S. had closed its consulate there. Authorities on both sides of the border warned Americans not to visit the area. "Tamaulipas is at war, and if there is no coordination between state and local governments, then the federal government will have a hard time waging a frontal attack on organized crime," PAN senator José Julián Sacramento Garza said. The American authorities agreed. "Some recent confrontations between Mexican authorities and drug cartel members have resembled small-unit combat, with cartels employing automatic weapons and grenades," read a warning from the U.S. State Department. "During some of these incidents, U.S. citizens have been trapped and temporarily prevented from leaving the area."

The situation became so dire that a Mexican military helicopter shot at gunmen from the air on the night of March 4. The following day, the Red Cross—an organization founded to tend to victims of war—ceased operations in the area because its volunteers had been shot at too often.

Criticism of the local media's unwillingness to put itself in the line of fire quieted down on March 8 when the Sociedad Interamericana de Prensa (SIP, or Inter-American Press Association) reported that eight local journalists had been kidnapped in Reynosa. One had been tortured and killed, two set free and another five were still missing. One of the men who was released told *Milenio*, a national newspaper, that his kidnappers identified themselves as *sicarios* and told him to warn his peers not to "stir things up." The reporter told *Milenio* that "they have decided that nothing more should be known or told . . . and we obeyed."

NEW ALLIANCES FORMED

The split between Los Zetas and the Gulf Cartel led to Mexico being basically divided between two warring factions. Los Zetas aligned with the Juárez Cartel, Tijuana Cartel and the Beltrán-Leyva Cartel, while the Gulf Cartel threw their lot in with the Sinaloa Cartel and La Familia. With the loss of Los Zetas, the Gulf Cartel formed a new enforcer unit, known as Los Escorpiones (the Scorpions).

On the afternoon of March 14, Arthur Redelfs was driving his pregnant wife, Leslie Ann Enriquez, home from a children's party thrown by the U.S. consulate in Juárez. They had their seven-month-old daughter with them in the back seat. One or both of them noticed that they were being followed, so Redelfs stepped on the accelerator of their white Toyota RAV4 with Texas plates. Their pursuers followed and, when the El

Paso family was trapped by traffic, opened fire. Redelfs, an El Paso prison guard, was killed by a bullet above his right eye and Enriquez, a ten-year veteran of the consulate, died from bullet wounds to her left arm and neck. Their daughter was screaming, but not injured.

Previously, American casualties in the Mexican Drug War had been accidental—people caught in the cross-fire, misidentified or simply in the wrong place when someone decided to shoot. But the assassination of Redelfs and Enriquez had all the hallmarks of a directed hit. "We know that the U.S. citizens were targeted," Juárez Mayor Jose Reyes Ferriz told CNN, noting that a police officer witnessed the car chase. "We know they were chasing them. We know they wanted to kill them."

Ten minutes before Redelfs and Enriquez were killed, Jorge Alberto Salcido Ceniceros—a supervisor at a Juárez factory who was married to Hilda Antillon Jimenez, a Mexican employee at the U.S. consulate—was found shot to death in his white Honda Pilot SUV, a car that looked a great deal like the RAV4 Redelfs was driving. His children—four and seven—were injured but survived. They had attended the same party.

"These appalling assaults on members of our own State Department family are, sadly, part of a growing tragedy besetting many communities in Mexico," Secretary of State Hillary Clinton said. "They underscore the imperative of our continued commitment to work closely with the government of President Calderón to cripple the influence of trafficking organizations at work in Mexico."

While the media concentrated on connections to the consulate, the Department of Homeland Security investigated and determined that the Redelfs/Enriquez murders were actually retaliation by an El Paso gang called El Barrio Azteca and that the target was actually Redelfs, not Enriquez.

Five days after the killing, the DEA and El Paso police launched Operation Knockdown against El Barrio Azteca, making 26 felony arrests. Ricardo Valles de la Rosa—a Mexican native who grew up in El Paso and became a member of the gang in prison—was among those charged. He admitted to both murders and said that El Barrio Azteca had a close relationship with the Juárez Cartel. The murder of Salcido Ceniceros had been a mistake. The American authorities found out that members of El Barrio Azteca worked on both sides of the border and carried out many different tasks for the Juárez Cartel, including contract killing. "Within their business of killing, they have surveillance people, intel people and shooters. They have a degree of specialization," said David Cuthbertson, head of the FBI's El Paso division. "They work day in and day out, with a list of people to kill, and they get proficient at it." It was also determined that another El Paso gang, the Artistic Assassins, did similar work for rival cartels.

MURDER NORTH OF THE BORDER

While much of the U.S. media's attention on the Mexican Drug War focused on Texas, a story emerged from Arizona that led to a national outcry, military mobilization and one of the most controversial laws in U.S. history. Robert Krentz was a well-known rancher. His family had established a cattle farm just outside Douglas, Arizona (a small, still mostly non-Hispanic town across the border fence from the much larger Mexican city of Agua Prieta) in 1907 and he had been voted into the Arizona Farming and Ranchering Hall of Fame.

After seeing what he described as literally thousands of illegal immigrants cross over his property, he became an outspoken critic of the contemporary border policy and called for more security. "A bear of a man with a reserved nature, he could seem imposing at first glance," read *The New York Times'* description of him. "But almost always rendered help to those who needed it, friends and family said."

He was doing just that at about 10:30 on the morning of March 27. A neighbor, Wendy Glenn, heard him broadcast a message to his brother Phil on a shared radio. "He says, 'I see an immigrant out here, and he appears to need help. Call the Border Patrol,'" recalled Glenn. "He was not frantic. He was not calling for help."

When nobody heard from him again after a few hours, his family and friends organized a search party. The body of Krentz's dog was found on a remote part of his ranch just before midnight. He had been shot several times. Searchers followed the tracks of Krentz's all-terrain vehicle and found his body at the wheel. His gun was still in its holster and his wallet was still in his pocket. Because it appeared as though Krentz was neither confronted nor robbed, Glenn came up with a theory for his murder. "There are a lot of people out here who are unarmed that need help, and I'm sure Rob didn't realize [the killer] was armed," she said. "I think he approached to see if he could help him and the guy thought maybe he was going to get arrested, that maybe Rob was the law . . . I don't know what the guy thought, but he never gave Rob a chance."

The Krentz family issued a statement in which they said they did not blame the Mexican people for the murder, but the governments of both countries. "Their disregard of our repeated pleas and warnings of impending violence toward our community fell on deaf ears shrouded in political correctness," it read. "As a result, we have paid the ultimate price for their negligence in credibly securing our borderlands."

The reaction to the Krentz murder was quick and huge. Locally, the first response people had was to arm themselves. Lynn Kartchner, owner of Allsafe Security, the most popular gun shop in Douglas, reported an immediate 20 percent increase in sales. "We've been selling a lot of the concealed type of guns," he said. "Most of these people who have been buying guns have told me if these people will shoot Rob, they will shoot anybody."

People in the state of Arizona made calls for federal help. "The federal government must do all it can within its power to curb this violence and protect its citizens from criminals coming across the border from Mexico," John McCain, the state's senior senator and a former Republican presidential candidate, wrote in a letter to Homeland Security Secretary Janet Napolitano, herself a former governor of Arizona. He pointed out that in the 262-mile strip of border known as the Tucson Zone, Border Patrol made about a quarter-million arrests in 2009. The request was bipartisan. McCain's sentiments were joined by those of Democratic Congresswoman Gabrielle Giffords, who said: "The federal government must respond appropriately. All options should be on the table."

Heeding their plea, Obama deployed 1,200 National Guard soldiers to help train and reinforce Border Patrol, immigration and customs agents along the border. McCain replied that 6,000 would have been a more appropriate number.

Mexico's ambassador to Washington, Arturo Sarukhán Casamitjana, used the opportunity to put a spin on the move that echoed much of what Calderón had been saying, by praising "additional U.S. resources to enhance efforts to prevent the illegal flows of weapons and bulk cash into Mexico, which provide organized crime with its firepower and its ability to corrupt."

The Krentz murder became a rallying cry for supporters of Arizona's controversial Bill SB 1070 (better known as the *Support Our Law Enforcement and Safe Neighborhoods Act*), which, if passed, would allow authorities to enforce a federal law already on the books that requires non-citizens to provide documentation upon request. The Act also bars state and local legislatures from restricting enforcement of immigration laws and increases penalties on anyone sheltering, transporting or employing illegal immigrants.

SB 1070's future was in doubt as the national (and international) media cast it as racist and many boycotts were threatened, but it was signed into law by Arizona Governor

Jan Brewer on April 23. Reaction to the law was negative in Mexico. Calderón said: "The Mexican government condemns the approval of the law [and] the criminalization of migration" and called it a "violation of human rights." But American journalist and Mexico specialist Chris Hawley pointed out that Mexico has essentially the same law on its books, allowing Federales to check the documents and even detain suspected illegal immigrants and that Federales and other Mexican police routinely engage in ethnic profiling when dealing with Central and South Americans.

BUSINESS AS USUAL IN MEXICO

While the central part of the border was caught up in political rhetoric, the northeast was still awash in violence. After a motorcade carrying the chief of police of a suburb of Juárez was shot up, tensions in Monterrey were high. On March 19, army soldiers engaged in a shootout with suspected Gulf Cartel members just outside the campus of *Instituto Tecnológico y de Estudios Superiores de Monterrey*, a prestigious university often referred to as Monterrey Tech. When the smoke cleared, authorities announced they had killed two *sicarios*. It was later revealed that the two dead men were actually accomplished graduate students at the school.

On the morning on March 28, 40 prisoners held at *Centro de Ejecución de Sanciones de Santa Adelaida*, a state prison in Matamoros, escaped without violence. Fifty of the prison's staff were arrested for complicity.

Two days later, just hours after authorities tried to douse rumors of impending violence after several key members of Los Zetas were arrested, the cartels surprised the military by staging seven different assaults on army bases throughout Nuevo León. It began when cartel members attempted to block the entranceway to a military compound near Matamoros by moving tractor trailers in front of it. In the end, 18 cartel members were killed in the ensuing gun battle, and authorities seized 54 assault rifles, 61 grenades, eight improvised explosive devices (IEDs), three rocket-propelled grenade launchers, and six armored SUVs. The only casualty suffered by the government forces was a soldier with an injured toe.

But like the Tet Offensive in the Vietnam War, while the attacks of March 30 were a military failure, they had an enormous psychological impact. Soldiers had been killed on patrol or in ambushes throughout the war, but these incidents marked the first time the cartels were willing to launch full-scale attacks on the military. It seemed just a matter of time before the cartels came out of hiding and confronted the police and military openly. The authorities, however, said that the brazen attacks were a show of desperation on the parts of the cartels.

Later that day, Federales in Villahermosa arrested Roberto Rivero Arana, nephew of Los Zetas leader Heriberto Lazcano Lazcano, and Daniel Pérez Galisteo, the acting police chief of Ciudad del Carmen, an oil refining town on the Gulf coast in the southern state of Campeche. Investigators determined that Pérez Galisteo had been receiving about $16,000 a month to allow Los Zetas to work in the city unmolested. "He's an agent who had been with the police force long before we took over the town government," Ciudad del Carmen mayor Aracely Escalante Jasso said. "We had given him our trust." Along with the men, the Federales seized 10 assault rifles, a grenade, ammunition, drugs and uniforms with police and Pemex insignia.

Another Gulf oil town, Tampico, was hit the next day. Masked gunmen attacked a police convoy as it approached El Moralillo bridge on its way out of town. Four officers—José Alfredo Ontiveros Romero, Federico Macías Hernández, Eduardo Robles Ramos and Salvador González del Ángel—were killed. That night, more gunmen forced their way into Club Mirage, a rowdy local strip joint favored by members of the Gulf Cartel. They shot the place up indiscriminately, killing five men and two women—including one dancing on stage. In the town square nearby, Jenni Rivera, a popular Mexican-American pop singer, was just about to take to the stage for an open-air concert when her entire audience of about 18,000 fled as a rumor spread that gunmen with grenades were coming to attack the show. As she was on the stairs to the stage, her crew stopped her from going on. "My security guys shouted at me not to go up and they pulled me and covered me," she said. "Everyone on my team is okay."

It was a spring of major discoveries for the Mexican authorities. The first came on April 23, when the Federales (supported by army soldiers) came upon a camp used by Beltrán Leyva Cartel to train assassins outside the town of San Dimas near the Pacific coast of Durango. After a brief firefight left seven *sicarios* and a man they had kidnapped dead, the Federales arrested 19-year-old José Natividad Ruiz Rodriguez. Several others escaped. They also seized about 1,000 pounds of marijuana, 11 AK-47s, three AR-15s, a shotgun, four handguns and 14 trucks, including two Hummers. They also discovered a .50-caliber Barrett special applications rifle. "The .50-caliber was interesting because we haven't seen that type of arm used in Mexico yet," said Scott Stewart, a former U.S. Army intelligence officer and an analyst for STRATFOR. The Barrett is an incredibly accurate long-range sniper rifle that can kill from well over a mile away. "The [Barrett's] 5.7 x 28 armor-piercing rounds are not available for sale to the general public and are probably coming from the Mexican military," he added. Three soldiers were wounded during the assault.

UNEXPECTED CORRUPTION OF A POLITICAL HERO

The second surprise came on May 26. Gregorio "Greg" Sánchez Martínez was regarded as a hero by many in southern Mexico. One of 15 children, Sánchez Martínez was born to a very poor family in Guerrero and grew up in Chiapas. At 16, he started his own lumber business and by his early twenties, he was wealthy and had made a name for himself as a popular gospel singer. He later moved to Cancún and dabbled in politics before being elected mayor of Benito Juárez Municipality, representing a coalition of four left-wing parties including the PRD. His populist, anti-corruption, anti-crime message resonated with his constituents (he had once disarmed and interrogated the entire Cancún police force), and Sánchez Martínez took a leave of absence from his job to run for governor of Quintana Roo.

Early in the campaign, Sánchez Martínez claimed on his website that he and other candidates from the "Todos por Quintana Roo" (All for Quintana Roo) coalition had received numerous threats. One he noted in particular read: "Resign from the race, or we are going to put you in jail or kill you."

He wasn't killed. But he was put in jail for money laundering and for aiding both Los Zetas and the Beltrán Leyva Cartel. "This takes us all by surprise," said his PRI opponent, incumbent Félix González Canto. "It is unprecedented." Sánchez Martínez, meanwhile, maintained that he was innocent and that the evidence was manufactured by political opponents. He has yet to be tried.

Evidence gathered from the investigation that led to his arrest later brought police to a *cenote*—a type of sinkhole common in Mexico and the Caribbean that are usually filled with water, but this one was dry—in Leona Vicario, just outside Cancún, that contained six bodies. The victims, four men and two women, had been asphyxiated and had cocaine in their bloodstreams. Three of the bodies had been stabbed multiple times in the chest, while the other three had the letter "Z" carved into their abdomens, a calling card of Los Zetas. Two of the bodies were identified. One was that of Isaías de Jesús Valenzuela Ruiz, head of security for the municipal government of Playas del Carmen, a small resort town just south of Cancún. The other was that of Francisco Silva Ruiz, who had recently moved to the area and made his living singing on public buses.

BODY DUMP

The third major discovery of the spring shocked and horrified even the most cynical people in a country beset by murder and decapitations. Taxco de Alarcón is one of Mexico's most beautiful cities. Nestled in Guerrero's densely wooded mountains, Taxco has been enriched by silver mines first discovered by Hernán Cortés. The early prosperity silver brought allowed the residents to dedicate themselves to artistic pursuits like architecture and landscaping.

But the town of about 40,000 had fallen on harder times. A strike had shut down the mines for almost three years. Workers accused its operator, Industrial Minera México (part of the Grupo México conglomerate owned by billionaire Germán Larrea Mota Velasco, whom *Forbes* rated as the 127th richest person in the world with a $7.3 billion fortune), of not honoring its contracts or promoting employee safety conditions.

Taxco had been largely untouched by the war until late May. Near the end of the month, townspeople began to report the presence of trucks around the shuttered mines after dark. Two Beltrán Leyva-associated gunmen arrested in a different part of Mexico revealed under interrogation that they had used Taxco as a place to dump three bodies. Further investigation led authorities to a mineshaft near a grazing pasture just outside of Taxco. To keep people out of the shaft opening, it had been surrounded by gray cinder-block walls that had been covered with a light application of graffiti. There was an opening protected by wrought iron bars, but they had been bent by some of the locals to provide access to the shaft so that they could throw trash down there. When the police and firefighters approached, they reported that the smell was so strong, they would have to delay the investigation until gas masks arrived.

Luis Rivera Terrazas, only 23 but already a senior state criminologist, tried to get police or firefighters to go into the 15-foot wide, 500-foot deep shaft, but they refused. Realizing he'd have to go down himself, Rivera Terrazas put on his office's only biohazard suit and climbed down the ladder. When it ended after 30 or so feet, he rappelled his way down to the bottom, careful not to let the jagged walls tear his protective suit. He described his slow descent as cold and wet. When he reached bottom, he was surprised when his feet sank into the floor, until he realized he was not stepping on a floor, but badly decomposed human remains. "It was like a quicksand, but filled with bodies," he said. "We were stepping on them—it was a very challenging working environment."

For six days, workers pulled body parts up from the shaft, often by hand, recovering what they could. The first reports from the site indicated that they had recovered pieces from 25 corpses; then it rose to 77. Rumors had the total going over 100 at one point. The problem for Rivera Terrazas was that many of the bodies were badly decomposed or in pieces. At least three were mummified. "There are headless bodies," said Rivera Terrazas said. "But some of the heads don't match the bodies."

Days of painstaking work allowed the forensics team to separate the mess into 55 individuals. Some of the victims had been bound and blindfolded. Some showed signs of torture. Many, it was determined, were alive when they were thrown into the shaft and some even survived on the bottom for at least a few moments. "The rocks in the shaft are sharp-edged and tore at the bodies," said Rivera Terrazas. "There were some who arrived alive at the bottom."

Identification was nearly impossible. Using tattoos and dental records, authorities were able to identify just eight of the dead after a month. One of them was Daniel Bravo Mota, a Guerrero state prison director, who had been missing for three weeks.

BARBIE, THE AMERICAN ENFORCER

The body dump was linked to a capo of the Beltrán Leyva Cartel—Edgar "Barbie" Valdez Villarreal. Growing up in a heavily Hispanic neighborhood in Laredo, Texas, the blond-haired, green-eyed Valdez Villarreal reminded the other kids of Ken, Barbie's boyfriend. They called him Barbie, and the name stuck when a high school coach started using it. His childhood was far from the rough upbringing most cartel members and associates endured. Valdez Villarreal grew up in a nice brick house with a manicured lawn and a wooden swing set in the back. His father, Abel Valdez Villarreal, owned a retail store and stressed hard work and a college education to his boys, taking them to church every Sunday. Barbie was popular and grew very large and strong. At 6-foot-5, he became something of a star playing both ways for the United High School football team.

And he had a wild side. His first arrest was at age 19 in 1992. While speeding down the wrong side of a Laredo road in his customized pickup, Valdez Villarreal collided head on with a Toyota Corolla driven by a middle school guidance counselor, killing him. Valdez Villarreal was charged with criminally negligent homicide. His clean record and pleas from his father convinced police not to indict him. His dad then offered to pay for college, but Barbie declined. A few weeks later he was arrested with a large quantity of marijuana. After his father bailed him out of jail, Valdez Villarreal fled to Mexico City.

Contacts he had made while dealing in Texas introduced him to Arturo Beltrán Leyva. The kingpin liked him and gave him a job as an enforcer with an allied gang in Nuevo Laredo, across the river from his hometown, called Los Negros (the Blacks). Originally formed in 2002 to protect the interests of the Sinaloa Cartel in northeast Mexico against Los Zetas and law enforcement authorities, Los Negros were among the best armed and trained gangs in the country. Aligned strongly with the Beltrán Leyva Cartel, Los Negros accepted Valdez Villarreal gratefully and he quickly rose through the ranks by showing brutal efficiency and even a little showmanship in kidnapping, torturing and killing his enemies.

Along with his skills as an enforcer, Barbie also succeeded as a trafficker. Although unable to cross the border himself after arrests and narrow escapes in Louisiana and Missouri, he had contacts with the Los Angeles–based Mexican Mafia and the brutal Mara Salvatrucha—a gang of Central American, mainly Salvadoran, immigrants better known as MS-13 with cells as far away as Colorado, Toronto and Washington D.C.—who worked with him.

Valdez Villarreal was also known for working the media. The newspapers in Mexico's northeast rarely reported on drug-related stories after the assassination by grenade of Roberto Javier Mora Garcia, a crusading reporter for Nuevo Laredo's *El Mañana* in 2002, but Valdez Villarreal would occasionally place ads in papers to get his message across. In 2004, he took out an ad in a Monterrey paper that said he was a "legitim-ate businessman" who had to move to the area from Nuevo Laredo because he was being unfairly harassed by police and politicians. After Mexican authorities named him as one of the most wanted men in the country in 2008, he took out another ad, acknowledging his leadership of Los Negros and calling on the government to stop Los Zetas, who he called a "cancer" and "narco-terrorists" and who he accused of kidnapping and killing women and children.

When Arturo Beltrán Leyva was killed at the end of 2009, Valdez Villarreal and his trusted lieutenant José Gerardo "El Indio" (the Indian) Álvarez Vázquez broke with the cartel, taking Los Negros—sometimes known as the Valdez Gang—independent. Álvarez Vázquez was arrested with 15 associates on April 21, 2010 at his home in Huixquilucan de Degollado near Mexico City after a prolonged gun battle. When he was presented to the media, he was incorrectly described as a high-ranking member of the Beltrán Leyva Cartel.

MURDER IN THE STREETS

Two weeks after the body dump was found, violence hit Taxco again. An anonymous complaint about noise coming from a downtown apartment drew state police at 10:10 a.m. As soon as they arrived, they were fired upon from inside the apartment. When more police and soldiers showed up, the firefight intensified. Forty minutes later, all 15 men inside the apartment were dead and three officers were injured. Police seized 16 assault rifles, six handguns and three IEDs. The authorities linked them to Los Negros.

The two weeks between the discovery of the Taxco body dump and the Taxco shootout were tumultuous ones for Mexico.

On May 31, a news crew from Channel 44 from Juárez was filming a piece at the Zaragoza bridge to Texas when shooting broke out. A white SUV had been in line to get over the bridge when the driver parked nearby and four of the six occupants got out of the vehicle. As they were headed to a white minibus that had been converted to prepare and sell burritos, all six of them were shot and killed by men in a nearby pickup truck who shot up both vehicles with AR-15s and sped away. While the news crew did not actually record any footage of the shooting or escape, they did manage to pick up a significant amount of video of Mexican Army soldiers a few feet away who did nothing to interfere with or pursue the gunmen.

Mass killing hit the north again on Thursday, June 10. It started in the afternoon when 30 masked, armed men claiming to be police forced their way into *Templo Cristiano Fe y*

Vida (Faith and Life Christian Temple), a second-floor drug rehabilitation clinic in Chihuahua. As soon as the men entered, they started shooting indiscriminately, killing 14 people including both staff and patients. One teenaged victim had enough time to call home, screaming "Mommy, they've come to kill us!" into his family's voice mail. When five others were discovered to be alive, they were lined up against the wall and killed. Four people survived the incident by pretending to be dead. The victims were between 16 and 63 years old. Despite arriving in trucks, the *sicarios* fled on foot. Police discovered a threatening message left behind, but would not reveal its contents.

Still, the message was clear to the people it was meant for. Within two hours of the *Templo Cristiano Fe y Vida* massacre, a series of seemingly unconnected shootings in Ciudad Madero, just outside of Tampico in Tamaulipas, left 18 men and two women dead. Social media was alive with threats of retaliation for both incidents.

Calderón, who was in South Africa attending Mexico's opening game in the 2010 FIFA World Cup was told of the incidents and commented: "[These] are outrageous acts that reinforce the need to fight with the full force of the law criminal groups carrying out such barbarism."

MAJOR LOS ZETAS TARGETS NABBED

At 5:30 in the afternoon of the next day, a heavily armored army unit set out for the quiet, residential Solidaridad neighborhood of Monterrey. They arrived at a cookie-cutter poured-concrete townhouse at 223 Avenida Fénix and surrounded the place. After tense negotiations, they emerged with two men. The fat one was Raúl Héctor "El Tory" Luna Luna and the thin one was David Eduardo "El Mantequilla" (the Butter) Fuentes Martínez. Luna Luna was said to be the leader of Los Zetas for the area and Fuentes Martinez was a major trafficker. Also seized in the townhouse were four AR-15s, another frightening Barrett .50-caliber, a handgun known in Mexico as the "cop killer," a grenade launcher, 45 pounds of marijuana and 58 ounces of cocaine. The state attorney general said that Luna Luna was Los Zetas' top man in the area and was connected with two kidnappings and at least six assassinations. He was also allegedly one of the two men who shot at the U.S. consulate in Monterrey back in October 2008. Fuentes Martinez was accused of trafficking and assisting Luna Luna.

As news of the arrests spread, armed, masked men set up 10 roadblocks in the city. On Avenida Universidad, members of Los Zetas commandeered a city bus and a three-ton truck to block traffic in both directions, while at Avenida Lincoln, two vehicles had their tires shot out in order to immobilize them and traffic around them. It took a combined military and state police force two hours to chase the gunmen away. There were no injuries, but at least two people complained to police that their vehicles had been robbed.

In the same city two days later, police made another huge arrest. A few months earlier, nine men had been arrested when they were discovered stealing thousands of gallons of gasoline from a Pemex pipeline they had tapped. Their sophisticated tools and methods indicated connections to organized crime. A subsequent investigation led police to Francisco Guizar Pavón, known as "El Rey de la Gasolinas" (the King of Gasoline). He had been a Pemex drilling engineer from 1974 to 1993, but was fired for alleged involvement in a plot to steal gasoline. Since then he had allegedly been supplying stolen fuel to Los Zetas and La Familia and enjoying their protection.

On Monday June 14, the violence began when two busloads of Federales headed to Mexico City were ambushed in Zitácuaro, a small city in the mountains of Michoacán. The resulting gun battle left 10 Federales and seven *sicarios* (believed to be associated with La Familia) dead.

Later that day, a riot erupted at a prison in Mazatlán, leaving 29 inmates dead, 18 shot and 11 stabbed. After the fighting stopped, it was revealed that a week earlier, 20 inmates who had been associated with Los Zetas had asked to be transferred out of the prison, which was deep in Sinaloa territory, but their request had been refused.

Confronted again by reporters, a visibly frustrated Calderón blamed the United States (and, by extension, Canada) for the need for a Drug War. "The origin of our violence problem begins with the fact that Mexico is located next to the country that has the highest levels of drug consumption in the world," he said. "It is as if our neighbor were the biggest drug addict in the world." He did not mention that his simile painted his own country as the world's biggest drug dealer.

Making matters much worse between the two countries was a June 9 border-crossing incident in which two people were killed. U.S. Border Patrol officers on bicycles intercepted a large group of Mexicans passing into El Paso over a railway bridge and moved in to stop them. Rather than acquiesce or attempt to flee, the group attacked the officers using a variety of methods, including throwing large rocks at them. The officers fired and two people were hit. One of them was 15-year-old Sergio Adrian Hernandez Huereka, who later died. Federales arrived, drew their guns and ordered the Border Patrol officers, who were still under attack from rocks and firecrackers, to leave.

The Mexican media went wild, turning Hernandez Huereka into a martyr for illegal immigrants. The Border Patrol issued a statement in defense of the officers, stating: "No agent wants to have to shoot another human being, but when an agent is assaulted and fears for his life, then his hand is forced. . . . The loss of this teenager's life is regrettable, it is due solely to his decision to pick up a rock and assault a United States Border Patrol Agent. We stand behind the actions of the agents who did their duty in El Paso, and are confident that the investigation into this incident will justify their actions." It also noted that the officers in question would undergo an investigation similar to the one that sent officers Ignacio Ramos and Jose Alonso Compean to prison for shooting an unarmed drug smuggler on the border in 2006.

All of the north was violent. As death threats increased, the police force of Guadalupe Municipality—a mostly rural region analogous to a county on the Rio Grande just east of Juárez—dwindled from 40 to just four officers. Guadalupe's staunchly anti-cartel PRI mayor, Jesús Manuel Lara Rodríguez, moved in secret to the quiet tree-lined Santa Teresa neighborhood in eastern Juárez. His government-in-exile did not last long, though. At 4:30 on the afternoon of June 19, as he was getting out of his car, he was gunned down and killed in front of his wife and daughter. Investigators found 11 spent cartridges in the driveway. Chihuahua's PRI governor José Reyes Baeza Terrazas—who claimed he had not been aware that Lara Rodriguez had moved to Juárez—immediately ordered 100 state police and Federales into the region to establish order and act as local police.

The Lara Rodriguez assassination came just two weeks before municipal and state elections, throwing the race for mayor into disarray. Thing got worse in the northeast on June 28, six days before the election. A convoy of two brightly decorated Chevy Trailblazer SUVs carrying Tamaulipas gubernatorial candidate Rodolfo Torre Cantú and some supporters to Ciudad Victoria's General Pedro J. Méndez International Airport was stopped by two Ford SUVs bearing Naval Infantry markings. According to witnesses, the politicians' bodyguards exited the vehicles to tell the masked men who they were transporting. The men posing as Naval Infantry disarmed the security detail and forced the others out of the SUVs before opening fire with a mix of AK-47s and AR-15s. Torre Cantú was killed at the scene, along with state congressman Enrique Blackmore Smer and bodyguards Gerardo Soltero Subiate, Rubén López Zúñiga and Francisco David López Catache. Severely injured were PRI congressional candidate Enrique de la Garza Montoto (Torre

Cantú's brother-in-law), Torre Cantú's personal secretary, Alejandro Martínez Villarreal, and bodyguard Aurelio Balleza Dante Quiroz. Torre Cantú's last-minute replacement—his older brother, Egidio Torre Cantú—won the election for a PRI/ Green coalition.

As had been true since the war began, politicians were not the only assassination targets. On June 26, a rumor spread throughout Mexico that Sonora-born, Phoenix-based *narcocorrido* singer El Shaka (José Sergio Vega Cuamea) had been murdered. It prompted him to write that the rumors of his demise were premature. "It's happened to me for years now, someone tells a radio station or a newspaper I've been killed, or suffered an accident," he wrote. "And then I have to call my dear mom, who has heart trouble, to reassure her." He also mentioned that he had taken extra security measures.

Hours after publishing the update on his site, El Shaka was on his way to a concert in Culiacán. He stopped his red Cadillac to pay a toll in the picturesque Sinaloa town of San Miguel Zapotitlán. As he headed out of the tollbooth, his car was showered in heavy weapons fire. He was killed immediately. His manager, Jesus Tirado Camacho, claimed that he could not understand why anybody would want to kill his client and that the 40-year-old had left behind at least 18 children.

As the summer of 2010 dragged on, the level of violence became almost constant. The day after El Shaka was killed, gunmen attacked another drug rehab clinic—the Fuerza Para Vivir (Strength to Live) in the mainly quiet Durango city of Gómez Palacio. They arrived in three trucks at about 2:00 p.m.

But unlike other attacks on rehab clinics, this one seemed directed. The assailants searched every room of the facility, shooting only those they recognized. Of the 49 people inside the building, only nine were killed and nine more injured. The dead ranged in age from 17 to 50. Surviving witnesses said that the masked men were looking in particular for the clinic's director, who they killed.

That same night, masked assailants entered a bar in Juárez and killed four men and a woman sitting together at a table. Witnesses could offer nothing to help the authorities, and the victims' family and friends could not explain why they were targeted.

But as routine as that shooting seemed by the incredible standards the country and that city in particular had seen in recent months, something happened on July 15 that spread even more terror by introducing a new weapon, one that had been deadly effective in other campaigns. And it was caught live on video.

CAR BOMBS—A NEW THREAT

At about 8:00 a.m., a call came into Chihuahua state police reporting shootings in Juárez in retaliation for the arrest of Jesús Armando "35" Acosta Guerrero, leader of La Linea and accused of the murders of at least two police officers. When a combined force of state and local police arrived, they found a man who had been shot in the head, but who was still alive. The video from Notimex news agency begins with paramedics in bright-red reflective vests treating the injured man. They are surrounded by a few cops all in black with masks on and weapons drawn. Off-screen, a pair of police officers check a suspicious car stopped in the middle of an intersection. Then boom! The screen goes first yellow, then bright red then finally gray as the cameraman runs away from the ear-splitting blast with the camera, still on, pointing at the sidewalk.

There are sirens, shouting and footsteps. When the cameraman is a safe distance away, he refocuses. The first thing he shoots is a paramedic, holding his ears, moaning in pain and wandering aimlessly. He then shoots the scene of the blast. The car that had been there is now a burning wreck with very little of its original structure intact. There are piles around the car—some burning, some not—that appear to be at least in part human remains. The cops, having shaken their initial shock, approach the scene. Some of them appear injured. Two others, without masks, help an injured man from the scene.

Two police officers, a paramedic and a bystander were killed at the scene. Nine other people, including the Notimex cameraman, were injured.

When the video was shown on national television (and CNN), it was an incredible shock. The entire nation saw that car bombs had joined the frightening array of weapons the cartels would use in public places. Comparisons to al Qaeda, Hezbollah and other terrorist organizations were common-place. "It's a lot like Iraq," said Claudio Arjon, the owner of a nearby restaurant and one of the first spectators on the scene, not realizing his city was already a more dangerous place than

Baghdad, at least statistically. "Now, things are very different. It's very different. It's very ugly."

The bomb had been triggered by a cell phone by someone watching the scene. They used a corpse as bait. "When (the two officers) went to check the car, there was a dead body in there, dressed up like a police officer, but it wasn't one of ours," said Juárez police spokesman Jacinto Seguro. "They put him in a civilian car, but dressed him up in a municipal police uniform. That's when the bomb went off. It's like an act of terrorism." An investigation determined that there was 22 pounds of C4 plastic explosive in the car.

The following day, graffiti appeared throughout the city, with the Juárez Cartel taking credit for the blast. One of them read:

> "What happened on September Avenue will keep happen-
> ing to all the authorities who keep supporting El Chapo.
> Sincerely, the Juárez Cartel. We still have car bombs."

"This is significant because usually it's La Linea, the Juárez Cartel's operatives, that sign the messages," said Juárez mayor José Reyes Ferriz. "It's as if to say: 'Now it's the big guys in charge, not the operatives.'"

Many media outlets, in particular the influential *Christian Science Monitor*, referred to this new method of terror as indicating this was the final stage of the "Colombianization" of Mexico, a reference to how drug cartels had terrorized that country in the 1990s. And the Colombians were watching.

Jose Ramirez Marulanda, a former Colombian army colonel and now principal of Bogotá-based Alpha Security, called the car bombing a "turning point" in the Mexican Drug War. "Because if they decide to start using car bombs one against the other . . . then the whole society, bystanders, innocent people could be affected," he said. "We could expect more sophistication day after day if they decided to go on with these car bombs."

As if to underline that comparison, three days later, in the Coahuila city of Torreón, a party was being thrown on behalf of a man who had been shot and injured on the city's streets earlier in the week. The guests at the party would not identify the man by name, instead calling him "Mota" (Speck), regional slang for marijuana. At 1:30 a.m., just as the party was beginning to climax, eight trucks pulled up outside the restaurant. A group of masked gunmen broke in and started firing indiscriminately. Twelve men, including Mota, and five women were killed immediately. Another 18 were severely injured. A cop, surveying the scene, told the only reporter who showed up, an American, "they shot anything that moved."

Chihuahua attorney general Arturo Chávez Chávez told reporters that he thought the killing was a message from one faction of the Juárez Cartel to another. "When the organizations are split, the strongest keeps what it already has and the splinter group goes in search of new latitudes, and that means they invade spaces that already belonged to somebody," he said. "That provokes conflicts and wars, which is what we're living."

But it was all part of a bigger war with small victories on

both sides. In the early morning rush hour, Jalisco state police spotted a luxury car with two men inside run a red light on Calle Patria in downtown Zapopan, a city that is part of the Guadalupe urban conglomerate. Reinforced by an army unit, the police gave chase into the suburban San Javier neighborhood. The car screeched to a stop in front of an ordinary-looking townhouse and both men jumped out of the car. The man in the passenger seat had an AR-15 and shot it at his pursuers, managing to kill one soldier and wound another. He was killed by a hail of gunfire. The driver ran inside the house and gave up after a half-hour of negotiations.

The dead man turned out to be Ignacio "Coronel Nacho" (Colonel Nacho) Coronel Villarreal. Head of the Coronel Villarreal Gang—whose job was to ferry drugs from Mexico's Pacific coast to the United States in variety of ways, mostly maritime—Coronel Villarreal answered only to Sinaloa Cartel chief Joaquín "El Chapo" Guzmán Loera himself. The other man was Coronel Villarreal's No. 2, Irán Francisco "Cachas de Diamante" (Diamond Handle) Quiñónez Gastélum. Both had outstanding warrants from the U.S. dating back to 2003.

Although the house was nondescript, police found $7 million in U.S. currency inside and a huge number of luxury items like watches and jewelry. It was linked to another safe house in the same neighborhood with a similar cache of riches.

It was a huge arrest and both the U.S. and Mexican governments treated it as such, congratulating themselves and pointing out how important Coronel Villarreal was to the trafficking industry. Two days later, President Calderón visited

Zapopan. While there, he gave a rousing speech about how Mexicans had to keep up with the good fight; that the days of a cartel-free country were not far off and that until then, the government would do what it could to protect law-abiding Mexicans. "We will continue working to strengthen the rule of law to achieve security, stability and tranquility of Jalisco families,' he said.

A year, or even six months earlier, that speech (and the death of Coronel Villarreal) would have meant a lot more. But after three-and-a-half years of war, most Mexicans knew that the removal of a capo really did little to alter the war or their way of life. The trafficking of drugs, cash and firearms didn't slow down. The violence on the street didn't slow down; if anything, it got worse. But there was still one hope. The one big boss was Guzmán Loera. Many believed that taking him down would be a huge step in defeating the cartels. Delighted by his nickname, the U.S. media began to call the strategy "Get Shorty."

CHAPTER 14

"A Phase of Very Intense Violence . . ."

Of course, while the hunt for El Chapo Guzmán Loera was the ultimate strategic goal, the Mexican government still had to keep peace and order as well it could, but the cartels were not going to cooperate.

The lion's share of the violence that had been suffered in Mexico had nothing to do with the police or army, but was a result of cartels fighting each other for territory. And since the death of Arturo Beltrán Leyva, the powerful Beltrán Leyva Cartel had split into two very distinct factions. One was based in Badirguato, Sinaloa, and was led by Héctor "El Ingeniero" (the Engineer) Beltrán Leyva, Arturo's younger brother. They called themselves the Cartel Pacifico Sur (South Pacific Cartel).

The other faction, based in Torreón, Coahuila, followed Edgar "Barbie" Valdez Villarreal. It was made up of his former gang, Los Negros, and some other members of the Beltrán

Leyva who found Hector's leadership less than inspiring. They went by a variety of names, but were usually known as the Valdez Cartel because of their leader's notoriety.

Of course, much of Barbie's allure to cartel members and media alike lay in the fact that he was generally regarded as the most ruthless capo in all of Mexico. So to counter that, Beltrán Leyva had to strike with an even more shocking blow.

It happened on August 22, 2010. Early morning commuter traffic in the Morelos city of Cuernavaca came to a standstill when drivers discovered four nude, mutilated corpses hanging from an overpass. Their index fingers and genitals were found strewn along the roadside, and their heads were piled up against the stucco walls of the bridge supports. Propped against them was a handwritten cardboard sign that read: "This is what will happen to all those who support the traitor Edgar Valdez Villarreal." It was signed "CPS," which authorities said stood for Cartel Pacifico Sur.

Later that day, police found a body in a car with Georgia licence plates on the Pacific coast highway Carretera 200 between Zihuatanejo and Acapulco. The U.S. State Department said that the victim was a U.S. citizen from Georgia, but gave no other details about the person's identity or any possible connection with the drug trade.

THE DEATH RANCH

Two days later, soldiers at a routine checkpoint just outside the city of San Fernando in Tamaulipas saw a badly injured man in ragged clothes step out of the scrub. When he saw them he started shouting in Spanish but in a dialect so thick they had a hard time understanding him. He eventually communicated that he was an Ecuadorean who had been approached by some coyotes who offered to help him sneak into the United States. Once he agreed, the coyotes took him to a ranch, took all his money and told him he had to work for a drug cartel as a *sicario* before they would take him over the Rio Grande. When he refused, they shot him and left him for dead. Once he was convinced they had left, he escaped. The man, an 18-year-old farmhand named Luis Freddy Lala Pomavilla, said he was not the only one the kidnappers were holding.

An armed convoy was sent out down Carretera 101 to investigate his claims. As soon as they were within sight of the ranch, the soldiers were subjected to assault rifle fire and grenade attacks. The resulting gunfight left one soldier dead and another severely injured. One cartel gunman was killed in the melée and another (a minor) captured, but "dozens" (according to contemporary press reports) managed to escape.

The overwhelming odor of the ranch gave away its purpose. Forensic investigators found the bodies of 58 men and 14 women in a sloppy pile against the cinder-block wall of a roofless building. Little or no attempt had been made to hide them. "The bodies were dumped about the ranch and were not buried," said a military spokesman who refused to be identified. "We are still investigating how long they had been there." Eventually, all 72 were determined to be illegal immigrants from Central and South America, who were traveling through Mexico as a group.

"They carry fairly large amounts of cash with them, in order to pay for the transport and every expense they need to make to reach the border," Miguel Molina, a Mexican immigration affairs analyst, said of immigrants who pass through Mexico. "All the drug cartels operating in Mexico also have a role to play in the kidnappings of illegal immigrants and otherwise regular people."

The military—who named Los Zetas as the likely culprit— also found 21 assault rifles, four bulletproof vests, police and army uniforms and four trucks, one with state police markings.

The next day, President Calderón addressed the incident on local radio. "Yesterday's crime, for example, shows (the cartels') beastliness, their brutality and their absolute lack of human scruples," he said. "I am sure we will still see a phase of very intense violence, principally among cartels."

THE ROAD TO BARBIE

Calderón would have better news to report in the following month, however. It began on May 25 with a raid at an Acapulco strip joint called XXXoticas, which many claimed was owned by Barbie, that ended with the arrest of eight men. They seized four AK-47s, a Smith & Wesson handgun, a fragmentation grenade and, most important, four cell phones.

Some of the men refused to speak, but others cooperated. One of their cell phones showed repeated calls to a man named Aarón Arturo Ginez Becerril, who one cooperative suspect acknowledged to be one of Barbie's top confidantes.

Ginez Becerril's phone was located via GPS in the parking lot of a shopping mall in southern Mexico City, but he was dead before the police arrived, shot once in the head. Using the same technology, they located the number most frequently called on Becerril's phone. It led them to the tranquil mountain village of Cañada de Alférez in the town of Lerma in the state of Mexico, just north of the capital.

Despite being aware that they might well find the notorious Barbie in the area, an elite U.S.-trained unit of Federales set up operations in the town, including a series of checkpoints, without military assistance. On their first day there, they stopped a trio of cars—a Chevy Cruze, a Ford Focus and a Chevy Malibu—they described as "exceeding the speed limit without discretion." When they pulled them over, the first person to exit the vehicles, who they described as a "large, white man," came to speak with them. It was only after they arrested him for traffic violations that they realized they had captured Valdez Villarreal—the second-most sought-after and certainly the most feared criminal in Mexico—virtually unarmed and unprotected. Six others in the cars drew weapons, but were arrested without gunfire. Besides Barbie, the Federales captured Maricela Reyes Lozada, Juan Antonio Lopez Reyes, Maritzel Lopez Reyes, Mauricio Lopez Reyes, Arturo Ivan Arroyo and Jorge Valentin Landa Coronado.

Barbie's arrest caused a media sensation on both sides of the border. In Mexico, the reasons were obvious. Valdez Villarreal was an incredibly violent warlord whose presence in custody made the entire country feel safer. And it showed

that the Federales could mount and finish a successful operation against a difficult target without military assistance. "The
capture of Valdez Villarreal is a high-impact blow against
organized crime," said Calderón spokesman Alejandro Poiré
Romero. "This is an important step in the national security
strategy."

Not everyone in Mexico was convinced that putting
Valdez Villarreal behind bars would actually change anything.
"The arrest of these drug lords does not have any significant
effects in terms of flow of drugs to the U.S. It did not happen in Colombia, where the government has dismantled the
big cartels, but they are producing *more* cocaine," said Jorge
Chabat, an expert on the drug war at Mexico City's *Centro de
Investigación y Docencia Económicas* (Center for Research and
Teaching of Economics). "In the long term, the dismantling of
these cartels would in principle produce a reduction in levels of
violence, but it is not going to happen in the short term. In the
shorter term, there is no significant change."

In the U.S., Barbie's arrest brought home how close the
drug war was. When he was paraded in front of the cameras,
it was clear to Americans that Barbie was one of their own.
Wearing an expensive green polo shirt with the word "London"
stitched on the front, the blonde, green-eyed and tall man was
actually quite photogenic (at least by cartel standards), looking far less like a Mexican gangster than a Texas high-school
baller who had let himself go a little. In fact, he was both. "He
seems to be a pretty bright kid, (but) very brutal and ruthless,"
said Scott Stewart, an analyst with the Austin, Texas-based

STRATFOR security consulting firm. "In a period of cartel warfare, the enforcers will tend to rise in the organization."

Even more compelling was his confession. Captured on video, Barbie is seen smiling and occasionally laughing. He keeps wiping perspiration from his head with a tissue and his sleeve, but he doesn't actually appear to be stressed or nervous. He admits that he became involved in the gang lifestyle because of the fast money and he decided to go hardcore because he was appalled at Los Zetas' habit of melting people's bodies and extorting local businesses, so he felt he had to fight them. Barbie quickly admitted to trafficking drugs, mainly from Panama, and that he had extensive "investments" in Colombia. When he is asked if they were drugs, he grinned and said yes. Barbie then boasts of receiving trailer loads of cash from the U.S. in return.

While other capos tend to mumble or stay silent in their taped interrogations, Valdez Villarreal was the opposite, talking openly, even bragging, about his career. He pointed out that he hired "some movie guys" to make a cinematic version of the story of his life, but had cut ties with them—despite a $200,000 investment—when he decided their script was too incriminatory. He said he regretted the violence in Mexico, but blamed it all on El Chapo, who he claimed broke a non-aggression pact agreed to by all the major cartels back in 2007.

One of the others arrested—a protected witness known only as "Jennifer"—revealed that Valdez Villarreal controlled the airports at Cancún and Toluca, a city of a million residents just north of the capital, by bribing the top federal agents there,

José Antonio "El Buen Hombre" (the Good Man) Rosales Carvajal and Edgar Octavio "El Chuta" (the Shooter) Ramos Cervantes. To gain access to the runways in Cancún, Barbie gave Rosales Carvajal $65,000 in cash and a new BMW. Jennifer also testified that the security detail at the airport was forbidden from inspecting Valdez Villarreal, his friends or their baggage.

And Jennifer dropped another bombshell. Earlier that year a video of four men, bound and obviously beaten, was shown all over Mexican media. The men are interrogated on the video. They reveal that they are members of Los Zetas and they have killed for the gang. At one point, the obvious leader of the quartet is asked "why did you kill my brother?" in reference to a gang member who was murdered. He doesn't answer. Then a handgun comes into the frame and the man is shot in the head. Jennifer testified that the men were kidnapped in Acapulco and brought to Valdez Villarreal, and that the voice of the interrogator was Barbie's.

Soon after his confession, Valdez Villarreal recanted it all, claiming it had been delivered under extreme duress. The DEA and Mexican government agreed that leadership of his gang passed to his father-in-law, Carlos "El Charro"(the Cowboy) Montemayor González.

As their rivals were weakened, Los Zetas, now fully independent of the Gulf Cartel and working hard to push them out of their territory, increased their aggressiveness in the northeast. On September 3, soldiers were fired upon as they approached a ranch near the small town of General Treviño in

Nuevo León. The resulting firefight killed five people, who the military claimed were members of Los Zetas.

TRAINING ASSASSINS IN CIUDAD MIER

Later that day, informants led authorities to believe that much of Los Zetas' operation was centered around Cuidad Mier, a Tamaulipas town of 6,000 a few miles from the Rio Grande. The town had been a staging area for Santa Anna's troops in the war for Texas and played host to Fidel Castro in 1956 when he set up a weapons smuggling operation there.

Aerial reconnaissance from a military helicopter revealed what appeared to be a marijuana farm at an old ranch locally known as "El Troncón" (the Stump). There were a number of large vehicles, temporary buildings and camouflage netting. The cameras from the helicopter also showed video footage of armed, masked men in front of the ranch house.

That prompted a combined force of army and naval infantry to stage a large-scale raid on the house. A gun battle that began at about 11:00 p.m. and lasted for about 90 minutes, left 27 accused Los Zetas members dead and two soldiers wounded. Two more suspected cartel members were injured and taken prisoner and three bound men who claimed to have been kidnapped were also taken into custody. Once inside, the soldiers determined that the ranch was not a farm at all, but a training facility for *sicarios*. They uncovered 25 assault rifles, 4,200 rounds of ammunition, four grenades and 23 vehicles, two of which were painted to look like military vehicles.

For many residents of Ciudad Mier, this was the last straw. Things had been tough there for a while. Armed masked men would occasionally engage in gunfights in the town's streets. Sometimes they would drive down the main drag and shoot assault rifles out the windows of their armored SUVs just for the sheer enjoyment of it. One of their favorite targets were transformers, which, when shot, could send whole neighborhoods into total darkness. In May, PAN gubernatorial candidate José Julián Garza Sacramento announced that his party would not field candidates in municipal elections in three towns, including Ciudad Mier, because of cartel-related violence. Later that month—in broad daylight—masked men tied a man to a tree branch and dismembered him alive. Also that summer, a shopping center had been burned out and the local water treatment plant had been attacked and disabled. Since workers were too frightened to return to the building, the region was left without tap water. The town's police station was burned and gutted. Nobody was hurt, but the entire force had long since walked off the job.

But it was the discovery of the assassins' training center that began the major exodus. Within a month, all but a few hundred of the town's 6,000 residents left. Those who remained were mostly elderly or for some reason unable to leave. "It's like we're in the Wild West," Santos Moreno Pérez, a Pentecostal minister, told reporters just as he was to join about 300 other former Ciudad Mier residents in the nearby city of Miguel Alemán, on the Rio Grande. "We have no mayor, no police, no transit system. We have been left to fend for ourselves."

MEXICO: THE NEW COLOMBIA?

That week, U.S. Secretary of State Hillary Clinton angered many Mexicans by stating that their country was "looking more and more like Colombia looked 20 years ago." Her comment drew support from Oscar Naranjo Trujillo, director of Colombia's national police and a four-star general who had spent his professional career fighting the cartels in his country. "They are headed there," he said.

The Mexicans disagreed. Alejandro Poiré Romero, chief spokesman on national security matters for the Calderón government, pointed out that Mexico's murder rate was still lower than Colombia's, and that the Mexicans were fighting a war against the cartels before they infiltrated the government to the extent they had in Colombia. He did not mention that 22 journalists had been killed in Mexico since Calderón had taken office, as compared to one in Colombia over the same period.

Obama went into damage control on Clinton's behalf the next day. He gave an interview to *La Opinion*, a Spanish-language newspaper in Los Angeles and stated: "Mexico is a vast and progressive democracy, with a growing economy, and as a result you cannot compare what is happening in Mexico with what happened in Colombia 20 years ago." Unlike other interviews with the president, the White House did not publish an English transcript of the discussion with *La Opinion*.

The day after Obama spoke, Juárez responded. Long the most violent of Mexican cities, the murder rate had gone down from 12 per day before the military had taken control of the streets and had stabilized at about six per day. But on

September 9, 25 people were killed in drug-related violence. At least four of them—two women and two men—were killed because they had witnessed another killing. At the sites of four separate attacks there were painted messages, all threatening the Sinaloa Cartel and El Chapo in particular. All of them were signed *El Diego*, which was the nickname for José Antonio Acosta Hernández, second in command of La Linea, the Juárez Cartel's enforcer unit. As police were investigating a murder in which the body was left in a car, they found a bomb in a nearby vehicle. It had failed to detonate.

Focus shifted farther down the Rio Grande on 11 when news broke that 85 inmates at the *Centro de Ejecución de Sanciones* (Sanctions Enforcement Center) in Reynosa escaped in a pre-dawn operation. Videotapes showed that a number of trucks drove down the long road—Calle Miguel Hidalgo—to the prison, which is surrounded by low scrub strewn with garbage, abandoned auto parts and piles of used tires, and stopped outside the concrete walls. Ladders being transported in the trucks were heaved over the prison walls. Inmates then climbed the ladders, got into the trucks and were transported to downtown Reynosa, where they mixed with the general public. There was no indication that anybody tried to stop them.

At 7:00 a.m., Federales arrested Warden Guadalupe Reyes Ortega, along with 43 other prison employees, including maintenance and nursing staff. The prison had been designed for 1,400 inmates, but was holding around 1,700. Tamaulipas Public Security Minister Antonio Garza García—who had assumed his position earlier that week—accused the Gulf

Cartel of the breakout, pointing out that they needed reinforcements (he called them "thugs") in their fight against Los Zetas.
"The guards evidently helped in the escape," he said. A riot in
the same prison in December 2008 had left 21 inmates dead
and another 34 injured.

By the time of the prison break, Reynosa had changed. It
had once had a reputation as a friendly, easygoing city, but in
the summer of 2010, it was rare to see anyone other than soldiers on the streets anywhere near sundown. "It's not officially
declared a war, but we are in a war zone," stated Eliacib Leija
Garza, state organizer of Tamaulipas for PAN. "Most of the
people stay home after six, eight at night. Just don't go out;
you take your precautions, because once in a while you hear a
bunch of shootings and things like that." He also told a reporter that because of the violence, the mayor and most officials
had moved to Texas. "And not only city and official people,"
said Leija Garza. "Investors—people who have businesses from
Tampico, Matamoros, Reynosa, Laredo—are going to the U.S.
because of this insecurity."

TROUBLE AT FALCON LAKE

The anarchic state of northeast Mexico started leaking over the
border a few miles up the Rio Grande from Reynosa. In 1953,
the two countries built Falcon Dam on the Rio Grande, which
provided a reliable source of water for drinking, irrigation
and hydroelectricity for the area. The resulting pool—known
officially as Falcon International Reservoir, but commonly as

Falcon Lake—was a very popular recreation spot and is regularly stocked with sport fish by the Texas government. It is also world-renowned for its birdwatching, with sizable colonies of rare species like the red-bellied woodpecker and black-chinned hummingbird.

Fierce territory wars between the Gulf Cartel and Los Zetas (as well as incursions by other groups, including the Sinaloa Cartel) had forced some of Los Zetas and their associates to seek refuge in and around Antigua Guerrero, the old part of Nueva Guerrero, a city on the shores of Falcon Lake. There were frequent reports—although more through social media and rumor than mainstream media—that members of Los Zetas were operating small boats and robbing people on the Mexican side of the lake. The mayor of Nueva Guerrero, Olga Juliana Elizondo Guerra, told *The Washington Post* that people on her side had frequently been harassed on their land, boats and vehicles had been stolen and tourists had stopped coming. "We hope this ends soon," she added.

On April 30, five Americans in two bass boats were fishing just outside the partially submerged Old Guerrero Church. It's known as a great spot for bass and is on the Mexican side of the border. They were approached by four "heavily tattooed" men with guns who boarded their boats, demanding money and drugs. The Americans rounded up about $200 in cash and gave it to the Mexicans. The armed men then returned to their boats and followed the retreating fishermen, breaking off their pursuit when it was obvious they were in U.S. waters.

After that, stories of Falcon Lake pirates—often claiming

to be Federales, but identified as members of Los Zetas by the "Z" tattoos on their necks and arms—began to surface more frequently. On May 6, three Americans fishing just north of a small island on the Mexican side of the lake were approached by two men with AR-15s who claimed they were Federales and that they had to search the boat for drugs and weapons; finding none, one of the men threatened to shoot them if they did not pay. They made off with about $400. Two days later, San Antonio dentist Richard Drake was approached by men he believes were pirates. "I turned and looked over my shoulder," he said. "Three guys in a bass boat with machine guns waving and yelling at me: 'Pull over! Pull over!'" He didn't. Instead, he outran them to the U.S. side.

By the Memorial Day Holiday at the end of May, four more armed robberies had been reported from the lake. One fisherman noted that the pirates had taken the memory disk from his digital camera in case it contained any incriminating evidence. The Texas Department of Public Safety (DPS) issued an alert telling Americans to look out for any boats with large prows, small outboard motors with the cover removed and hulls with no identification numbers. A Border Patrol boat had encountered one such boat filled with masked men and gave chase, but it proved too fast and made it safely back into Mexican waters.

Normally, Memorial Day draws 200 or more bass boats and tens of thousands of visitors to the lake. But in 2010, there were only about two dozen boats. Dwayne Deets, a Houston-based fisherman whose electronics-laden bass boat is worth about $50,000, spoke with reporters about how he was avoiding the Mexican side of the lake even though everyone knew that's where the bigger fish were. "We've all heard about the pirates, and we're all sticking to the American side of the lake, because those are some bad boys out there," he said, pointing out that firearms are legal for fishermen to carry on the U.S. side, but not on the Mexican side. "I just pray no one gets killed out there."

Tom Bendele, owner of Falcon Lake Tackle, took American reporters on a tour of the lake, include Salado Cove, near the island where the May 6 incident took place. "Until this started, we fished everywhere, and we never cared about the border, Texas to Mexico. But now? No. Hardly anybody is fishing the Mexico side of the lake," he said. He pointed out how parts of Mexico are just swimming distance from Texas and that Mexicans often use nets (which are illegal on the lake) to catch large quantities of fish to sell. "You could see how it would be easy to get jumped in here," he added. "Notice you don't see any Americans?"

Though precautions were taken, incidents of piracy—always following a similar script—continued. Another Border Patrol vessel encountered a boat that fit the DPS's description on August 31. Ominously, it had the words "game warden" on it. It was misspelled, and the letters were made of duct tape. That boat also fled to Mexico before it could be intercepted.

Local fear turned to national hysteria on September 30 when 29-year-old Tiffany Hartley of McAllen, Texas, told a story that everyone found shocking and more than a few found incredible. She and her 30-year-old husband, David Hartley, had been riding their personal watercrafts (although the media has referred to them as "Jets Skis," a brand from Kawasaki, they couple were actually riding Bombardier Sea-Doos) on the Mexican side of the lake to take photos of the Old Guerrero Church. They were planning on moving to Tiffany's hometown in Colorado and wanted to have some souvenirs of their time in Texas. At about 2:30 in the afternoon, the couple had finished shooting and decided to head back. "When we were coming out, we saw them," she said in a nationally televised interview. "They just waved at us, like we were—you know, friendly, very friendly wave. We were on our way—so we just continued, took a few more pictures, continued out. And we were, I don't know, maybe halfway to the U.S. I can't really give you a great idea of where exactly."

When the three boats began to approach them, Tiffany said the American couple decided to head back to Texas. As they gathered speed, Tiffany said she heard gunfire, seeing the impact of at least two shots hit the water to her left. She then said she looked back to check on David only to see him face down in the water. "And I, of course, no questions asked, not even thinking, just went right back to him to make sure and check and see, check on him to make sure he was okay," Tiffany said. "When I flipped him over, he was shot in the head." She actually had to go past her pursuers to get to him.

She said that she then attempted to lift his body onto her Sea Doo, but couldn't because he was "so much bigger" than she was. Tiffany is a thin 4-foot-10 and David weighed about 250 pounds. As the men in the boats approached her with weapons aimed at her, she said she gave up the struggle and raced past them, back to Texas as quickly as she could and called 911 from a nearby payphone.

An eyewitness came forward and said he saw Tiffany return, but did not see the gunmen or hear any shots. "I saw the 'Jet Ski' come around an island," he told ABC News. "There was something wrong actually. The way I saw her come around it looked like something terribly wrong happened. I mean, she was jittery, frantic. . . . She was crying, sobbing."

Although the pirates had been known locally for some time, the death of David Hartley made them international news and Tiffany made the media rounds calling for a complete investigation and for both governments to work harder to make the border safer. And experts weighed in as well. "Piracy on Falcon Lake is an incredible story, especially when Somali piracy has been so much in the news," said Robert Chesney, a national security and terrorism expert at the University of Texas School of Law. "It's amazing to think that it's actually happening on the Texas border."

Divers searched the American section of the lake and found no evidence. Mexico launched its own investigation, which the Hartley family criticized as insufficient. A spokesman for the state of Tamaulipas pointed out that Tiffany had yet to file a complaint in Mexico, and she had produced no evidence aside from her word.

After no physical evidence was found by either side, doubts of the veracity of Tiffany's claims began to emerge on both sides of the border. Marco Antonio Guerrero Carrixales, Tamaulipas district attorney, told *The McAllen Monitor* that he was not sure events unfolded as Tiffany claimed. Rumors in the towns around Falcon Lake focused on the idea that Tiffany murdered her husband and concocted the story to clear her name. "It certainly feels better to imagine that a young good-looking married couple was blissfully in love, and that they were simply having fun in the sun when dark forces struck," Wendy Murphy, a law professor at New England Law/Boston and author of *And Justice for Some* told Fox News. "But let's remember the Scott Peterson and Charles Stuart cases. Two men seemingly head-over-heels in love with their beautiful pregnant wives when they claimed an unknown killer ruined their picture-perfect lives."

The congressman for her area, Democrat Aaron Peña, leapt to Tiffany's defence. He called Guerrero Carrixales' comments "a convenient excuse for the sorry response" by his investigators. "Everything tells me that she's being truthful," said Peña. "There was a witness, its fits with other criminal activity seen in the area, and how do you make assumptions without having evidence, and the only evidence is what she's saying." Her biggest supporter has been David's family, particularly his sister, Nikki Hartley, who has been outspoken in Tiffany's defence through the media.

Although no physical evidence was ever recovered, Mexican authorities were making a case based on testimony from people on their side of the border as well as Tiffany. On October 10, Homicide Detective Rolando Armando Flores Villegas went on local television to discuss the case and mentioned the names of two suspects, both known to be associated with Los Zetas. On the morning of October 13, his head was found in Ciudad Miguel Alemán, just feet away from the bridge to Roma, Texas.

The discovery sparked outrage and fear in Texas. "The beheading has such strong resonance with Islamic fundamentalism that it raises the specter of groups in Mexico being as fanatical and as bloodthirsty as Osama bin Laden and his gang," said Gary Freeman, a political science professor at the University of Texas. "They seem to be copying some of their techniques, and that might be deliberate." The Tamaulipas police issued a statement that pointed out that Detective Flores Villegas was working on a number of cases and that they saw no link between his assassination and the Hartley case.

CALIFORNIA DEBATE ON THE LEGALIZATION OF MARIJUANA

While fear of Mexican violence spilling over the border was growing in the U.S., attitudes towards drugs—at least marijuana—were changing. In California—with 37.3 million residents, it had more people than any other state or Canada— possession of small amounts of marijuana was still illegal, but was punished by a $100 fine and no chance of jail. That changed slightly on October 1, when Republican Governor Arnold Schwarzenegger signed a bill introduced by Democrat Senator Mark Leno decriminalizing the offence. Under the new rules, people caught with small amounts of marijuana would still pay the $100 fine, but the offence would be treated much like a parking ticket with no court appearance (unless the accused demanded it) and no criminal record. Schwarzenegger, who admitted to marijuana use when he was younger, said that the new legislation changed little aside from freeing up the state's courts and saving a lot of money on trials. "The only difference is that because it (was) a misdemeanor, a criminal defendant (was) entitled to a jury trial and a defence attorney," he said. "In this time of drastic budget cuts, prosecutors, defence attorneys, law enforcement, and the courts cannot afford to expend limited resources prosecuting a crime that carries the same punishment as a traffic ticket."

That legislation came into effect during the hotly contested debate on California's Proposition 19, better known as the *Regulate, Control & Tax Cannabis Act*. It was a bill that, if passed, would legalize sales of marijuana to Californians 21 and older, and allow county governments to regulate and tax its use. It was an unprecedented document as no legislature in the world has legalized recreational marijuana use—not even the Netherlands or Jamaica, where the sale of marijuana and its use have been open for decades.

Supporters—who included former U.S. Surgeon General Joycelyn Edwards, Vicente Fox, many notable California politicians, police chiefs and newspapers—claimed the law would generate at least $1.4 billion in revenue for the state annually and would save a similar amount on enforcement. Critics—who included Schwarzenegger, former Governor Jerry Brown, both California senators, U.S. drug czar Gil Kerlikowske and

Mothers Against Drunk Driving—claimed that the current law was permissive enough and that legalization of marijuana would not affect organized crime. The RAND Corporation determined that Proposition 19 would lead to at most a 20 percent drop in the revenues of the Mexican cartels (perhaps promoting more violence as cartels fought for what remained of the revenue) and that if California replaced Mexico as the major supplier of marijuana, cartels exporting it to other states could relocate or be formed there.

The November 2 election, in which Democrat Brown regained the governor's office over Republican Meg Whitman (who also opposed Proposition 19), saw the proposition defeated 5,333,359 votes (53.5 percent) to 4,643,761 (46.5 percent). Notably, none of the seven counties closest to the Mexican border voted in favor of Proposition 19. Similar propositions failed by even larger margins in Oregon, Arizona and South Dakota.

According to published reports, none other than El Chapo officially thanked the U.S. government for keeping drugs illegal. "Whoever came up with this whole War on Drugs," one of his top lieutenants told a reporter, "I would like to kiss him on the lips and shake his hand and buy him dinner with caviar and champagne. The War on Drugs is the greatest thing that ever happened to me, and the day they decide to end that war, will be a sad one for me and all of my closest friends. And if you don't believe me, ask those guys whose heads showed up in the ice chests." According to the report, El Chapo elaborated, saying: "I couldn't have gotten so stinking rich without George Bush, George Bush Jr, Ronald Reagan, even El Presidente Obama; none of them have the *cojones* to stand up to all the big money that wants to keep this stuff illegal. From the bottom of my heart, I want to say, *gracias amigos*, I owe my whole empire to you."

TIJUANA TROUBLES

Desperate for some good news after the Falcon Lake incident and the defeat of Proposition 19, Mexican authorities announced a huge bust on October 18. It started in the morning when a tractor trailer surrounded by SUVs approached a routine Tijuana police traffic stop. When it became clear the convoy was not going to stop, a short gunfight broke out, injuring one suspect and one cop. The police called for reinforcements, and once the convoy was surrounded by superior firepower, the 11 men in it surrendered. The trailer, bound for the U.S., was full of neatly packaged marijuana. Under interrogation, they revealed the whereabouts of the warehouse at which they had loaded the trailer.

When the raid on the warehouse was finished, General Alfonso Duarte Mujica claimed that they had seized 105 tons of marijuana, which they valued at $334 million. Alejandro Poiré Romero, Mexico's spokesman for national security affairs, called it "the largest seizure in the country's history of marijuana prepared and packed for sale and distribution." He pointed out that Mexico had confiscated more than 7,400 tons of marijuana already in 2010 and echoed comments

Calderón had made about Tijuana—with huge reductions in violence in recent months—being something of a success story. "This administration has maintained an important effort in the eradication and confiscation of illicit substances," he said. "This is an important milestone that demonstrates the ability of the Mexican state when security forces in three levels of government coordinate and take responsibility around a common goal."

About a week after Mexican authorities were congratulating themselves for turning Tijuana around, the city became the site of the latest drug rehab massacre. Melquiades Hernández Esperanza, head of *El Camino a la Recuperación* (The Way to Recuperation), an unlicensed drug clinic, was in a dormitory counseling nine patients when she heard gunshots. When she got to the second-floor window to see outside, Hernández Esperanza said she saw four masked men with assault rifles leave the building. They left behind 13 dead men. A patient who had stepped out for a bite to eat just before the attacks told reporters that other surviving patients had told him they were all ordered to lie face down on the floor while the gunmen killed the people they recognized.

Although some tourists had returned to Tijuana in recent months as violence levelled off, the Americans and their comparatively free spending habits, had stayed away. After the most recent massacre, many businesspeople in Tijuana resigned themselves to the idea tourists were not coming back. "It is something really troubling," said Edmundo Guevara Márquez, president of the city's Business Coordinating Council. "Above all, since various authorities say we are among states that, in terms of security, have advanced and done it strongly."

A few hours before the attack in Tijuana, an unknown voice over police radios threatened that Tijuana would get "a taste of Juárez" that night. It wasn't just an idle taunt, and could be interpreted as an announcement that the Juárez Cartel was moving into the area, or just a harbinger of terror from Mexico's most violent city.

FRIGHTENING THE YOUTH

Just the night before the Tijuana shooting, in a working-class neighborhood of Juárez, a boy named Francisco López Arteaga was celebrating his 14th birthday with family and friends in a small concrete house at 2069 Calle Félix Candela rented by the boy's father for the celebration. Masked gunmen stormed their way in—it's still one of the few houses on the block without wrought iron gates—and opened fire indiscriminately. Fifteen partygoers between the ages of 12 and 30 were killed and 20 more were injured, the youngest a 9-year-old boy. López Arteaga and his father survived, but his mother was killed. Her 3-month-old daughter—sleeping in a stroller beside her—was unharmed. "I feel so much pain and rage," Francisco López Arteaga's father—who had hidden his son and six other children in a closet during the attack—said. "I am sure they will never catch the people who did this."

Social media was on fire throughout Mexico as people—who felt they could no longer rely on media reports for any explanations—discussed the shocking massacre in real time. The majority of them agreed that the killing was a signal to youth throughout Mexico, especially places like Juárez where the cartels held sway, that if they didn't work with the cartels, they too would be targets. It was like the *plata y plomo* offer the police had been given. López Arteaga and his friends, mostly older than him, had reputedly rebuffed offers to work for the cartels in the past.

Three days later, in another chilling demonstration of what happened to people who didn't join—at least according to social media—the cartels shocked Mexico. Tepic is the capital and largest city in the sleepy Pacific coast state of Nayarit. Long an agricultural backwater, Nayarit had for a few years received federal funds to develop and market itself as a tourist destination, with miles of largely undiscovered beaches. The marketing campaign pointed out how safe Nayarit's beaches were in comparison to others in Mexico as it actually had seen very little of the violence suffered by its neighbors, particularly Sinaloa, Jalisco and Zacatecas. The only time Nayarit came into national consciousness during the Drug War was on April 22, when 12 bodies, eight of them incinerated, and several destroyed SUVs were found on a remote part of a ranch near a small village called San Jose de Costilla. Authorities claimed they were members of the Gulf Cartel whose bodies had been dumped there by the Sinaloa Cartel.

But at 9:45 on the morning of October 27, a local man on a small motorcycle pulled up to the *Auto Lavadas Colima* (Colima Carwash) on Avenida Ignacio Potrero, a few blocks from Rio Suchiate, the main drag of the Lázaro Cárdenas neighborhood. While they were chatting outside the open-air car wash (it's really just a small cinder-block office with about 40 feet of corrugated metal leaning from its roof to a shorter building nearby and some hoses) at 9:57, three SUVs pulled up and the men inside them opened fire. The man on the motorcycle, all 13 Colima employees and a bystander who was leaving the Mini Super Lupita fruit market across the street were killed. Two other passers-by were injured.

Of the dead, only the man at the fruit market was older than 23. According to police, most of the victims had been associated with a nearby drug rehab clinic. Social media throughout Mexico was filled with stories and speculation that the victims were killed because they refused to work with the cartels. In a speech, Calderón agreed that the three massacres were linked and that the victims were targeted because they had chosen not to be part of the drug trafficking industry. "These are acts perpetrated by unscrupulous criminals who snatch life from innocent people, most of them young people with life ahead of them, young people struggling to build a future, to overcome addictions, to study," he said.

BEHEADING THE GULF CARTEL

With little positive to report over the last violent two and a half weeks, Mexican authorities made a headlines again on November 5. After a six-month investigation, they managed to track down Antonio "Tony Tormenta" (Tony Storm) Cárdenas

Guillén, leader of the Gulf Cartel, in the Fraccionamiento Victoria neighborhood of Matamoros. With a force of 150 Naval Infantry supported by a small army unit, Federales, state and local police, they moved in. When Cárdenas Guillén and his men saw three helicopters circling their hideout, they moved to another safe house, but were caught on surveillance video.

As the land force approached, the Gulf Cartel members greeted them with assault rifle fire and grenades. Almost as soon as the battle started, area residents captured it on video and uploaded it to YouTube. Many started tweeting updates, telling relatives they were safe and warning others not to come to Matamoros. One, typical of those sent that day, read: "Shelter, everyone! Don't leave your houses please. Pass the word." The gunfire could be heard across the Rio Grande and the University of Texas at Brownsville and Texas Southmost College told their students to go home, rescheduling several weekend events.

After a number of his bodyguards—said to be members of Los Escorpiones—were killed. Tony Tormenta made a desperate attempt to flee. His armored SUV had been considered bulletproof, but it was no match for .50-caliber shells. Almost as soon as he turned the key, he was hit by 20 of them.

Cárdenas Guillén was dead, as were four of his men, two Naval Infantry and journalist Carlos Guajardo Romero. A crime reporter with the local daily *Expreso Matamoros*, Guajardo Romero, was leaving the scene to speak with a contact in the federal government when soldiers mistook his unmarked pickup truck for that of a fleeing *sicario*. He too was shot 20 times.

Records taken from the building they fled from indicated that Cárdenas Guillén had enjoyed the protection of many officials in Tamaulipas for years. Despite years of purges and desertions, as many as half of the state police were still thought to have received some kind of payment linked to the Gulf Cartel. Authorities said that leadership of the Gulf Cartel was assumed by Jorge Eduardo "El Coss" Costilla Sánchez. He was best known for a 1999 incident in which he helped detain DEA and FBI agents at gunpoint.

November 2010 was a tumultuous time for Mexico, with crises on both coasts. Fears that oil from the Deepwater Horizon oil spill were headed towards Mexico's Gulf coast were joined by news that the *Carnival Splendor*—a luxury cruise ship with about 4,500 passengers and crew—was stranded without electricity, food or fresh water in the Pacific not far from Ensenada, Baja California.

Inside the country, however, it was business as usual. Nice weather in Chihuahua on the weekend of the November 6 and 7 led to a great number of the city's residents stepping out to enjoy it. Thirty of them and 25 people in Juárez were murdered.

THE SEESAW CONTINUES

A number of announcements in November showed that there seemed to be no end in sight for the seesaw battle for control of Mexico.

The first was a shocker from Denver on November 8. Retired fire department lieutenant David Cordova and Ronal Rocha, an assistant basketball coach at Regis University, were among 35 Sinaloa Cartel associates arrested for trafficking in a cross-border investigation. Twenty-one others were arrested in Denver, seven in Juárez, two in El Paso and one each in Alabama, Nevada and Illinois. Three other suspects were listed as fugitives. Officials seized 117 pounds of cocaine, 17 pounds of marijuana, nine firearms, $650,000 in cash and 15 vehicles. The Denver-based group operated in a number of cities, purchasing drugs from Sinaloa Cartel contacts in El Paso, then distributing it to street-level dealers. "If you purchased cocaine in the Denver area in the last two years, it's a very good probability that you purchased it from this supply chain," said Dan Oates, chief of the Aurora, Colorado police force, which aided in the operation.

Information from the Denver arrests allowed authorities to find and arrest Manuel "La Puerca" (the Sow) Fernández Valencia and 17 other Sinaloa Cartel members and associates. After a 20-minute standoff in Culiacán without a shot fired, La Puerca and his men surrendered. Eight tons of marijuana were found in the house. La Puerca told police that his son had been assassinated after being mistaken for El Chapo's son because he was driving a white Ferrari. El Chapo's boy had a similar-looking white Lamborghini. He also stated that a month later, El Chapo had caught and killed the murderer.

And on the same day, Gregorio Barradas Miravete (who had recently been elected as a PAN mayor of Juan Rodríguez Clara, a largely rural municipality in the state of Veracruz) was kidnapped. He and two supporters—former PAN mayor Omar Manzur Assad and driver Ángel Landa Cárdenas—were stopped and forced out of their car by masked gunmen who had set up a military-style checkpoint just outside the village of Isla at about 4:30 p.m. The three men were then forced into the back seat of a blue-gray Hummer SUV. Their tortured bodies were found a few hours later inside the bullet-riddled truck about 60 miles away just outside the Oaxaca city of Tuxtepec. Their hands had been bound in duct tape and they were accompanied by a bright green sign. Written on it in black Sharpie was: "This is what will happen to all those who support Los Zetas."

Many in the area had predicted the Barradas Miravete assassination, especially after he promised a complete investigation of the transactions of outgoing PRI mayor Amanda Gasperín Bulbarela.

Also on the November 9, U.S. inspector general Glenn A. Fine published a 138-page report on gun trafficking from the U.S. to Mexico. In it, he praised the joint ATF-Border Patrol Operation Gunrunner for seizing more than 5,400 firearms and 400,000 rounds of ammunition since 2006, but he also pointed out 15 ways to further decrease the supply that had not yet been implemented. The ATF said it welcomed the report and would consider his proposed initiatives.

YOUNG ASSASSINS FOR THE CARTELS

Outside of Mexico and the U.S. border states, the Mexican Drug War rarely made international headlines. Worldwide media paid attention to stories like the arrest of Valdez Villarreal or the Taxco body dump and treated them almost as though they were isolated incidents. But there was one arrest on December 4 that caught the world's attention and demonstrated exactly how violent and entrenched in the culture the Mexican Drug War had become.

The shocking video that was seen all over the world begins with two masked soldiers with bulletproof vest escorting a schoolboy out of a building at Cuernavaca Mariano Matamoros Airport and up against a brick wall. It's 9:00 p.m. and dark, but the area is well lit. The boy, who comes up the soldiers' shoulders, looks scared. He's slight, with a wide face and closely cropped curly hair. His lip is swollen and he has a bruise on his forehead. He's wearing a loose black shirt and baggy cotton pants. He looks for all the while like he's about to cry until he starts to answer questions with a tough-guy smirk. Though it was widely reported in the news that the boy was 12, he was actually 14, but small for his age. As reporters' cameras constantly flash and advance, he then tells the soldiers that his name is Edgar Jiménez Lugo, and that he was born in San Diego, in the U.S. He then goes on to tell a story that is both shocking and sickening. As he tells it, his smirk goes away and his voice begins to shake as though it was the first time he articulated the facts of his life to himself.

His parents were illegal immigrants and crack addicts. When his father was arrested and sent back to Mexico, he was sent with him. Jiménez Lugo lived in a crowded home with his father, an aunt and uncle, his grandmother and five siblings.

He dropped out of school after third grade. He spent his time hanging out with other boys of various ages until the gang recruited him. They trained him to be a *sicario*. "I participated in four executions," he said, admitting to beheading his victims. "When we don't find the rivals, we kill innocent people, maybe a construction worker or a taxi driver." A reporter asked him if killing people scared him. "No," he replied. "They drugged me and forced me to do it."

Jiménez Lugo, better known as *El Ponchis* (literally, the Cloak, but it's also local slang for barrel-chested, and is a joke on how slight Jiménez Lugo was) was arrested along with his 19-year-old sister Elizabeth while attempting to board an airplane to Tijuana. Once there, they intended to cross the border on foot to join their mother in San Diego. He admitted that he worked as a *sicario* for the Cartel Pacifico Sur (CPS) and his boss was *El Negro* (whom police knew to be Jesús Radilla Hernández, leader of the CPS), and his sister, who claimed to be one of *El Negro*'s girlfriends, was in charge of disposing of bodies. Pictures and videos on one of El Ponchis' cell phones show him posing with AK-47s and even beating tied men with a stick marked CPS, chatting and giggling the whole time. In the background of one video, as El Ponchis is beating a man suspended from the ceiling, you can hear a child singing "Hit him, hit him, hit him. Don't lose your aim"—a play on a traditional song from children's *piñata* parties. The victims were later identified as the men whose bodies were hanging from the overpass in Cuernavaca in August.

El Ponchis told them that he had been kidnapped by the

CPS—then the Beltrán Leyva Cartel—when he was 11 and had worked for them ever since, with a starting salary of $2,500 a murder. He, Elizabeth and 23-year-old sister Ericka were the ringleaders of a gang called *Las Chabelas* (the Isabels) based in Jiutepec, a poor Cuernevaca neighborhood.

Six other men arrested in connection with the case said that it was El Ponchis who cut off the victim's heads, fingers and genitals. He denied it, but did admit to multiple murders. "I've killed four people. I slit their throats. I felt awful doing it," he said. "They forced me, told me if I didn't do it they would kill me. I only cut their throats, but I never went to hang [bodies] from bridges, never." Both Lugo and his sisters were convicted and imprisoned.

One person the arrest did not shock was Morelos Attorney General Pedro Luis Benitez Velez. He told reporters that it's not uncommon for cartels to recruit children. They are easily fooled, he said, and can be coerced into violent acts without complaint. "They're persuaded to carry out terrible acts," he said. "They don't realize what they are doing." He also pointed out that unlike the U.S. and Canada, Mexico has no protocol for trying youths as adults. The cartels, he said, are aware of that and use children and teenagers for the dirtiest jobs, knowing they'll be free again soon. In the El Ponchis case, the maximum penalty for his actions was three years in a juvenile detention center. "Even if he killed a hundred people, the maximum he could get is three years," said Armando Prieto, the juvenile court judge who presided over Jimenez Lugo's trial. "That's the constitution."

When asked about the arrest, Calderón said that "in the most violent areas of the country, there is an unending recruitment of young people without hope, without opportunities."

A noted Mexican psychologist told media that the whole family had been transformed into psychopaths by their environment and lack of family structure. "In this case there is no mother figure, nor a father, to guide them. There is no one to rescue them because they don't go to school, they have no master or psychologist," said Peggy Ostrosky, head of Laboratory of Neuropsychology and Fisicopsicología of the Faculty of Psychology, National Autonomous University of Mexico. "They like to kill, to steal, and they don't need to conform to society because they are mistreated and become very hostile from a young age." She reported that it is likely they were abused, probably sexually, at an early age and that there is no effective cure or even treatment for their mental condition.

Mexican children's rights advocates pointed out that the drug war had led to thousands of orphans turning to street gangs for some semblance of family and security. Many of them turn to crime at very young ages. "Youth prisons in Mexico are now full of minors who have been arrested for crimes linked to the drug war. Most of the inmates had been convicted of drug-related murders, kidnapping and drug trafficking," said Oswaldo Hogaz, Juárez prison's director of inmates. "These kids are cheap, bloodthirsty, and they know the government can't punish them much."

Mexican authorities released a video of *El Ponchis*. In the video of his confession, he looks small and thin, with his curly hair almost as wide as his narrow shoulders. They ask him how much he was paid for an assassination. He replied "$3,000 for a head." At the end, the interviewer asked Jiménez Lugo what his future plans were. "I know what will happen to me now," he said. "I regret getting involved in this and killing people. But when I'm released I want to go straight. I'll work, do anything, as long as it's not a return to this."

It might not be that easy. "Whether he's found guilty or not, he can't come back here," said David Jiménez, his father. "The families of those he is said to have killed will want their revenge."

CHAPTER 15
Mexican Cartel Violence Moves North

Mainstream media in North America frequently pose questions asking when the Mexican cartels will bring their war north of the Rio Grande. The simple answer is that they already have.

Effective law enforcement has kept much of the violence at bay, but—as Americans saw in the crack-fueled territory wars of the late '80s and early '90s—when there is competition for drug sales, violence follows.

As early as 2008, the U.S. Department of Justice declared that Mexican cartels "are the dominant distributors of wholesale quantities of cocaine in the United States, and no other group is positioned to challenge them in the near term," in its annual *National Drug Threat Assessment*. The Mexicans had in fact replaced the traditional Italian and Irish mafias and motorcycle gangs at the top of the cocaine-trafficking pyramid, and in many places, members of those groups work in the employ of Mexicans. The report linked the cartels' ascendance to a number of factors, including higher quality drugs, a seemingly unending supply of workers and the threat of violence.

The two big differences between the drug trade in Mexico and North America are the level of violence and the widespread corruption of authorities. Despite just being a few yards away from Juárez—one of the most dangerous cities in the world—having masses of illegal immigrants and some of the most relaxed gun-control laws in the nation, El Paso is one of the safest cities in the United States. In 2010, there were 5 murders in El Paso, compared to 223 in similarly sized Baltimore, which is nowhere near Mexico and has very strict gun laws. In fact, more El Paso residents have been murdered in Juárez than in their own city in the past decade. In the same period, Juárez suffered 3,111.

Many sociologists have attributed the comparative safety of U.S. border cities to the number of legal immigrants in them. "If you want to find a safe city, first determine the size of the immigrant population. If the immigrant community represents a large proportion of the population, you're likely in one of the country's safer cities. San Diego, Laredo, El Paso—these cities are teeming with immigrants, and they're some of the safest places in the country," said Jack Levin, a criminologist at Northeastern University. "Overall, immigrants have a stake in this country, and they recognize it. They're really an exceptional sort of American. They come here having left their family and friends back home. They come at some cost to themselves in terms of security and social relationships. They are extremely success-oriented, and adjust very well to the competitive circumstances in the United States."

Throughout North America, the cartels are in charge of trafficking, but we have not seen the kind of megaviolence Mexicans have. And when there has been violence—as with the five men whose throats were slashed in Hoover, Alabama—it has been carried out not just by illegal immigrants, but against them. Jack Killorin, head of the federal Atlanta High Intensity Drug Trafficking Area Task Force, said that the Atlanta area, particularly suburban Gwinnett County, is a major hub for Mexican cartels. But their presence has not affected the larger community with violence. "The same folks who are rolling heads in the streets of Ciudad Juárez are operating in Atlanta. Here, they are just better behaved."

That "good behavior" means fewer murders. "We're not seeing violence across the cartels," he said. "They're just not in conflict. Some people would say that at this end of the distribution chain they're more interested in cooperating and making money than in conflict. Others would say there's plenty [of business] to go around, so there's no need for conflict."

But while murder rates in border cities are not increasing, kidnapping is. But again, the victims are almost entirely illegal immigrants involved in trafficking. "We don't know how many have been kidnapped, but guesstimates by local law enforcement put abductions in border towns at four to eight a week," said Fred Burton, STRATFOR's vice-president in charge of counterterrorism studies. "They are snatched in the U.S. and taken to Mexico."

That relative calm seemed to ebb in the summer of 2008. With gunfire from Mexico sometimes heard on the U.S. side of the border and the Red Cross having abandoned its efforts in places like Reynosa, it was a tense time for border cities. On August 25, the El Paso police department received an alert from the Department of Homeland Security that violence could well slip over the border soon. "We received credible information that drug cartels in Mexico have given permission to hit targets on the U.S. side of the border," said El Paso police spokesperson Chris Mears. While police forces in border cities and the Border Patrol were on heightened levels of security, nothing major occurred.

MEXICO ON THE EDGE

In November, the still-new Obama administration commissioned a report on national security from the U.S. Joint Forces Command. It said that Mexico and Pakistan were at risk of a "rapid and sudden collapse" and stated that: "The Mexican possibility may seem less likely, but the government, its politicians, police and judicial infrastructure are all under sustained assault and pressure by criminal gangs and drug cartels. How that internal conflict turns out over the next several years will have a major impact on the stability of the Mexican state."

Retiring CIA director Michael Hayden agreed. He described the Mexican drug cartels as the biggest concern to the U.S. after Iran and ahead of al Qaeda, North Korea, Iraq and Afghanistan.

Not surprisingly, the Mexican government tried to downplay the idea that it was in danger of collapsing. "It seems inappropriate to me that you would call Mexico a security risk," Interior Secretary Fernando Gómez Mont said. "There are problems in Mexico that are being dealt with, that we can continue to deal with, and that's what we are doing."

That following February 2011, the U.S. State Department issued its most strongly worded warning about traveling to Mexico. It particularly warned spring breakers, many of whom go to Mexico's beaches every year, and, in an unprecedented move, also warned people traveling to vacation spots on the U.S. side of the border, like South Padre Island, Texas. It advised visitors to border areas to "exercise common sense precautions such as visiting only the well-traveled business and tourism areas of border towns during daylight and early evening hours."

HOME INVASIONS ESCALATE IN ARIZONA

While little violence has spilled over into Texas, it is another story in Arizona. The city of Tucson, not far from the Sonora border, has seen a rash of home invasions with more than 200 in 2008, a crime, authorities said, that was "unheard of" in Tucson just a few years ago. "The amount of violence has drastically increased in the last six to 12 months, especially in the area of home invasions," said Pima County Sherriff's department Lieutenant Michael O'Connor. "The people we have arrested, a high percentage are from Mexico."

Tuscon police sergeant David Azuelo was investigating one such home invasion with a reporter from *The New York Times* in tow. In this particular attack, masked, armed men burst into a Tuscon home and pistol-whipped the father until he was unconscious. Upon finding a mother bathing her three-year-old son, they demanded money and drugs. "At least they didn't put the gun in the baby's mouth like we've seen before," Azuelo told the reporter. Azuelo also told the reporter about a similar home invasion in which a 14-year-old boy was abducted and another in which the attackers got the wrong house and shot a very surprised woman who was watching television.

While Azuelo was asking the pistol-whipped man questions, he determined that the attack—like the bulk of Arizona home invasions—was linked to the cartels. A quick search of the house revealed a blood-stained scale, marijuana buds and leaves and a bundle of cellophane wrap. Police acknowledge that most home invasions are to collect debts, but there is a growing number that are simply robberies. When dealers find out that another dealer has received a large shipment, Azuelo claimed, they will just go and take it from them and sell it themselves.

Azuelo said that the assailants he saw "were not very sophisticated." But they had an easy time escaping because the victims frequently refused to cooperate. "For me, the question is how much they got away with," he said. "The family may never tell."

One of his detectives predicted that the trend in home invasions would continue to increase. "I think this is the tip of the iceberg," Tucson detective Kris Bollingmo said. "The problem is only going to get worse."

And, as had been the modus operandi in Mexico for years, the home invaders in Arizona were beginning to masquerade as police. "We are finding home invasion and attacks involving people impersonating law enforcement officers," said Commander Dan Allen of Arizona's State Department of Public Safety. "They are very forceful and aggressive; they are heavily armed, and they threaten, assail, bind and sometimes kill victims."

INTERNATIONAL DRUG DEALING

According to Homeland Security Director and former Arizona governor Janet Napolitano, it was getting worse. Appearing before a senate panel on February 19 asking for authorization for National Guard troops to help the Border Patrol, she pointed out that the cartels had established themselves in at least 230 U.S. cities. "The cartels have fingertips that reach throughout the United States," she said.

The cartels' major center for export, according to the DEA, is Dallas. "We've got some of the major cartel members established here dealing their wares in Europe," said James Capra, head of the U.S. DEA's Dallas office. "[The cartels] are dealing with Italy, Spain, you name it. They can operate their logistical center from here and coordinate between Mexico, Central America and Europe."

This information came after a 23-year-old Dallas-area

jail employee named Brenda Medina Salinas illegally used the jail's database to check up on two ex-boyfriends who had been arrested on drug charges. The two men—Moises Duarte and Henry Hernandez—were questioned and agreed to cooperate with police. Wiretaps revealed that the men (and others) had been importing cocaine to Dallas, then moving it to the eastern United States and Europe in coordination with the Camorra (Neapolitan Mafia).

In April 2010, the U.S. military announced that it would be using the techniques it had acquired from fighting in Iraq and Afghanistan to assist the Mexican military in combating the drug cartels. "We've learned and grown a great deal as we've conducted operations against networks of terrorists and insurgent fighters," said U.S. Air Force General Gene Renuart, commander of Northern Command. "Many of the skills that you use to go after a network like those apply . . . to drug-trafficking organizations." He pointed out that the Mexican military had been much more successful fighting the cartels than police had, and that their tasks were not unlike urban warfare.

But while the effort was well publicized in the U.S., it was largely kept quiet in Mexico. "The Mexican Army doesn't want to be seen in the press as cooperating too closely with the U.S. Army," said Craig Deare, a professor at National Defense University. "One of the conditions of the cooperation is staying out of the visibility of the press." Not only was the Mexican military's pride at stake, but many people south of the border remembered how the U.S. and other sophisticated militaries had trained the soldiers who later became Los Zetas. If the best-trained and armed members of the Mexican military had left for the cartels' higher pay a few years ago, there would be little, they speculated, to prevent it from happening again.

GUNFIRE IN THE DESERT IN PINAL COUNTY

Just a week after the passage of Arizona's controversial law regarding illegal immigrants on April 23, 15-year-veteran Pinal County deputy sheriff Louie Puroll was patrolling a lonely stretch of Interstate 8 on April 30. The region, known as the Vekol Valley, is true desert, where vegetation is sparse and plants over a foot high are very rare. He said he came across five men, two with rifles, and what appeared to be bales of marijuana in heavy backpacks. He followed them discreetly for about a mile to a trash-strewn area known by locals as an illegal immigration route just under Antelope Peak. He lost sight of them, then as he crested a ridge he came face to face with the smugglers. One shot at him with an AK-47. The bullet sliced through his back, just above his left kidney, but caused only a superficial wound. He fled and the men kept firing, but missed him. He called 911 from his cell phone. Shots could be heard in the background of the call. Puroll gave his location coordinates from a handheld GPS, then shouted "Triple 9s!" the universal police code for an officer in danger and requiring assistance. Then he said: "I'm taking fire! Get me some help! Send Ranger [the force's helicopter]! I've been hit! I've been hit! I've been hit!"

The following day, 17 illegal immigrants were rounded up

as the sheriff's office collected suspects in the Puroll case. None had AK-47s or backpacks full of marijuana.

Of course, the incident caused a firestorm of controversy in the media. Supporters and opponents of the new law rallied on each side of the Puroll case. Many people claimed Puroll was lying to further the state's clampdown on illegal immigration. One of them was *Phoenix New Times* reporter Paul Rubin, who wrote an article called "Pinalcchio: Renowned Forensics Experts Say a Pinal County Deputy's High-Profile Tale About Getting Shot After Encountering Drug Smugglers Doesn't Add Up." In it, he accused Puroll of embellishing the story and Sheriff Paul Babeu of using it as leverage for his own political aims.

After the story appeared, Rubin met with Puroll again. This is how he described the meeting:

> After four hours of dialogue, I shut down my tape-recorder at the truck stop. Puroll tells me: "Now that that's off, let me tell you something. You're lucky to be alive right now." The deputy explains that a friend of his, a "rancher of Mexican descent," recently offered to murder me because of what I wrote in "Pinalcchio." I ask the deputy what he'd said to his pal. "I said that it wouldn't be a good idea, not to worry about it," he says evenly. I ask him why he's telling me this. He sees me taking notes, but continues. "Thought you'd like to know some people were upset with you, that's all," the deputy replies, smiling slightly.

Puroll was later fired for remarks made to another reporter that he had been approached by cartel members who offered him cash to cooperate. "They didn't want me to sell or buy the stuff," he said. "Just that they'd make it worth my while to look the other way out in the desert if I bumped into them." Although he did not say he took the bribes, he did not follow police procedure by arresting the men, reporting the offers or calling for backup.

While Puroll's integrity suffered serious setbacks, Babeu was still making hay with the event. In June, he appeared on television to discuss the deaths of two alleged drug smugglers (one of whom had been caught and deported seven times) in the same part of the desert Puroll had been shot in. He showed night vision videos of men with assault rifles carrying backpacks he alleged were full of drugs to vehicles parked on Interstate 8 in an area of Pinal County well known to be a highway for illegal immigrants. "How is it that you see pictures like these, not American with semi and fully automatic rifles. How is that okay?" he asked, claiming that he had lost control of large parts of the county to the cartels. "We are outgunned, we are outmanned and we don't have the resources here locally to fight this." He pointed out that many areas of Arizona that had been popular recreation spots now had signs warning that dangerous drug smugglers frequented the area.

He was not alone. While the mainstream media and many other politicians argued that Babeu was overstating the cartels' presence on U.S. soil, his supporters went online with their observations. One of them, syndicated conservative radio host

Roger Hedgecock, published photos of warning signs posted by the U.S. federal government that read (in part): "Danger—Public Warning Travel Not Recommended" and pointed out that the U.S. Fish and Wildlife Service had closed off a 3,500-acre section of the Buenos Aires National Wildlife Refuge to visitors because of what he called cartel activity. The staff at Buenos Aires played the incident down. Bonnie Swarbrick, the park's outdoor recreation planner and spokeswoman, said that the closure was to allow "National Guard and construction workers to patrol the area" without encountering the public. She also said that since the park had replaced its old barbed-wire fence with a 12-foot wall in 2006, there had been fewer sightings of illegal immigrants in the park. She did not explain what exactly the National Guard was doing in the park, however.

Babeu and his supporters were not convinced. When asked if the 1,200 National Guard troops promised by President Obama to reinforce Border Patrol would help, Babeu replied: "It will fall short. What is truly needed is 3,000 soldiers for Arizona alone."

A month later, another Arizona sheriff—Maricopa County's Joe Arpaio, a nationally known opponent of illegal immigration who styled himself "America's Toughest Sheriff" after his treatment of inmates had been challenged as cruel and unethical—made the news. A man who wished to remain anonymous told local news that his wife had received a garbled Spanish message on her voice mail that offered a $1-million bounty on Arpaio's head and $1,000 for anyone who wanted to join the Juárez Cartel. "She showed it to me. I was kind of disgusted," he said. "I reported it to the sheriff's department yesterday . . . they said they were going to direct the threat squad on it." It also gave instructions to pass the threat along, and soon other people in the area were reporting that they had received the same message.

The sheriff's office took the threat seriously. "Arpaio gets threats pretty routinely, but obviously with this heightened awareness of his role in the immigration issue we've got to take this one a little bit more seriously with a million-dollar contract out on him," said county spokeswoman Lisa Allen. "It's going so many different places that our folks are looking at it and thinking well at any given point in time it could land in front of some crazy person who thinks 'I can do that.'"

CARTEL INVOLVEMENT IN THE BANKING CRISIS

Any thought that the Mexican cartels' presence in the U.S. was local and small-time were shattered in the summer of 2010. As part of a widespread investigation into U.S. banks after the economic collapse of 2008, financial giant Wells Fargo made a plea bargain with the federal prosecutors. The deal was made in March, but only made public in July.

As financial institutions all over America were failing in 2008, Wells Fargo had purchased North Carolina-based Wachovia, which the federal government had forced to sell its assets to prevent a failure. According to a report by Bloomberg World News (which broke the story), investigators found that

Wachovia "didn't do enough to spot illicit funds in handling $378.4 billion for Mexican currency exchange houses from 2004 to 2007. That's the largest violation of the *Bank Secrecy Act*, an anti-money-laundering law, in U.S. history—a sum equal to one-third of Mexico's current gross domestic product." In a three-year period, one loosely run American bank had in effect laundered as much money for the cartels as was legally earned in all of Mexico in a year.

The investigation began in April 2006 when Mexican soldiers seized a DC-9 cargo jet at the Ciudad del Carmen airport. Inside were 5.7 tons of cocaine in 128 identical briefcases. The cocaine was linked to the Sonora Cartel (which had since been absorbed by the Sinaloa Cartel), and the jet had been purchased by money that had been laundered by Wachovia and then deposited into accounts in North Carolina-based Bank of America.

"Wachovia's blatant disregard for our banking laws gave international cocaine cartels a virtual carte blanche to finance their operations," said the lead investigator, federal prosecutor Jeffrey Sloman. His team also uncovered more cartel deposits at Bank of America and London-based HSBC, and that Miami-based American Express Bank had paid a fine in 2007 for a smaller version of the same problem.

Later, an investigation of Arizona outlets of Colorado-based Western Union, the world's biggest money transfer firm, showed widespread corruption when it came to dealing with cartel cash. Undercover officers visiting more than 20 Western Union offices were allowed to use multiple names, pass fictitious identification and smudge their fingerprints on documents, investigators said in court records. "Their allegiance was to the smugglers," said Arizona's assistant attorney general Cameron Holmes. "What they thought about during work was 'How may I please my highest spending customers the most?' In all the time we did undercover operations, we never once had a bribe turned down."

As 2011 opened, there was little hope the war would end soon. Statistically, things were actually getting much worse. The death toll in 2010 was 15,273—a 59 percent increase over 2009 and an incredible 42 people killed per day.

But perhaps even a bigger toll was the widespread feeling that Mexico had drawn itself into a war without an end. "After the news of El Ponchis broke, the whole country just kind of got depressed," said Jaime R, a former Juárez shop owner who now lives in El Paso. "It just seemed like the stories were all the same; you'd just see that the numbers and places had changed, but it was always the same." Like many Mexicans, Jaime R checks Facebook and Twitter frequently to ensure that his family and friends are safe. "You can't trust the news," he said. "So you have to trust your family."

Not long after El Ponchis was arrested, the news was dominated by a huge gunfight in Apatzingán. It began on the morning of Thursday, December 9, 2010, when masked gunmen opened fire on Federales. The armed men then confiscated cars, used them to barricade all five road entrances into the city and set them on fire. While they were collecting the cars, they killed the teenage daughter of a former Apatzingán mayor and an eight-month-old baby who was riding in the back of a taxi with his mother.

The firefight went on for two solid days. Five Federales and one more bystander were killed. Videos of cartel members carrying away their dead showed one body that police claimed belonged to Nazario "El Más Loco" (the Craziest) Moreno González, leader of La Familia Cartel.

After the shooting stopped, one of the captured cartel members, Sergio Moreno Godinez, confirmed that El Más Loco had indeed been killed in the fighting, but he did not know where his body was. He also claimed that La Familia was in decline and that an e-mail campaign that was sent to reporters all over the state of Michoacán in which La Familia promised to quit trafficking in exchange for total amnesty was real.

Whether they were ready to give up or not, they were implicated in a massacre not long after. At 1 a.m. on January 8, 2011, police were called to Acapulco's Plaza Sendero, a shopping mall on the east side of the city, which is rarely seen by tourists, to investigate a fire. When they arrived, they found a group of cars, some of which had been set ablaze. Once they had doused the flames, authorities found the decapitated bodies of 15 men in the twenties. In another car at the other end of the parking lot, they found another body of a man of 30, head intact. They also uncovered two notes signed by "El Chapo's people" that threatened Los Zetas and La Familia. As morning broke in Acapulco, 13 more bodies were found, including six stuffed in the backseat of a taxi parked behind a supermarket a block away from Plaza Sendero.

In fact, since the capture of Teodoro "El Teo" García Simental last January led to a drop-off in violence in Tijuana, Acapulco had been getting more violent as rival cartels fought for the Pacific port. On the day before the Mexican Open tennis tournament was to be played there on February 21, broad-daylight shootouts killed 13 people. Three heads were found just outside a traffic tunnel downtown on March 7.

Tourism from North America fell off sharply, down 50 percent from the almost-as-violent year before. But Acapulco's hotels reported 90 percent occupancy rates as Mexicans—eager to take advantage of bargain prices and perhaps desensitized to the violence around them—flocked to the resort.

And Acapulco was hardly alone. At 4 a.m. on February 28, seven naked, tortured, decapitated bodies were found hanging from three separate bridges in Mazatlán on the Mazatlán-Tepic highway. The next day, a collection of bodies (authorities said 20, social media said 70) was uncovered in the village of La Gavia in the municipality of San Miguel Totolapan in Guerrero. It created little buzz in the media and was often reported as "another narcofosas," a word coined by Mexican media to refer to a mass grave filled by the cartels. The following week, a gunfight broke out between elements of Los Zetas and the Gulf Cartel at 6:50 a.m. in the town square of Abasolo in Tamaulipas. Before the army came to stop it, 18 men were dead. And two days later, on March 10, curious people in Santiago Tangamandapio in Michoacán approached a car that they found stopped in the middle of a busy intersection at 6 a.m. Inside was the dead body of the city's director of public security, Jorge Hernández Espinoza.

Violence was relatively constant in Juárez, but it was silenced for a brief period on February 3 when a storm that sent blizzards through much of North America, dumped a few inches of snow on the city. There were 28 auto accidents in Juárez that day, but no fatalities.

ARIZONA CANDIDATES FOR GOVERNOR FACE OFF

As the Arizona gubernatorial election approached, political tensions and rhetoric started to become more intense. Democratic challenger Terry Goddard accused incumbent Brewer of spreading false information regarding Mexican cartels beheading illegal immigrants in the Arizona desert. "I'm astonished, frankly, everybody who [has] studied this knows there are no beheadings," Goddard said, citing a survey of state medical examiners. "Arizona has the lowest violent crime rate we've had since 1983, our law enforcement has done a great job, and why the governor won't simply say I was wrong, there were no beheadings, Arizona is safe, I do not understand, this is hurting us incredibly."

Brewer did not answer Goddard's accusations directly. Instead, on October 10, 2010 a discovery was made that convinced many in Arizona that the Mexican Drug War had indeed moved north of the border. Martin Alejandro Cota Monroy lived in Perris, California, a predominantly Hispanic city in Riverside County. He was an illegal immigrant and professional drug trafficker, working in association with the Sinaloa Cartel.

That spring, he was ferrying a shipment of 400 pounds of

marijuana and a small amount of meth for the cartel when he decided to keep it, and sell it himself. When his contacts in U.S. asked him where the drugs were, Cota Monroy told them that they had been intercepted by the Border Patrol.

They weren't convinced for long and Cota Monroy was kidnapped the next time he was in Mexico. The men who kidnapped him were hired to kill him, but he managed to bargain with them, saying he would pay them back for the shipment, putting his house in Perris up as collateral.

They released him, but when they found out that Cota Monroy did not actually own the house, his fate was sealed.

At about 5:00 a.m., a man talking to his girlfriend at a row of townhouses in Chandler, Arizona (a suburb of Phoenix that had been named to *Forbes* magazine's "most boring cities in the U.S." list) noticed some Hispanic men arguing a few doors away and then leaving in a Ford Expedition SUV with California plates. He called police. They arrived at the house at about 5:30 and found the door open. Cota Monroy's body was just inside and his head was a few feet away. His body and head both showed signs of significant trauma and torture. "It was a very gruesome scene," Chandler police detective David Ramer said. "Anytime you see a headless body stabbed multiple times, obviously that's gruesome. And this is a message being sent— not only are they going to kill you but they're going to dismember your body, and 'If you cross us, this is what happens.'"

An investigation into Cota Monroy's death led to the arrest of Tuscon-based illegal immigrant Crisantos Moroyoqui, who worked for the PEI Estatales/El Chapo organization, better known as the Sinaloa Cartel. Three other men—including one identified as "El Joto" (the Queer) were QMAT fugitives. It was alleged that the men were part of El Gio, an enforcer unit operating on behalf of the Sinaloa Cartel. "The cartel hired hit men specifically to kill him," said Detective Dave Ramer, spokesman for the Chandler police. "He lied his way out of being killed the first time. He said he was going to put up his house for collateral to pay for the drugs, but he didn't own a house. You're going to say whatever you can to save your life."

Brewer won the election and incidents related to the trafficking of both drugs and humans continued to be attributed to the cartels. In February 2011, a bus traveling in Nogales, Arizona, a few feet from the international border was stopped when a section of road collapsed underneath it. Police then discovered a hand-dug tunnel under the border that they said was used to smuggle immigrants and drugs into the U.S. It was just 19 feet long, beginning just on the Mexican side of the fence and exiting in the employee parking lot of the Dennis DeConcini Port of Entry building. It was, police said, the 25th such tunnel that had been uncovered since the summer of 2008.

On the same day, Babeu publicly responded to a letter signed by several mayors of towns in Arizona's border counties that had asked him to tone down his rhetoric. He said:

Pinal County is the number one county in the United States for drug and human trafficking. Our pursuits and drug seizures tied to drug and human trafficking far exceed those of the four border counties. The threat from an unsecured border, where 241,000 illegals were apprehended last year by the border patrol and an additional 400,000 got away. Those are failing grades by anyone's score card.

Some speak of improved safety, while we have doubled the confiscation of drugs, calls to the Border Patrol and had 340 vehicle pursuits this year—up from 286 the year before and 142 the year prior. We have a serious public safety threat in my county, due to an unsecured border with Mexico and our nation should be highly concerned about the more dangerous national security threat that is presented with OTMs [an acronym meaning illegal immigrants "other than Mexicans"] and persons from countries of interest (that harbor/sponsor terrorists or speak ill of the U.S.A).

Just this week, the U.S. Department of Homeland Security confirmed that Pinal County has a minimum of 75-100 mountains or high-terrain features that are occupied by Mexican drug cartels. How have we arrived at this point in America that this is acceptable to have foreign-born criminals controlling safe passage in an entire region of our state?

If these mayors were serious about dialogue with me, they would have called, or at least waited for (their) letter to arrive by mail at my office, prior to releasing their letter to the media. They have done the very thing they accuse me of doing. I do not represent these mayors or their citizens, yet I do represent the nearly 400,000 citizens of my county and the overwhelming majority of Arizonans, who laugh at Secretary Napolitano's suggestion that our border is more secure than ever.

On that same day, Jaimie Zapata, an agent with the U.S. Immigration and Customs Enforcement agency (ICE) and another unidentified agent were stopped at a roadblock in Mexico City. Men masquerading as soldiers fired upon the men, killing Zapata and badly injuring the other agent.

The attack was met with a strongly worded statement from Homeland Security Director Janet Napolitano. "Let me be clear: Any act of violence against our ICE personnel . . . is an attack against all those who serve our nation and put their lives at risk for our safety," she said.

That led many people in the U.S. to believe that their government would be more active in the Drug War. "You start killing U.S. officials and that really turns up the heat," said George Grayson, a Mexico expert at the College of William & Mary in Williamsburg, Virginia. "There's going to be great pressure on the Mexican government to find out who was behind this killing, enormous pressure."

Just as the rhetoric was reaching its highest levels, French videogame developer Ubisoft released a violent *Grand Theft Auto*-style videogame called *Call of Juarez: the Cartel*. In it, players must travel from Los Angeles to Juárez "taking the law into your own hands." As first, the company defended the game. "*Call of Juarez: the Cartel* is purely fictional and developed by the team at Techland for entertainment purposes only," a Ubisoft press release said. "While *Call of Juarez: the Cartel* touches on subjects relevant to current events in Juárez, it does so in a fictional manner that makes the gaming experience feel more like being immersed in an action movie than in a real-life situation." After much controversy, Ubisoft eventually pulled the game, recast it in the Old West and relaunched it as *Call of Juarez: Bound in Blood*.

On March 1, ICE announced that its Operation Southern Tempest had resulted in the arrests of 678 people throughout the southeastern United States who were involved with the Mexican drug cartels. ICE Director John Morton pointed out that those arrested represented 133 individual gangs, including the Salvadoran MS-13, the Latin Kings, the Bloods and the Jamaican Posse.

And two days later a raid occurred that convinced many Americans that the war had indeed spilled over the border. In Columbus, New Mexico—the very town that Pancho Villa had attempted to take over in 1916—11 members of local government, including Mayor Eddie Espinoza and Police Chief Angelo Vega, were arrested in a conspiracy to import weapons into Mexico. In the 84-count indictment, the accused were alleged to have purchased at least 200 firearms—specializing in 9mm pistols and a shortened form of the AK-47 that can be fired using just one hand—and 1,500 rounds of ammunition to resell in Mexico.

"I couldn't tell you for sure that the firearms would ultimately be put in the hands of people who were going to hurt other people, but because we believe the firearms were destined for Mexico, we feel we made a big difference today," said District Attorney Kenneth J. Gonzales. "Presumably these folks are engaging in this activity because there is money to be made. We're very disappointed that we have among these

11 people three people in government positions—a police chief sworn to protect the public and a mayor sworn to lead and provide for the public safety and a village trustee that has that duty as well. That was part of the tragedy here—we're actually having to search a police department."

So before the spring of 2011 had arrived, many features of the Mexican Drug War had clearly been seen north of the border. Mass arrests of drug-trafficking gangs were being arrested with no disruption of the flow of drugs on the streets. Rough justice had been handed out by cartel members in the form of throat slashings and a beheading. American financial institutions (some of whom received government assistance for their own mismanagement) had been shown to have aided the cartels. And to complete the cycle, elected officials and the police had been found to be corrupt—running illegal firearms to the cartels for profit.

• • •

Of course, it's impossible to predict what will happen next in the Mexican Drug War. The two sides in Mexico appear to have reached a bloody equilibrium in which forces loyal to President Calderón make mass arrests, sometimes of top *capos*, which seem to have no effect on the level of violence or trafficking.

There are no easy answers. Acceptance of marijuana usage in North America is growing, but trafficking is still illegal. While legalization could be an option in the future, at this point it would be against the wishes of the majority of North Americans, and it would have little or no effect on the trade of cocaine, methamphetamines, heroin, MDMA and other drugs. And mere legalization is no guarantee that smuggling would stop. When the Canadian government increased taxes on cigarettes in 1991, thousands of Canadians risked arrest—and many even risked their lives with dangerous night-time waterborne border crossings—to smuggle cheaper tobacco across the border. When the legislation was hastily repealed in 1994, it had cost Canadian taxpayers $4.8 billion, according to a University of Ottawa study. Taxed marijuana, if significantly more expensive than contraband, could have a similar effect. Trade to those for whom marijuana sales would still be prohibited—minors, for example—would also contribute to illegal trade.

While many groups, including the quasi-governmental RAND Corporation, have advocated rehabilitation and education programs instead of interdiction, it should be noted that while they may reduce drug use and especially dependency, they do not eliminate it. A rough analogy can be found with unplanned pregnancies: although sex education is universal and contraceptives are cheap and easily accessible, millions of North American women still experience unplanned pregnancies every year.

Any of these actions can help reduce the effect of trafficking, but as long as there are outrageous sums of money to be made, there will be people who are willing to intimidate and kill to get their share. The combination of factors that incubated the Mexican Drug War—poverty, ignorance, hypocrisy, corruption and the contempt it breeds—made it an ideal place for war to emerge. Before the Fox and Calderón initiatives, there was much less violence, but there was also an environment in which the government essentially took orders from criminals.

It seems that there are two paths Mexico can take. It can continue with the War Against Drug Trafficking in hope that it will subside much like the crack wars did in the U.S. Or they can go back to collaborating with the cartels, allowing them to keep the peace in their own way.

NOTES

The standard Mexican naming convention is usually that the given names are followed by the paternal surname and then the maternal surname. For example, former Mexican president Vicente Fox Quesda's father was named José Luis Fox Pont and his mother Mercedes Quesada Etxaide. For the most part, I have usually included both surnames to reduce confusion. The exceptions are those personalities—like Fox or Lydia Cacho (Ribeiro)—who are well known to North Americans by one surname. With them, I use two surnames for first reference and one for subsequent mentions. Many sources, including the Drug Enforcement Administration (DEA), hyphenate Mexican surnames, as in Fox-Queseda. A second given name is sometimes given when two people share the same first name and surname, as in Francisco Javier "El Tigrillo" Arellano Félix and Francisco Rafael "Frankie O" Arellano Félix. Mexican-Americans, like Jenni Rivera, are generally referred to by one surname if it is their preference. Some historical figures like Francisco I Madero (González) have their second surname listed in parentheses on first reference if it is not commonly used. One exception is that of journalist Jesús Blancornelas, who was born Jesús Blanco Ornelas, and conflated his name.

Nicknames are given between the given name and first surname in quotation marks. English translations are provided where appropriate. Some liberty has been taken with the translations, as in examples like "El Gordo," which literally translates as "the fat one," but I think is better expressed as "Fatso." Some nicknames, like "El Kalis" have no literal English translations, while others, like "El Puma" are self explanatory. In published reports, Edgar Valdez Villarreal is often called "La Barbie" because the doll he is named after is feminine and just as often "El Barbie" because he is masculine. Mexican sources I have spoken to recommend using just "Barbie." Although translating Zhen-Li Ye Gon's nickname "El Chino" as "the Chinaman" may sound culturally insensitive, I think it accurately reflects the way it was used by Mexican media.

With place names, I use local spellings and accents, unless the place in question is a commonplace English word. For example, I use Mexico City for Ciudad de México, but Culiacán is spelled with its accent. For place names that are used in more than one place, like Hidalgo, the state is also given. The exception is Juárez, because of the importance to the narrative of Ciudad Juárez in Chihuahua.

Civilian versions of the AK-47 and M-16 assault rifles are known as the WASR-10 and AR-15 respectively, but when they are illegally brought back to military standards, I refer to them as AK-47 and AR-15 as is commonplace, if not strictly correct.

Although the official name of Mexico is Estados Unidos Mexicanos (the United States of Mexico) and that of America is the United States of America, in the book, as with convention, the phrase "United States" refers to America. For reasons of convenience, North America refers to the United States and Canada, not Mexico, and Central America refers to Belize, Costa Rica, El Salvador, Guatemala, Honduras, Nicaragua and Panama, not Mexico.

The preferred spelling of the consumable product of the cannabis plant is marijuana, but the United States government uses the older spelling "marihuana." I retain their spelling when quoting official documents. Cocaine refers to powdered cocaine and crack cocaine is simply called crack.

Drug cartels often have multiple names—such as the Tijuana Cartel, which is often known as the Arellano Félix Organization or AFO—I prefer to use geographic names to avoid confusion. The exception is the Beltrán Leyva Cartel (also known as the South Pacific Cartel) because of the importance of the Beltrán Leyva family in its founding and organization and La Familia (instead of Michoacán Cartel), because that's what they are more commonly called and it befits their quasi-religious philosophy.

The river separating Texas and Mexico is called the Rio Grande in the U.S. and Canada and Rio Bravo in Mexico. I use the name Rio Grande.

Although it is controversial, I frequently use the term "illegal immigrant" because of its commonplace usage and because undocumented migrants are indeed breaking immigration laws.

SOURCES

Because of the nature of the conflict in Mexico and the pressure put upon journalists who risk being kidnapped and murdered for reporting what they see, many of the sources used in this book would be put into grave danger if their names were published. Because of this, most individuals referred to in this book are given assumed or partial names. Sources are named where the source is deceased, imprisoned, well known (such as politicians or pop stars) or already exposed by the media (as in the case of people such as Tiffany Hartley).

Officially, much of my research has come from the U.S. Embassy to Mexico, the U.S. General Accounting Office, the U.S. State Department, the U.S. Department of Homeland Security, U.S. Bureau of Citizenship and Immigration, the Federal Bureau of Investigation, the police departments of El Paso, Tuscon and other cities. Some information has also come from the Royal Canadian Mounted Police,

Citizenship Canada and various Canadian police forces. Even more came from The Center for Latin American and Border Studies, the Pew Research Center and many other nongovernmental organizations.

More information came from the reporters and editors of *International Herald Tribune*, *El Universal*, *The Houston Chronicle*, *Milenio*, Alertnet, *El Mañana*, Reuters, BBC, CNN, *The Washington Post*, *The New York Times*, *The Los Angeles Times*, The Associated Press, Bloomberg, Yahoo!, *The Christian Science Monitor*, *Nueva Leon Enlinea*, *El Diario*, Fox News, *The Times* of London, CBC, ABC, MSNBC, *The Star-Tribune*, *Time*, *The Chicago Sun-Times*, *The El Paso Times*, *Newsweek*, *The Washington Examiner*, *Crónica*, *Diario Eyipantla Milenio*, *Diario Xalapa*, *El Dictamen*, *Excélsior*, *Frontera*, *El Imparcial*, *El Informador*, *La Jornada*, *La Voz de Michoacán*, *El Vigia*, *El Nacional*, *El Norte*, *Notimex*, *Novedades de México*, *Novedades de Quintana Roo*, *Novedades de Tabasco*, *Novedades de Yucatán*, *El Occidental*, *Periódico Vanguardia*, *Publico*, *La Prensa*, *Reforma*, *Siglo 21*, *El Siglo de Torreón*, *El Zócalo* and many other media outlets. Special thanks to Eric, Joe, Karen and Javier.

INDEX